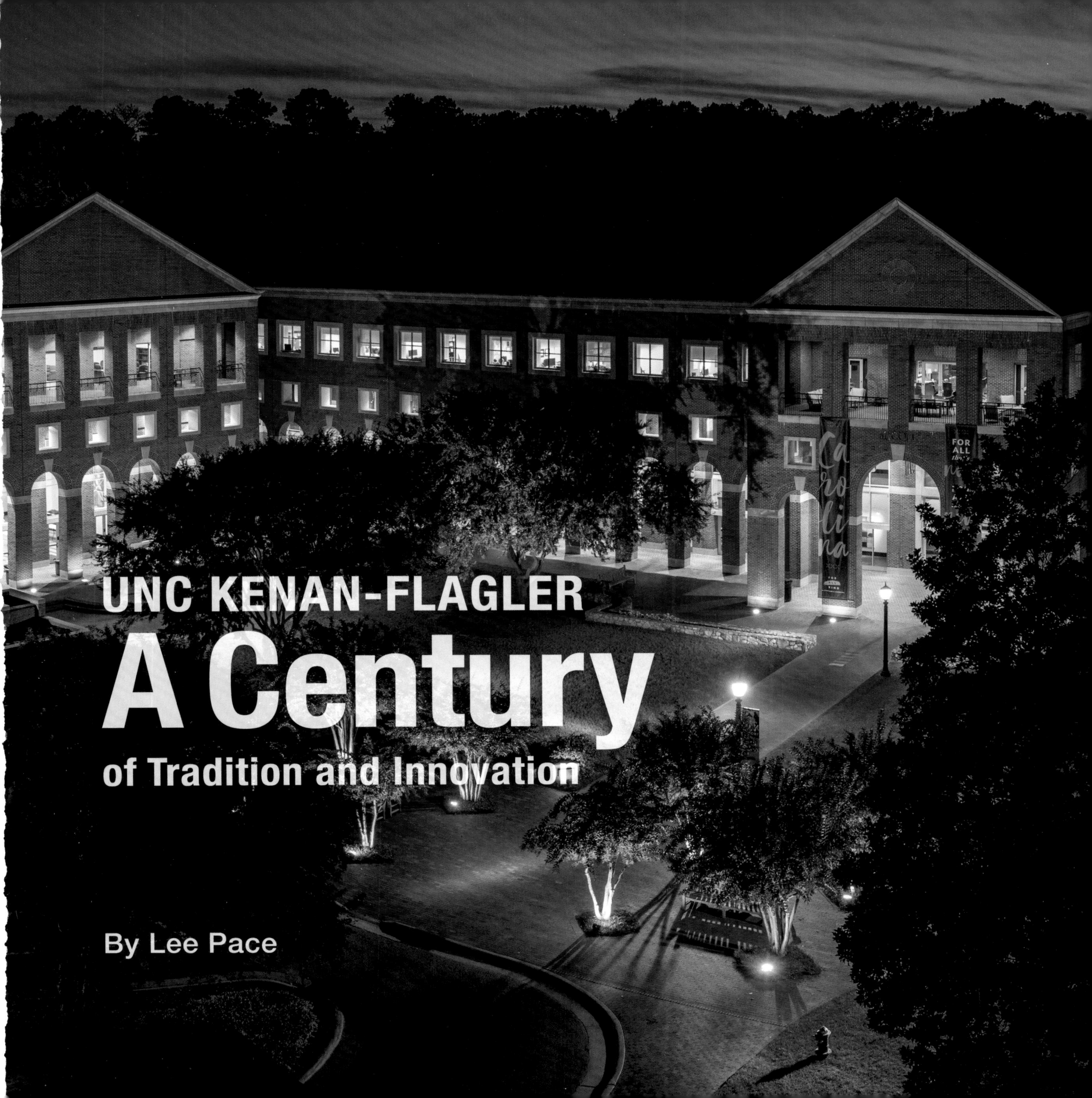

UNC KENAN-FLAGLER

A Century

of Tradition and Innovation

By Lee Pace

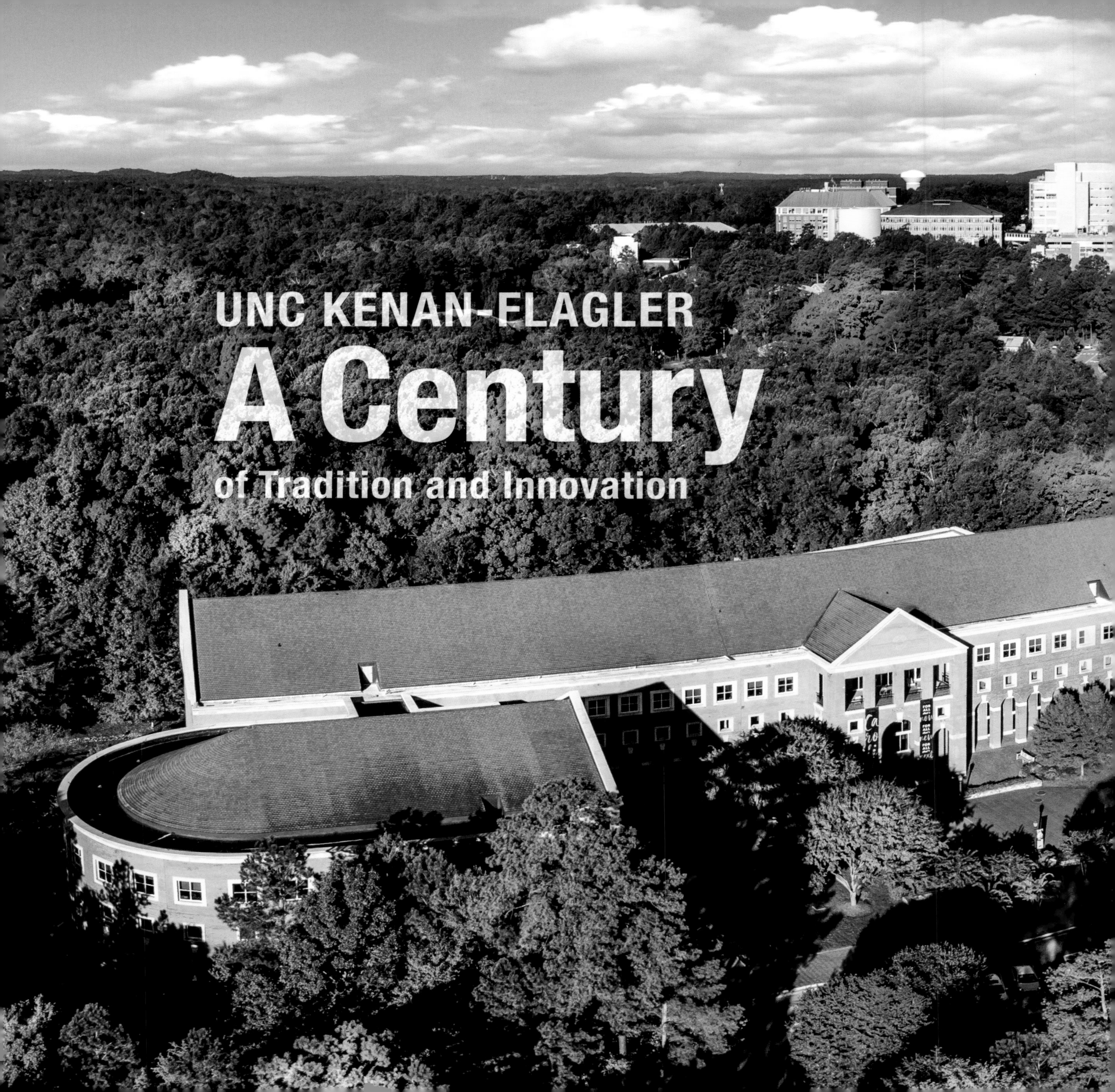

UNC KENAN-FLAGLER

A Century

of Tradition and Innovation

UNC KENAN-FLAGLER

A Century of Tradition and Innovation

ISBN-13: 978-0-578-44868-8

**Library of Congress Control Number:
2019900446**

Printed in Canada by Friesens Corporation

Book Design and Production by Sue Pace, Chapel Hill, N.C.

Photo on title page and rear end sheet by Steve Exum; photo on front end sheet from North Carolina Collection, Wilson Library, UNC-CH; aerial photo on pages 2-3 by Ryan Montgomery of Monty Aerials.

UNC
KENAN-FLAGLER
100

"The spirit of camaraderie and collaboration was remarkable. There was never a sense of it being a zero-sum game, and I think that's key and one of the lessons I've applied in leadership."

Stevie McNeal (MBA '87)

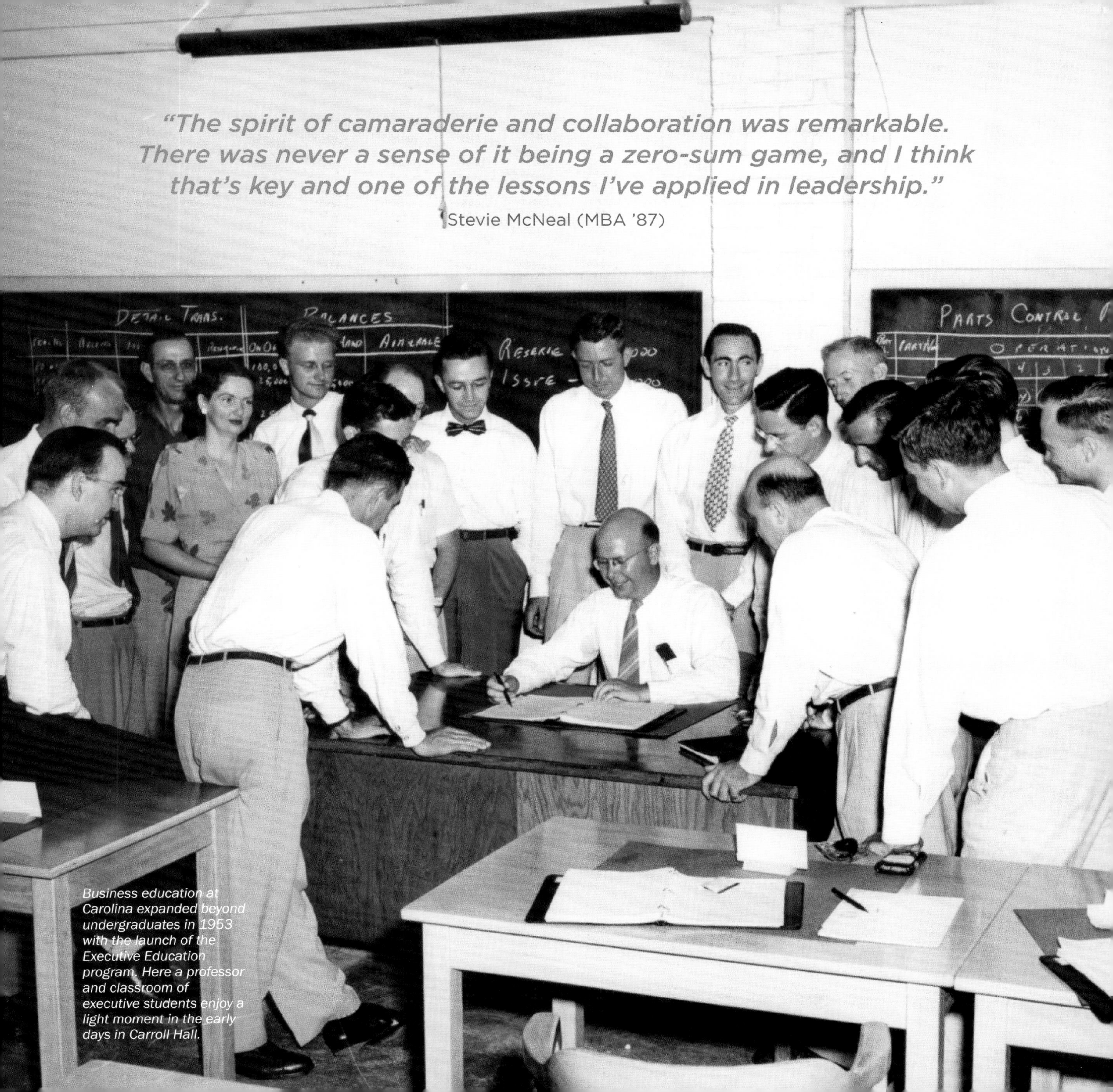

Business education at Carolina expanded beyond undergraduates in 1953 with the launch of the Executive Education program. Here a professor and classroom of executive students enjoy a light moment in the early days in Carroll Hall.

"Some men seem to be slaves of duty. Dudley Carroll hastened to it like a war-horse at the sound of a trumpet."

Chancellor Robert House

Carroll (front row, second from left) gathers with the Business School faculty in the 1940s, a decade before a new building named in Carroll's honor opened on the west side of Polk Place.

DUDLEY DEWITT CARROLL HALL

CONTENTS

SIDEBARS

FOR ALL that's next
Carolina
FOR ALL KIND
225 YEARS
UNIVERSITY OF NORTH CAROLINA
LVX
LIBERTAS
CHAPEL HILL
DONATED BY
THE SENIOR CLASS
1989

INTRODUCTION

I am a proud member of the 1979 School of Journalism graduating class at the University of North Carolina, and I have many fond memories and lessons garnered from the classrooms at Howell Hall. My favorite professors spanned the gamut in specialties and personality—from the curmudgeonly Jim Shumaker to the Pied Piper-esque Walter Spearman to the orderly and precise Richard Cole—but each was an outstanding teacher and helped usher me into the real world with an array of functional skills.

Yet through four decades in the working world, I have developed more of a connection and affinity for Kenan-Flagler Business School as, since 1987, I have operated as a tiny business in the media, publishing and broadcasting worlds, an independent contractor at first and then officially a corporation later at the advice of my accountant.

My balance sheet has ebbed and flowed through three recessions. I have had to adapt from paper and ink to the Internet-of-Things. I have submitted invoices to companies that promptly went bankrupt. I have lost sleep over not having enough work and pounded the caffeine when having too much. I have hatched ideas that came to blissful fruition and wryly chuckled in hindsight over others that crashed and burned. I have filled out quarterly tax reports and learned to take credit card payments on an iPhone. I have figured out that nothing ever goes according to plan—that Idea A soon becomes A-1 and the final product is a half dozen iterations down the road.

And I have done it all by trial-and-error and by instinct. I have often wondered if a business education might have served me better.

Which is why writing and orchestrating this book to celebrate the first century of Kenan-Flagler Business School had so much appeal. The two years it took to plan, research, write and organize these 208 pages gave me a fascinating glimpse behind the curtain of the operation and functioning of one of Carolina's most important assets—and hopefully a dollop of wisdom might have rubbed off as well. The photo at left of South Building so handsomely draped in banners celebrating the University's 225th birthday was taken in October 2018, one day following University Day festivities when Chancellor Carol Folt remarked: "Today, Carolina is one of the world's greatest global, public, research universities. Creativity flourishes. The artistry and intellectual power of our faculty, staff and students produce game-changing discoveries that save lives and drive innovation." And the Business School is Exhibit A.

This book is built around three legs of a tripod and a chapter for each—the school's history and evolution; the legacies of its namesakes, the Kenans and Flaglers, and why their stories are germane to education and business today; and the culture that permeates the bricks, mortar and people and stresses a blend of the art and science of conducting commerce. Interspersed throughout are sidebars highlighting noteworthy professors, alumni, events and programs within the school.

I am confident what we have assembled within the covers of this book will make for good reading, fond reminiscing and entertaining browsing. I am confident the important bases—ranging from Alumni Hall a century ago to McColl Building today, from Dean Carroll to Dean Shackelford, from the days of teaching rural economics to sending graduates out into North Carolina's high-tech business environment—have all been covered.

But the danger in these projects, of distilling a century into two hundred-plus pages, sixty thousand words and two hundred images, is who and what do you overlook? Who is missing who shouldn't be? It was one thing to capture the history of Kenan-Flagler. It was another to offer a slice of life into today's energy and brilliance, to reflect something of the bright eyes and bushy tails of students with boundless energy, ideas and ideals. The story lines can simply become overwhelming. For the oversights, I offer a preemptive apology.

So what we have here is a slice of a century, if you will—hopefully one that satisfies and piques the interest of all those involved to begin working on the story for 2119. It was the great entrepreneur Walt Disney who said, "The way to get started is to quit talking and begin doing." Indeed, with the dreams and drawing boards emanating from Kenan-Flagler today, there's another book to be written. And it won't take a hundred years to fill it up.

Lee Pace

The Business of Next

By Doug Shackelford

The power of education to improve lives is a universal story.

Our story began one hundred years ago when UNC's leaders envisioned a role for business at a liberal arts university. It was an unlikely idea at an unlikely time—the country was recovering from World War I—in an unlikely place as North Carolina sat on the bottom economic rung of American states.

That vision set the Department of Commerce on a trajectory to become UNC Kenan-Flagler Business School—one of the best business schools in the world. It is reflected today in our teaching, research and impact on society. It is the foundation of our approach to preparing students with the enduring knowledge and skills they need to thrive in the complexities of 21st century commerce.

Our Centennial story shows how far we have come and what enabled us to reach this point. It is a story of tradition—what is enduring and important to who we are and will remain. It is a story of innovation that will set the stage for the next 100 years.

Great people, greater impact

The Department of Commerce was approved on January 14, 1919, and opened its doors on October 2. The first degrees were awarded to twelve male students in 1921.

A century later our students, faculty and staff come from around the state, the country and the world. We have approximately 900 Undergraduate Business students, 1,800 MBA students, 400 Master of Accounting students and seventy PhD students, and serve 5,000 executives annually in our Executive Development programs. We have almost 37,000 alumni living and working in fifty states and eighty-six countries.

We have become more diverse every year, making us better than ever. By increasing the size and number of our programs, we multiply the impact of a Carolina education on improving the lives of our students, their families and their communities as we fulfill UNC's mission of teaching, research and service.

Our core values are excellence, leadership, integrity, community and teamwork. They both reflect and form our unique culture. They enable us to attract dedicated faculty and staff and talented students who contribute to our community. They are ingrained in our passionate alumni who share their time and treasure with the school because they want others to have the transformational education they did—and because they want to see UNC Kenan-Flagler reach new heights.

Preparing the next generation

Our culture shapes how we prepare future business leaders. The school's general management approach dates back to its founding as a department in the College of Arts & Sciences. As you will read, our first dean, Dudley Dewitt Carroll, imbued "the young department, its students and faculty with a standard of ethics and broad view beyond the dollar signs of profit that would endure over its first century."

The original curriculum included ethics, practical French and Spanish, English composition, technical writing and psychology, sales management, commercial and industrial geography and Latin American history. Later we were among the first business schools to instill in students how to work in teams—long before it was as common at other schools or valued by business as it is today.

School leaders stayed true to the goal of preparing students with enduring knowledge and skills to contribute at graduation and during long, successful careers as they navigate a complex future.

Now our students can expand their studies to build on standard business areas, such as finance and marketing, to include entrepreneurship, global business, real estate, leadership, energy, family business and much more. In 2019 we celebrate the twentieth anniversary of our Center of Sustainable Enterprise and the first year of our Center for the Business of Health.

Today our graduates are CEOs, entrepreneurs, investors, active military and veterans, civic leaders, brewers, book authors and filmmakers. They put their expertise to work in world capitals, emergency rooms and from home offices. They are volunteers and parents. They use what they learn at Carolina to lead and change organizations from Main Street to Wall Street—to create, build and lead businesses, to fulfill their dreams and improve their companies, communities and countries.

Creating knowledge

We have long required our faculty to excel at both teaching and research, which is not common at most business schools. "The school looks upon the two major activities—teaching and research—not as separate entities, but as mutual and reinforcing ways of educating students to learn, to understand, to practice and to be better prepared," the *Durham Morning Herald* reported in 1964. "It is a very striking fact that often the best teachers are the best research scholars," said Dean Maurice Lee, and the best researchers "are also the best teachers."

Our faculty are stronger than ever, having a broader impact—on the state and around the world—than ever before. They examine important problems and bring those insights into the classroom and to the business community. Their work provides the foundation for students and business leaders to look beyond the short-term to anticipate challenges and develop solutions—shaping the future state of business.

Innovating from the start

Our story is one of innovation. Responding to the environment and looking to the future are a part of our fabric. Historically we've been quick to adapt in terms of the courses we offer, how we teach them and creating new programs.

"Interviews with key faculty and several students reveal a 'theme' that can be identified in the structure, the work and the spirit of the school," that same *Durham Morning Herald* article reported almost sixty years ago. "This theme could be expressed by stressing the open-mindedness, the flexibility, and the willingness of faculty and students to venture—and even pioneer—in new programs of business learning."

Part of that innovation is teaching using whatever ways are the most effective for learning. The most dramatic example is our ability to see and seize the promise of technology—online programs and more—to improve learning. At a time of tectonic change for business education as a whole, technology is enabling us to revamp learning at Kenan-Flagler and continue to develop new ways to educate future business leaders. Our commitment to excellence in teaching puts us at the forefront of using innovative methods to improve students' and executives' learning and outcomes.

The next one hundred years

As we celebrate the first one hundred years of business education at Carolina, we are excited about the future. We have the privilege and obligation to shape people's lives through education. What does that mean for the next century?

Our community has long had a special sense of place. Today it extends beyond Chapel Hill, across state lines and national boundaries. Increasingly our sense of place is derived from our values rather than our geography. The Business School is no longer a building in Chapel Hill—it is a community of people bound by shared values and common goals.

This Centennial helps us look back at our roots, to understand and honor the vision and commitment of the people who built this school and contributed ideas, labor and financial support. Our students, alumni, faculty and staff have the opportunity to follow in their footsteps to create the kind of impact that will live on for another century.

We are stewards of an institution that has already changed the lives of thousands of people, directly and indirectly, over these many years. We want to deepen and broaden our impact on people's lives and the wider society.

We have changed dramatically in the last century, but what makes us special is ingrained in our very roots and so remains constant. Our story is one of community—rooted in our core values. It is one of tradition—a tradition of innovation. And it is one of ambition—to become the best business school of the 21st century.

Our first 100 years have prepared us to achieve that ambitious goal. Join us on our journey to define what's next. The best is yet to come.

Thank you for being part of our success,

Douglas A. Shackelford (BSBA '80)
Dean and Meade H. Willis Distinguished Professor of Taxation

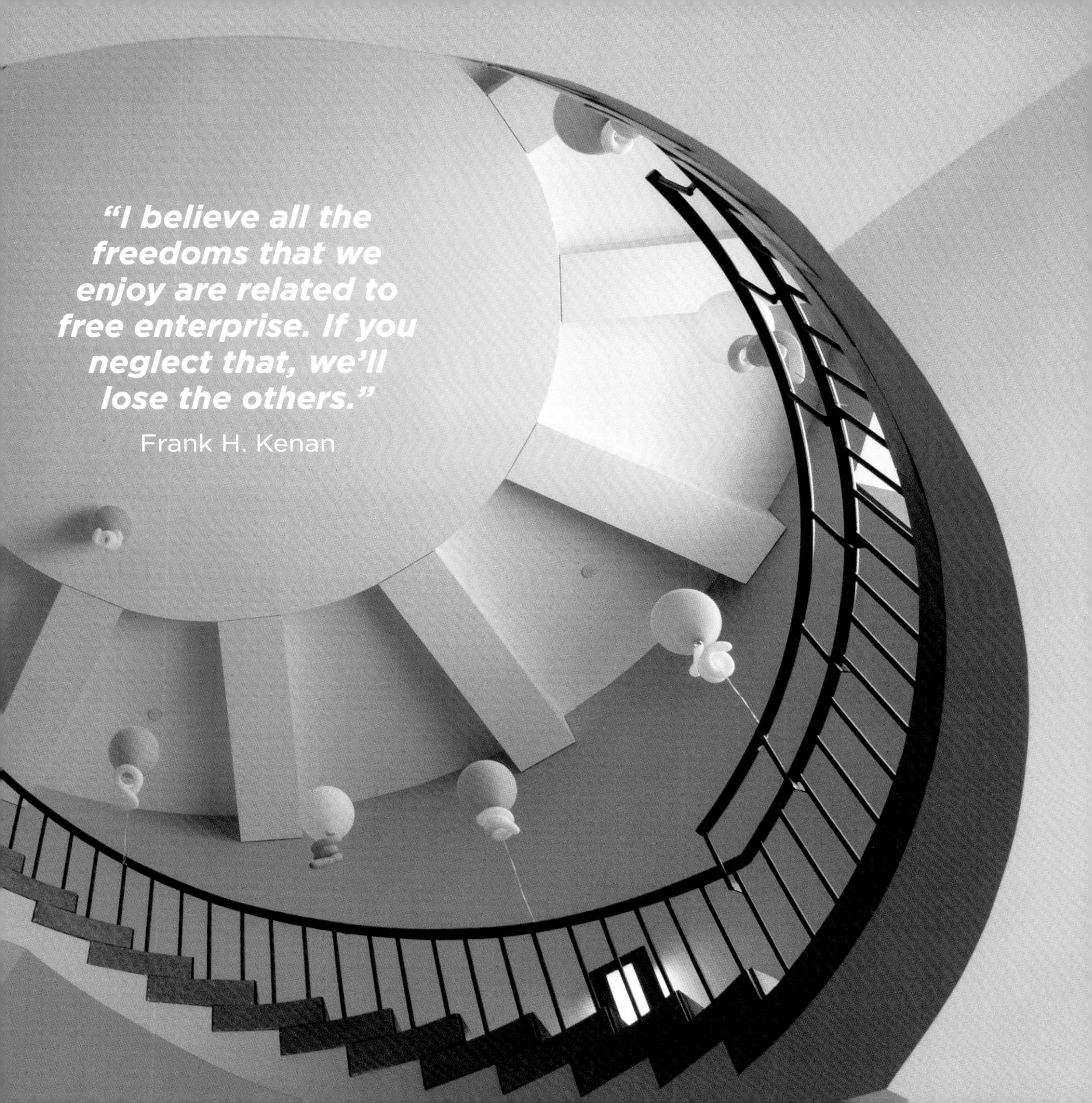
"I believe all the freedoms that we enjoy are related to free enterprise. If you neglect that, we'll lose the others."
Frank H. Kenan

South Building and the Old Well as they looked in the late 1910s (opposite) when the Department of Commerce was formed at the University of North Carolina at the behest of University President Edward Kidder Graham (above).

Open for Business in Chapel Hill

The United States had just declared war on Germany and entered the great World War in the spring of 1917, but fortunately the nation's exposure to the conflicts in Europe would last only eighteen months before armistice was signed on Nov. 11, 1918. Edward Kidder Graham was the forty-year-old president of the University of North Carolina in 1917, and he was patiently arranging his chess pieces for the eventual end of the war.

"Educationally, the decade that follows the war will be, I believe, the richest and most fruitful in the nation's history," Graham said.

One of Graham's priorities was to make the University more responsive to the opportunities and needs of North Carolina's agricultural and industrial bastions of tobacco, cotton, textiles and furniture. One evening in the summer of 1917, Graham was visited at home by a young man named Lenoir Chambers, who would later be a prominent newspaper editor in Norfolk, Virginia. Chambers had to leave after a short stay, and Graham asked, "What is your rush?"

"I'm taking a course in economics under a man named Carroll, and he doesn't seem to know anything but work," Chambers said. "I have to get ready for him."

"I'd like to see a man like that," Graham said. "Will you please ask him to come see me in my office tomorrow?"

The professor in question was Dudley Dewitt Carroll, who taught summer classes at Carolina in 1916 and '17. Carroll did indeed visit Graham, and the president outlined his plan for merging education and business at the Chapel Hill campus to Carroll, a native of Stokes County who was teaching economics full-time at Hunter College in New York City. Already the University had a Department of Economics and Finance, which had been established by President Francis Preston Venable in 1901, but Graham sensed an urgency for a program geared more toward the needs of a statewide business and industrial community that was expanding and was hungry for sharp leadership and cutting-edge ideas. He knew what was transpiring at other universities around the nation, that Joseph Wharton in 1881 had endowed the first collegiate business school at the University of Pennsylvania and that in 1916 seventeen institutions had bonded to form the American Association of Collegiate Business Schools, among them Pennsylvania, California, Chicago, Dartmouth, Northwestern and Harvard. Graham wanted Carolina to offer a business curriculum as well.

"About sixty percent of our students go into some kind of business," Graham said, "no matter what occupation they think they will follow when they graduate. I am looking for a man who can give them a liberal education and sound business principles in a four-year course. Would you be willing to undertake it?"

Carroll said he had one more year on his contract with Hunter College, but if Graham could wait, he would relish the opportunity.

"The job will be waiting," Graham said.

Graham never lived to see his vision consummated as he died in October 1918 from the massive flu pandemic that swept the globe and infected an estimated one-third of the world population. "The University lost her greatest leader, one whom she could ill afford to lose at this trying time," noted the *Yackety-Yack*, the UNC student yearbook. "But his spirit is with us yet and animates the heart of every man who had the good fortune to know him."

"The University has lost a virile young leader of the new era who brought the University he loved into a more intimate relationship with people all over the state," *The Daily Tar Heel* added. "At the same time, he placed it in the forefront as one of the universities of the nation alive to educational requirements of today."

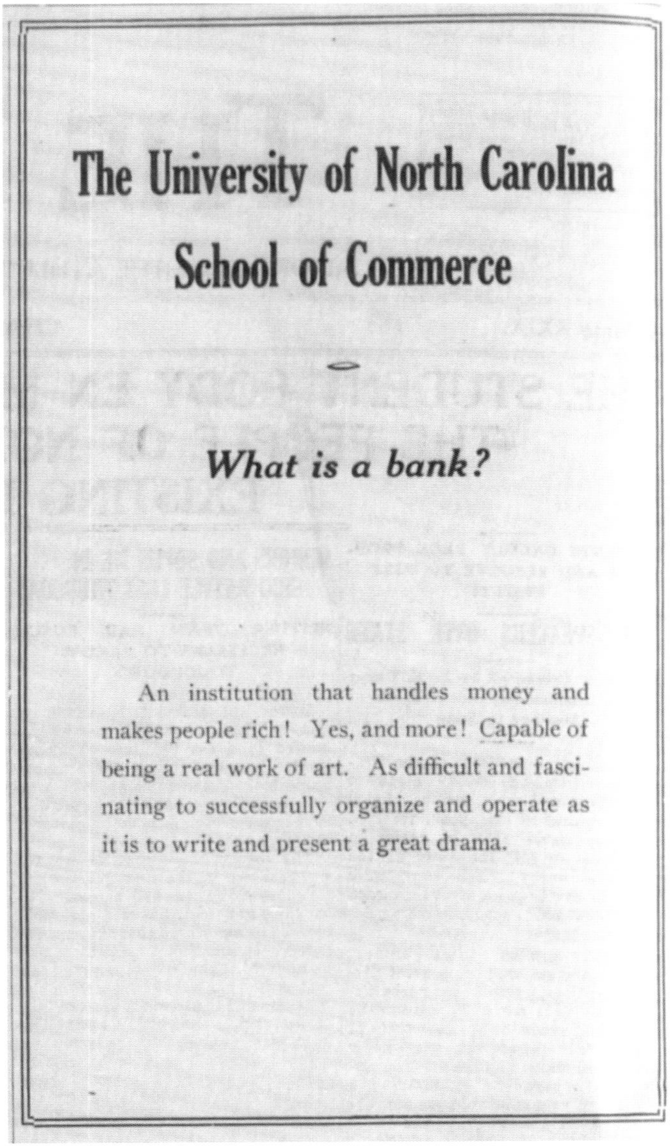

The University of North Carolina School of Commerce

What is a bank?

An institution that handles money and makes people rich! Yes, and more! Capable of being a real work of art. As difficult and fascinating to successfully organize and operate as it is to write and present a great drama.

PHILLIP HETTLEMAN
Goldsboro, N. C.

Age, 21; Weight, 160; Height, 5 feet 10 inches

Phi Society, Secretary (2), Reporting Clerk (2), Vice-President (3); Freshman Intra-Society Debate (1); Freshman Inter-Society Debate (2); Sophomore Inter-Society Debate (2); Associate Editor *Magazine* (2), Assistant Editor-in-Chief *Magazine* (3); Winner Preston Cup in Journalism (2); State Reconstruction Committee North Carolina Club; Circulation Manager *Tar Baby* (2); Associate Editor *Tar Heel* (2), Business Manager (3); German Club, Amphoterothen.

WELL, he came over here three years ago, and finding that board was high, books higher, and time dear, decided that four years was too much chronological tax for a diploma, so he has extracted one in three. Meanwhile he has fiddled around with the Tars—*Heel* and *Baby*—and the Carolina *Magazine*, usually in a business-like fashion, but occasionally in a literary effort, making no insignificant record for himself. Philip believes in work, spending very few idle hours.

WILLIAM DONALD CARMICHAEL
Durham, N. C.

Age, 20; Weight, 160; Height, 5 feet 9½ inches

Phi Society; Durham County Club; Glee Club (1); Minstrel (1); Secretary Class (2); Winner Preston Cup in Journalism (2); Varsity Basketball (1, 2, 3), Captain (3); Class Executive Committee (3); Writer Last Will and Testament (4); Editor-in-Chief *Tar Baby* (3); Secretary Pan-Hellenic Council (4); Leader Fall German Club Dance (4); Chief Commencement Ball Manager (4); German Club; Coop; Gimghoul.

Σ Υ; Κ Σ.

"BILLY" can play, play on the basketball court like an Hawaiian in water; can work, work for the *Tar Baby* like Horace Greeley weeding college men from "other horned cattle;" can write, write to the tune of the Journalistic Cup; can pull those provoking practical jokes—jokes that associate him and Will Ruffin with Tom Sawyer and Huck Finn; can make love, make love like Romeo subjected to a shower of moonbeams reflected by Juliet's radiant face while Hymen smiles in peace around the corner.

Phillip Hettleman and Billy Carmichael were in the first graduating class of the Department of Commerce, the former in later life endowing a professorship at Kenan-Flagler and the latter running the University's business affairs for many years.

Marvin Hendrix Stacy, a 1902 UNC grad and later a mathematics professor and dean of the University, was tabbed as the interim president, and on Jan. 14, 1919, the University Board of Trustees approved Stacy's recommendation for the formation of a School of Commerce. One week later, Stacy was dead, another victim of the flu. His successor, Harry Woodburn Chase, followed through on the idea for a business school and spoke upon its launch of the needs the new curriculum would meet.

"The business training of former times, acquired through the prolonged and wasteful process of simple experience, is inadequate to meet the changed conditions of the present day," Chase said. "The courses of study are designed to give a general grounding in the fundamentals of business and, at the same time, a definite and practical preparation for those who expect to engage in any of the great lines of industrial and commercial activity."

Carroll delivered a talk on campus in March 1919 on the importance of business education and cited the recent

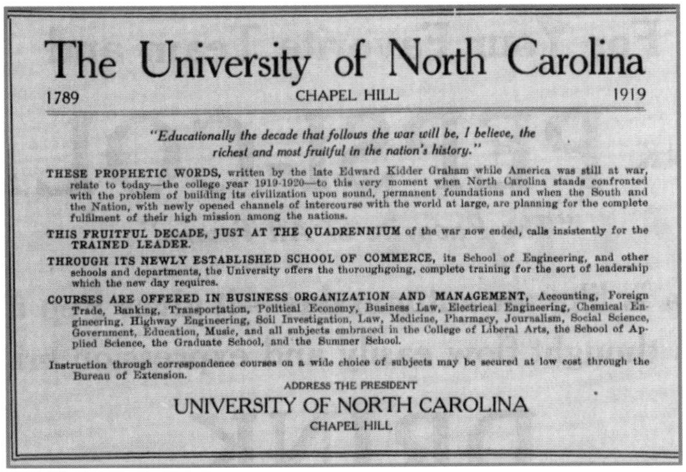

The University of North Carolina

1789 CHAPEL HILL 1919

"Educationally the decade that follows the war will be, I believe, the richest and most fruitful in the nation's history."

THESE PROPHETIC WORDS, written by the late Edward Kidder Graham while America was still at war, relate to today—the college year 1919-1920—to this very moment when North Carolina stands confronted with the problem of building its civilization upon sound, permanent foundations and when the South and the Nation, with newly opened channels of intercourse with the world at large, are planning for the complete fulfilment of their high mission among the nations.

THIS FRUITFUL DECADE, JUST AT THE QUADRENNIUM of the war now ended, calls insistently for the **TRAINED LEADER.**

THROUGH ITS NEWLY ESTABLISHED SCHOOL OF COMMERCE, its School of Engineering, and other schools and departments, the University offers the thoroughgoing, complete training for the sort of leadership which the new day requires.

COURSES ARE OFFERED IN BUSINESS ORGANIZATION AND MANAGEMENT, Accounting, Foreign Trade, Banking, Transportation, Political Economy, Business Law, Electrical Engineering, Chemical Engineering, Highway Engineering, Soil Investigation, Law, Medicine, Pharmacy, Journalism, Social Science, Government, Education, Music, and all subjects embraced in the College of Liberal Arts, the School of Applied Science, the Graduate School, and the Summer School.

Instruction through correspondence courses on a wide choice of subjects may be secured at low cost through the Bureau of Extension.

ADDRESS THE PRESIDENT

UNIVERSITY OF NORTH CAROLINA

CHAPEL HILL

Dudley Dewitt Carroll was the man charged with creating and supervising the first concentrated business curriculum at Chapel Hill, and the new department as it evolved beginning in 1919 published a series of ads in "The Daily Tar Heel" to tell its story.

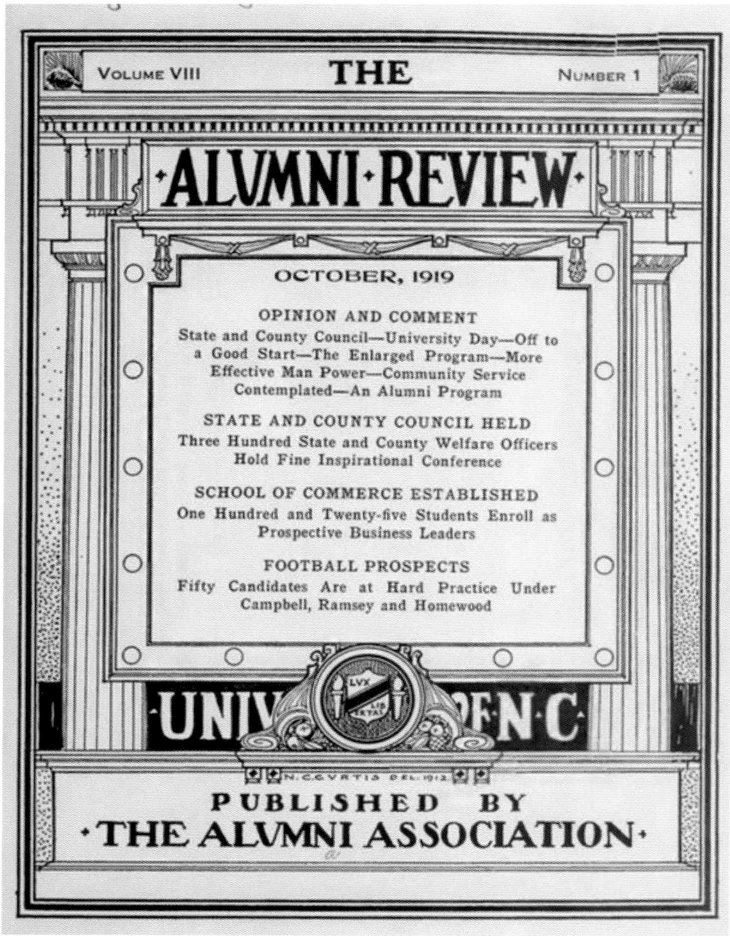

VOLUME VIII THE NUMBER 1

·ALUMNI·REVIEW·

OCTOBER, 1919

OPINION AND COMMENT
State and County Council—University Day—Off to a Good Start—The Enlarged Program—More Effective Man Power—Community Service Contemplated—An Alumni Program

STATE AND COUNTY COUNCIL HELD
Three Hundred State and County Welfare Officers Hold Fine Inspirational Conference

SCHOOL OF COMMERCE ESTABLISHED
One Hundred and Twenty-five Students Enroll as Prospective Business Leaders

FOOTBALL PROSPECTS
Fifty Candidates Are at Hard Practice Under Campbell, Ramsey and Homewood

UNIV N·C

PUBLISHED BY
·THE ALUMNI ASSOCIATION·

The cover of the "Alumni Review" in 1919 included a reference to the new School of Commerce, and over the 1920s the operation would grow along with the University; the first degrees were awarded in 1921.

challenges of World War I. He noted that Herbert Hoover, at the time the head of the U.S. Food Administration and the man in charge of the logistics and systems of moving perishables around the nation, said that fifty percent of fruits and vegetables produced in the United States were wasted before they could be consumed.

"A comprehensive study of business is no easy thing," Carroll said. "Unbusinesslike methods were used when we first entered the war, but it was soon discovered that experienced business men must be put in charge to produce the most efficient results."

The School of Commerce at the University opened its doors on Oct. 2, 1919 in two rooms in the Alumni Building. There were 125 students according to a story in *The Daily*

Tar Heel and three faculty members—Carroll as the dean of the school; Charles Lee Raper, head of the Department of Economics and dean of the graduate school; and Roy B. Cowin, an associate professor of accounting. Within one year, two more professors were added, both in the realm of rural economics: Eugene C. Branson as a full professor and Samuel H. Hobbs as an assistant professor. Among the staff additions the following year was J.W. Matherly, who had been at the University of Chicago and Georgetown College as a professor of economics. One of the goals of the fledgling operation was addressed with this passage from the 1919-20 course catalogue: "The forces and influences operating in this field are so far-reaching and baffling in their complexity that to master them requires both broad and intensive teaching."

Chapel Hill at the time had under 1,500 full-time residents, and the campus was concentrated in the grounds to the west and east of McCorkle Place, down to Cameron Avenue and the environs around South Building. The University had a total of 1,300 students register for classes in the fall of 1919, and they bought their books at A.A. Kluttz Co. University Bookstore, their film at Foister's Camera Shop, their prescriptions at Patterson Brothers Druggists and ate many meals at Gooch's Cafe.

Thomas Wolfe was editor of *The Daily Tar Heel* in October 1919 and his roommate, William D. Carmichael Jr., was one of first students enrolled in the new Department of Commerce. Carmichael, a sophomore that year, was also the captain of the basketball team, which posted a 7-9 record playing on its home court of Bynum Gymnasium (now Bynum Hall), a venue with the curious feature of having a running track suspended over the hardwood court. The Carolina football team reassembled for 1919 after a two-year hiatus because of the war—"sacrificed to military training," said the *Yackety-Yack*—and posted a 4-3-1 record, including a 6-0 win in the season finale over arch-rival Virginia. Trinity College, the forerunner to Duke University, did not yet field a football team.

Carroll wrote in a "Report of the Dean" that the school made remarkable progress in its first year given a number of handicaps—among them "inadequate quarters, lack of equipment, a dearth of qualified teachers, a considerable number of students attracted by mere curiosity to try out a new thing, and a lack of confidence on the part of the administration of the University itself that the school could be of any practical use in actual business operations."

The *Yackety-Yack* for the 1919-20 school year devoted four pages near the front of the book to business and industry in the state, displaying a collage of images representing all manner of enterprises from Manteo to Murphy—including the obvious ones but hitting also on ship building, quarrying, tanning, bark harvesting and cotton ginning. A passage of text referenced labor strife and "bloodshed" in Charlotte, Concord and Albemarle and suggested a "college-trained man" would provide the necessary skills to face new business challenges.

"This year in the life of North Carolina will stand for the ripening of our industrial life into the fullness of self-reliant young manhood feeling its strength and ready for new and larger tasks," the *Yack* offered. ".... As it has responded in times past, the University would prepare itself to advance to meet this new call for a trained and consecrated leadership in the field of industry."

One issue of the *Carolina Alumni Review* in 1920 said the school was borne "out of the demands of the people of the state for more and better business training, more intense, more comprehensive acquaintance with the keen business world of present-day industrialism." *The Daily Tar Heel* added that the initiative evolved from the "desire to serve the special needs resulting from the phenomenal industrial growth in the South in recent years." By September 1920, the department had 140 registered students among upperclassmen, and thirty percent of incoming freshmen were business majors. "The results thus far are extremely

BINGHAM HALL

School of Commerce

The School of Commerce was established in September, 1919. It was developed in response to the need of a large number of students who are going into business and who can spend at most only four years in college. The problem was to determine the best use which could be made of this four year period. The two basic requirements of happy and successful living in the modern world demanded that a part of the course should be devoted to the study of business principles and practices. On the other hand, it was equally clear that competence in making a living would be useless unless it were attended by an enlarged capacity to enjoy life. The four year course of study is therefore about equally divided between subjects which expand outlook, and lay a basis for intelligent citizenship and subjects which develop understanding and mastery of modern business principles and procedures.

Dean Dudley DeWitt Carroll, M.A.

D.D. Carroll, Dean.

DEPARTMENT OF ECONOMICS AND COMMERCE

The "Yackety-Yack" devoted one page to each key school or department in the early days; this is from 1933.

encouraging," noted *The Daily Tar Heel.*

The launch of the new school wasn't met with universal support, however.

One high-ranking dean thought a business program would be too easy and drag down the standards of the University.

"Don't you worry one bit about that," Dean Carroll responded. "We are going to make our courses tough, and nobody looking for crips will be coming to us."

The first two years of study were designed to be broad and general before a commerce major began in his third year focusing on courses in accounting, business organization, money and banking, insurance, transportation, corporate finance, commercial law, labor problems, rural economics, practical French and Spanish, advanced English composition, technical writing and psychology.

Included in the fourth year were theories of economic reform, advanced accounting, industrial management, public finance, foreign trade, international law, markets and marketing, salesmanship and sales management, advanced commercial and industrial geography, Latin American history, social psychology and ethics.

Students would spend the summer between their junior and senior years in an internship, ideally one matching their eventual career interest. The University already had an established relationship of sending interns to National City Bank of New York, and this continued under the auspices of the School of Commerce.

The Daily Tar Heel in February 1920 noted that Carroll was working to set up a series of eight lectures for the spring from "representative businessmen of the state and the nation." The story noted the lecture series launch had been delayed "because of the influenza situation." One such lecture occurred in March when J.E. Latham of Greensboro spoke on the subject of "Merchandising in Cotton." Other lectures were arranged with representatives of the Tariff Commission, Federal Trade Commission and Census Bureau.

A series of ads promoting the new business curriculum ran in 1920 in *The Daily Tar Heel* under a headline for The University of North Carolina School of Commerce.

One tactic appealed to the idea that successful businesses trickle down and have a positive effect on other areas of University life:

"Did you ever stop to think that the only possible source of funds for a more adequate provision for better roads, better schools and a larger and better equipped University must be the surplus product of North Carolina's industries? Then why not get ready to help expand these industries and make them more efficient?"

Another approach at a University geared at the time toward arts and the humanities drew a parallel between running a bank and staging a play:

"What is a bank? An institution that handles money and makes people rich! Yes, and more! Capable of being a real work of art. As difficult and fascinating to successfully organize and operate as it is to write and present a great drama."

And yet another message appealed to the simple desire to make money and, yes, get rich.

"What about the price of cotton? Could it have been foreseen? If so, some person could have served his section well, and incidentally made himself a fortune. If you are interested in such vital scientific problems, why not study them?"

Just two years into the program, Carroll noted a sixty-percent increase in business enrollment from year one to year two and told his superiors he needed more space, certainly for classrooms and a library but also for an "industrial museum" where the state's rapid industrial revolution could be chronicled; he also wanted space for a student-run bank that would provide practical training for advanced banking classes.

The first degrees of Bachelor of Science in Commerce were awarded in 1921. Twelve students received them, and it's appropriate that one of them would later play a key role in the University's development. Billy Carmichael was born in Durham and after graduating from Chapel Hill moved to New York City, where he first worked in advertising and later founded his own brokerage firm, Carmichael and Carson. Carmichael returned to Chapel Hill in 1940 to serve as vice president and financial officer for the consolidated University and, over the next two decades, played a significant role in raising money for an expanded medical school, a new teaching hospital and what would become a public broadcasting system. He died in 1961 and, four years later, the new basketball arena for Coach Dean Smith's team would be named in his honor.

Another of the graduates in that 1921 class of business majors was Phillip Hettleman, who followed a financial career in New York City and during the 1980s endowed the Hettleman Professorship in the Business School. The first holder of this chair was Richard I. Levin.

Matherly spoke in a 1922 lecture of the growing

appreciation for business education: "Business today is unquestionably a profession and is being run upon a scientific basis—we need scientific methods in business as in chemistry or medicine; and we propose to teach the rules of the game in the School of Commerce and to inculcate the scientific principles of business."

Matherly cited a Danish immigrant living in Iowa who, two years before, had conceived the idea of covering small bricks of ice cream with melted chocolate and that in two short years the Eskimo Pie had "taken the country by storm." Matherly said that inventor Kent Nelson was "penniless ninety days ago and at present is making over $6,000 per day with his new pie industry." Matherly said such an achievement is an indication of the many possibilities for "trained men in business."

The neophyte operation soon outgrew its tight environment in Alumni Hall and was the beneficiary of an ambitious new building campaign that started in 1921 and addressed the University's post-war growth. The Board of Trustees asked the North Carolina Legislature for funds to build three classroom buildings, five dormitories and several houses for members of the faculty. A building committee was appointed to oversee the $1.5 million appropriation, and the renowned New York firm of McKim, Mead and White was retained as consulting architect. The architects' master plan included preserving a mall of open space south of South Building—which did in fact happen and is the space known today as Polk Place—and their first buildings were a cluster of three that would sit in a court to the east of the mall. A new home for the UNC School of Law that would be named Manning Hall sat at the head of the court, flanked by Saunders Hall to the north and Murphey Hall to the south. The latter two opened in 1922, and *The Daily Tar Heel* in October 1922 reported the school was in "new headquarters" on the second floor of Saunders Hall and had a registration of about four hundred for the fall session.

****

Carroll & Commerce Perfect Fits

Times were good for the School of Commerce in its first decade and it had the perfect man to lead it from infancy to maturity during the healthy economic climate of the Roaring Twenties.

Dudley Dewitt Carroll was born on a farm in Stokes County, North Carolina, on July 28, 1885, the fourth of eleven children. A profile on Carroll in a 1955 volume on the Kenan Professorships edited by A.C. Howell, secretary of the faculty at UNC, noted the values instilled in him from an early age from his rural upbringing: "His youth was spent in an atmosphere common to most rural communities, made up of hard physical labor, simple living facilities, limited educational opportunities, but also close family life, strong community cohesion and uncompromising training in integrity and devotion to duty."

He attended Guilford College and earned his degree in 1907 and then spent five years as an instructor in history and economics and the last two years as dean of the college. He moved to New York City for three years of graduate work, earning a master's degree in 1916 at Columbia and beginning a two-year assignment as assistant professor of economics at Hunter College. He was thirty-three years old in 1918 when he was asked by President Graham to run a new Department of Commerce at Carolina.

Carroll would imbue the young school, its students and faculty with a standard of ethics and broad view beyond the dollar signs of profit that would endure over its first century. He wrote in a passage for the 1934 *Yack*: "In the attempt to give the student a practical basis for his life, care is taken that he shall not lose sight of the social obligations or his cultural needs." The yearbook six years later described Carroll as an "earnest thinker, sundown golfer, and vigorous participant in the business and civic life of Chapel Hill." In

FACULTY OF COMMERCE SCHOOL

First Row, Left to Right—SHERRILL, CARROLL, LEAR, EVANS, SPRUILL, BLAINE.
Second Row, Left to Right—BUCHANAN, WOLF, HEER, WOOSLEY, BERNSTEIN, PEACOCK, ANSON.
Third Row, Left to Right—ANDERSON, HOBBS, COWDEN, WINSLOW, LIMMERMANN, TAYLOR, DONOVAN, KUHLMAN, BUNTING.

The faculty in 1938 outside Bingham Hall with Dean Carroll front row, second from left.

November 1919, he spoke during a Red Cross fundraising drive on the wonders of that humanitarian organization, saying "for the negligible sum of one dollar the privilege of participating in a world movement for the alleviation of suffering could be obtained." He insisted on students learning at least one foreign language because of the "lessening to a great degree of international barriers and distances."

As part of a series of lay lectures at the Chapel of the Cross Episcopal parish on Franklin Street in December 1925, Carroll, a devout Quaker, spoke on "Religion and Business." He cited the Biblical story of Judas Iscariot in making one point, noting that Judas was "the business manager of the affairs of his Lord." When he betrayed Christ for thirty pieces of silver, Carroll said, he was letting the "means in life get between himself and the ultimate end or goal as people often do today.

"Many people today are doing just the thing that Judas did," Carroll said. "They are selling their Lord, when they think they are only making a harmless and perhaps advantageous business deal. However, business and religion are easily reconciled. The two should be a help to each other. Religion of the right sort tries to help the business leader create a better economic order, and business of the right sort tries to help spread the great truths of religion. The greatest thing in life is to strive to keep the means in life from getting between us and the ultimate goal."

Carroll sought to expand his personal horizons and spread the University of North Carolina name by spending eight months from October 1924 through the following May traveling across Europe on the Kenan Traveling Professorship. He visited England (spending time at the London School of Economics), France, Italy,

Czechoslovakia, Austria and Germany. He wrote home to colleagues saying he "is having a wonderful time hobnobbing with European notables," according to *The Daily Tar Heel*, and another newspaper account mentioned etchings and rare manuscripts he bought for the School of Commerce. "There is doubtless some very valuable and excellent material on European social and economic problems stored away in the numerous trunks and boxes Dean Carroll brought back to this country with him," the newspaper reported.

He consistently stressed the two-fold mandates of a college education—to prepare oneself to make a living and to learn how to enjoy the cultural side of life. To civic and campus groups he warned against the tendency to judge a man by his income and not developing the ability to relax. The ultimate aim of life, he said, wasn't the accumulation of wealth but "the capacity to enjoy and appreciate the beauty and culture of the world."

Carroll was an avid baseball fan and was known by his faculty to never schedule a meeting during a Tar Heel baseball game. Bingham Hall, which was built for the Department of Commerce and opened in 1929, sat beside Emerson Field, the original baseball diamond, and Carroll would slip out of his office on spring afternoons to catch the final innings of home games. His house was located on Laurel Hill Road near the first tee of the old Chapel Hill Country Club (an area today occupied by the Outdoor Education Center and Cone Tennis Complex), and Carroll played a combination game of golf and track that exhausted his opponents.

"He stroked and literally ran after the white ball from the first tee to the ninth green," one colleague said upon his death in 1971. "Playing and keeping up with him was a challenge even to his youngest companions."

He regularly joined other Chapel Hill dads to lead a group of youngsters not yet of Boy Scout age on regular hikes, campus tours and sports outings on Saturday mornings. One *Daily Tar Heel* account of the group's activities cited Carroll's "drawling voice, pleasing to the ear, and infinitely slow."

Carroll served three decades as chairman of

the Orange County Building and Loan Association and also a stint as chairman of the Alcoholic Beverage Control Board of Orange County. A strict teetotaler, Carroll managed the board to fight alcohol abuse and ensure that profits from the system were channeled to public schools.

He was a member of a small but active Quaker community in Chapel Hill that had, as part of its agenda, a humanitarian concern for the Jews being persecuted in Germany in the 1930s and into World War II. Carroll, Economics Professor Edward Bernstein and University President Dr. Frank Porter Graham were welcoming and helped Jewish refugees settle in Chapel Hill. One, it was the right thing to do. And two, it was good business.

"As a Southerner I feel the South has suffered because it has not been in the tide of immigration," Carroll said. "Fine immigrants from Europe have avoided the South because of industrial and racial problems, and this has caused a stagnation in the South's economy. An infusion of new blood would be one of the greatest blessings for the South."

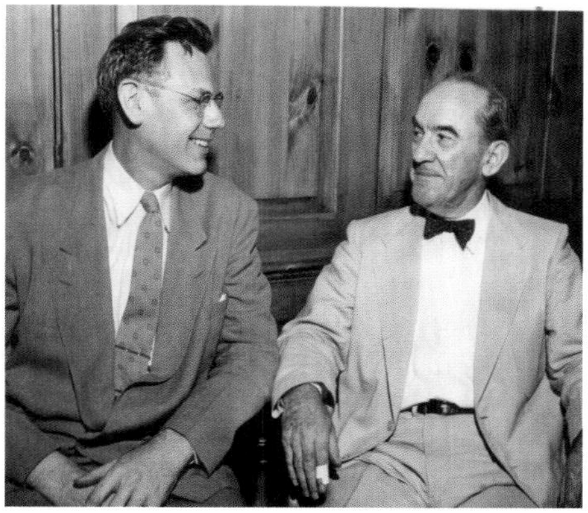

Deans Thomas Carroll (L) and Dudley Carroll in the early 1950s and the brand new Gardner, Carroll and Hanes Halls (opposite).

One of the immigrants that Carroll helped find a home in the South was a Viennese candy maker named Edward Danziger, who moved to Chapel Hill in 1939 and opened Danziger's Old World Candy Shop at 155 Franklin Street, the location that had been Gooch's Cafe. "Papa D," as he was known, sold Viennese coffee and candy and in time turned it into Danziger's Old World Restaurant, modeled after an Austrian tavern. His son Ted dug out the basement under the restaurant and conceived another restaurant with a European flair. The Ram's Head Rathskeller would become a Chapel Hill institution along with other Danziger eateries such as the Ranch House, Villa Teo and Zoom Zoom.

"That story alone tells me that I know who is the best dean we've ever had at the school," says Douglas A. Shackelford (BSBA '80), Kenan-Flagler dean since 2014 and Meade H. Willis Distinguished Professor of Taxation. "We might have had another dean who raised more money. We might have another dean that started a cutting-edge program. But Dean Carroll was fighting *genocide*."

So highly regarded was Carroll among his fellow faculty members that in 1955 he was elected chairman of the faculty, the highest honor a professor at Carolina could receive. He was also named Kenan Professor of Economics that year. He was described in one *Daily Tar Heel* missive as "a hard-boiled dean" and the paper observed that the Department of Commerce was "a mighty tough school for those seeking crips."

Robert B. House, chancellor of the University from 1945-57, remembered Carroll respectfully and fondly, noting Carroll's perfectionism and task-masker mentality.

"While under his discipline, students fretted," House said. "But under the harsher discipline of successful mature life, they came to love him for the sternness they thought in youth they hated.

"Some men seem to be slaves of duty. Dudley Carroll hastened to it like a war-horse at the sound of a trumpet."

****

The Tillman Tour

ROLLIE TILLMAN

Rollie Tillman poses in front of the Kenan Center during construction in the mid-1980s; opposite, Kenan-Flagler grad Jeff Tucker was among the many who thrived in Tillman's classes and years later created the Rollie Tillman Jr. Development Fund.

The ultimate business laboratory just might well be the campus at the University of North Carolina. Rollie Tillman Jr., longtime professor and Kenan-Flagler Business School administrator, thought so and often began his talks introducing the school to new students, faculty and other groups by pointing to the names on streets and buildings around Chapel Hill.

"We begin with an entrepreneur and end with a cluster of entrepreneurs," Tillman liked to say. "A tour of this campus is a tour of business and industrial accomplishment in North Carolina."

Tillman would begin by showing a slide of Franklin Street and a street sign with the word *Franklin*—named for Ben Franklin.

"Ben Franklin was among the colonies' quintessential entrepreneurs," Tillman said. "Newspapers, magazines, insurance companies, patents on bifocals, fireplaces, insane experiments with lightning, capped off by a stint as a venture capitalist in France raising funds for that upstart called 'The United States of America.'"

His tour would continue with an image of the Morehead Planetarium, a gift from UNC graduate and chemist John Motley Morehead III (1891), who helped found Union Carbide Company. Then Tillman would show an image of Hill Hall, the current headquarters for the Department of Music that, when it opened in 1912, was Carnegie Library, built with funds from the steel fortune of Andrew Carnegie.

There would be references to Carmichael Auditorium, named for an early Business School graduate, William D. Carmichael Jr., who went to Wall Street and returned in the mid-1900s to run the University's business affairs .... to Skipper Bowles Drive, named for the investment banker and businessman who led the fund-raising drive to build the basketball arena named for Coach Dean Smith .... The Lineberger Cancer Center, constructed from the generosity of the Gaston County family so prominent in the state's textile industry dating back to the mid-1800s.

And then Tillman would tie it up by getting to South Campus with a synopsis of Henry Flagler, William R.

Kenan Jr. and Frank Kenan—whose names adorn the Business School at Carolina and who each were remarkably successful in business.

"That was such an inspiring speech Rollie used to give," says Kenan-Flagler professor David Ravenscraft. "It was amazing. It was just as good the tenth time you heard it as the first."

"His orientation speech was wildly entertaining because he was such a great storyteller," adds Jeff Tucker, a 2000 MBA graduate.

Once Tillman gave his talk to a group of alumni and friends in Charlotte and a woman came up afterward and said, "Dr. Tillman, I teared up listening to your talk, it was so good," she said. "And I went to *Clemson*."

Tillman graduated from Carolina with a business degree in 1955, then went to Harvard for his MBA and PhD degrees. He returned to Carolina as an assistant professor in business administration, soon became a full professor and later ran the MBA and Executive Development programs and was the founding director for Frank Hawkins Kenan Institute of Private Enterprise. He retired in 2003 and over more than four decades left an indelible mark on countless students.

"Rollie has an inquisitive mind, his judgment is solid, and he's interested in solving problems and helping folks," said Erskine Bowles, a 1967 Kenan-Flagler graduate and later a prominent investment banker and president of the University of North Carolina System. "He's all about rolling his sleeves up, making a difference and making people more efficient."

Tucker, managing director with Century Bridge Capital, a private equity firm based in Beijing, China, and Dallas, Texas, developed a close relationship with Tillman and fondly remembers the classes he took under Tillman.

"Those who took him really loved him," Tucker says. "Some professors make your blood pressure rise before you get to the classroom. Then there are those you just look forward to going to class and you know you'll walk away with something. It will be interesting and it will be a safe place to be. He was that kind of professor."

Tillman grew up in Florida and followed a cousin to Chapel Hill in the early 1950s. He was happy to be back at Carolina after his graduate work at Harvard but was getting some pressure from his family to return to Florida and help tend to some family business interests there.

"He was struggling with that because he had fallen in love with Chapel Hill," Tucker says, recounting conversations with Tillman. "At some point, his father came to visit, and they spent three or four days together and wound up sitting somewhere on campus. His father turned to him and said, 'Rollie, this place is good for you.' In telling the story, Rollie smiled like the weight lifted off his shoulders. He knew then it was okay.

"Like so many people who come for undergrad or graduate school, they ***get*** that connection," Tucker says. "I always felt this place was good for me, too. I think of that because of Rollie's story."

Maturity Through Mid-1900s

Dean Carroll's longevity was remarkable as he nurtured business education at Carolina from infancy to adolescence and into maturity, with the major themes of the Roaring Twenties, the Depression and World War II impacting the University and all its departments and schools. By 1927 the School of Commerce had mushroomed to five times its original size in less than a decade and had an enrollment of 552 and staff of thirty. It also had its first women students, among them Virginia Harrison Maloney (a 1934 graduate) and Eliza Rose Bagby ('37).

Business education had become important enough at the University by this time that it warranted a new building all of its own—Bingham Hall, which opened in the spring of 1929. The three-story building was constructed of red brick with limestone trim, matching the other new buildings along Polk Place as the campus crept ever southward. The structure cost $160,000 and was named for Colonel Robert Bingham, who received his degree from the University in 1857 and later became a noted educator as head of a prep school in Asheville bearing his name.

The Great Depression of the first half of the 1930s provided the Business School and its Rural Economics faculty a veritable Petri dish in the heart of an agricultural and industrial based state to study the issues that led to such painful economic times. Half of the total population of the state by 1930 still lived on working farms, and the overproduction of cotton and tobacco led to dwindling prices going into the Depression. The introduction of new man-made materials such as rayon and increased competition from foreign textile mills ravaged the cotton market as well, and technological advances made during World War I resulted in mass production of new labor-saving machines that cut into the need for a strong work force.

"Many of our North Carolina farmers are desperately poor, live in wretched houses, and are scantily provided with even the necessities of life," one UNC sociologist wrote in 1929.

Carroll announced in 1933 that a new elective for upperclassmen called Economics 96 would be taught, offering an introduction and examination of the National Recovery Administration launched by President Franklin D. Roosevelt to stimulate business recovery in the United States.

The next major developments in the school's evolution occurred in the mid-1940s, just as World War II was ending and soon after as the University grappled with the enormous influx of students studying under the G.I. Bill in the post-war resurrection of the American economy.

The North Carolina Business Foundation was created in 1946 by some 250 business and political leaders from across the state to act as a fundraising arm to support the school. Its purpose, said its founding statement, was to "aid and promote, by financial assistance and otherwise, all types of education, service and research for business and industry at or through the School of Commerce and other departments at the University." One of the leaders was Robert M. Hanes, a 1912 Carolina graduate and the president of Wachovia Bank; Hanes served two years as foundation president when it was conceived.

It was important, these scions of the statewide business community believed, to keep local-grown talent at home.

"Too many North Carolina boys have gone to northern schools for business education and were persuaded by northern institutions to take positions outside our state," said the founding statement. "We have in this manner lost some of our best business leaders." Consequently, another of the objectives of the Business Foundation was to see the school eventually develop an MBA Program.

The school also during this period fine-tuned its mission

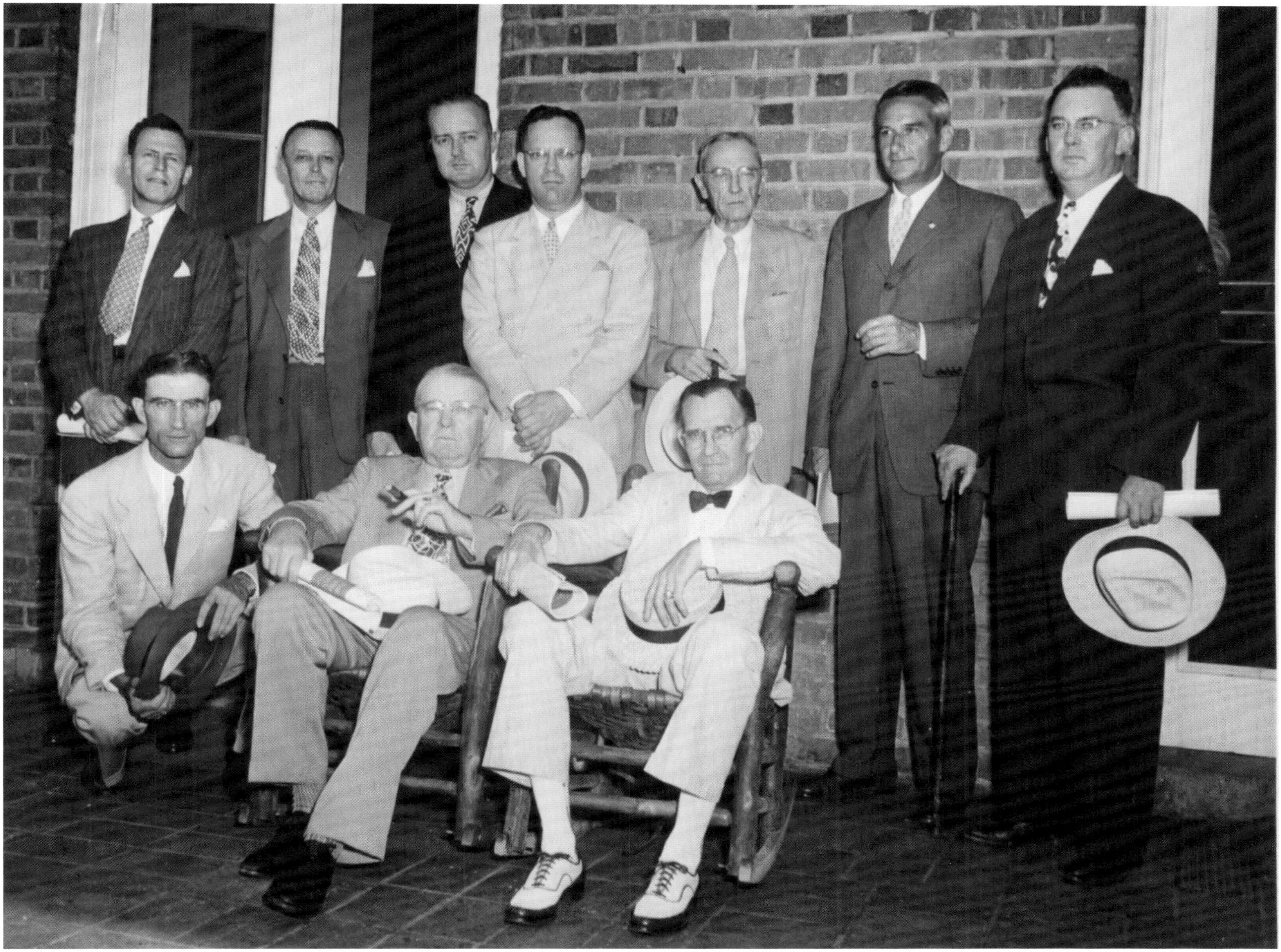

A group of Durham businessmen attending the inaugural meeting of the Business Foundation gather outside the Carolina Inn in 1946. Among them is David St. Pierre DuBose (back row, second from right), whose Meadowmont home would years later be donated to the University and then to Kenan-Flagler.

As business machines evolved through the mid-1900s, the School of Business Administration was diligent about keeping up and having students master their applications.

to produce well-rounded graduates who could handle a myriad of challenges and skills in their working lives.

"The main emphasis in education is to shift away from doing a 'thing,'" said Associate Dean Robert S. George in 1946. "We live in a dynamic economy. The way we do a thing today may be discarded tomorrow; thus our new program is designed to help students meet these changes and make more rational decisions in such a highly dynamic environment."

The nation was on the cusp of entering the Second World War in 1940, but already Carroll was sending warning flags to University administrators that the School of Commerce had, in just over one decade, outgrown Bingham Hall. Carroll said the school would have to cut enrollment if it didn't have bigger quarters and noted that enrollment had doubled over the decade. The building accommodated four hundred commerce majors plus many economics majors. It had nine classrooms, one seminar room, three laboratories and a small auditorium to seat 150 students. Seven professors were required to use one classroom between them.

But it took nearly another decade for Carroll to get what he wanted. The Board of Trustees building committee voted unanimously in August 1949 to ask the state legislature to appropriate $1.98 million for a new business complex, formed as a three-building court on the west side of Polk Place. The buildings were designed to match the opposite court of Manning-Saunders-Murphey halls that opened three decades earlier, with administration, faculty offices, a large auditorium, seminar rooms and lounges contained in the center structure with classrooms and laboratories mainly located in the two wing buildings.

"The possibility that the three separate buildings might hinder the efficient operating of the School of Commerce was carefully investigated, and all facts obtained gave the green light to the proposal," noted a *Daily Tar Heel* story.

That approval would prove to be Carroll's crowning

Dean Carroll Stresses Need For New Commerce Building

To Cut Enrollment If Space Not Given

By Orville Campbell

"Requirements to enter the school of commerce have already been increased, and we will have to limit registration in the future unless we get a larger building," Dean D. D. Carroll, head of the school of commerce, stated yesterday in a special TAR HEEL interview.

Pointing out that enrollment in the commerce school has more than doubled in the past ten years, Dean Carroll gave several specific examples showing the need of the proposed new commerce building that is included in the new university budget.

The present commerce building, Bingham hall as it is commonly known, accommodates over 400 commerce students and many economic majors. The building has but nine classrooms, one seminar room, three laboratories, one machine room, and a small auditorium or large lecture room that will seat 150 students.

The building is so crowded that seven

See COMMERCE, page 4.

Westminster Choir Scheduled

The Westminster Choir, of Princeton, N. J., which is scheduled to appear in concert here on March 1 under the auspices of the Carolina Playmakers, will broadcast at 10 o'clock tonight with the National Broadcasting Company Symphony orchestra under the direction of Arturo Toscanini.

The radio performance Saturday evening, which will include Verdi's "Te Deum" and "Requiem," is the first in a series of choral performances for which Toscanini has selected the Westminster Choir. Second in the series will be a program on Saturday, December 28.

Following the appearance with Toscanini on the 28th, the Choir will begin their southern tour to Havana, Cuba, which will include an appearance here. The Choir has just returned from a successful fall tour, which included a performance with the Rochester Symphony orchestra, of Rochester, N. Y., under the direction of Jose Iturbi.

This story in "The Daily Tar Heel" in November 1940 reported of Dean Carroll's desire for more space for the Business School.

achievement as he planned to step down in 1950 after three decades running the school to focus on teaching and research. The head building would be named in his honor, with the two wing buildings named for Robert M. Hanes, a 1912 Carolina graduate from Winston-Salem and the president of Wachovia Bank, and O. Max Gardner, the former governor and an ardent supporter of the University.

Construction hit a snag in January 1951 as bricklayers went on strike for a raise of twenty-five cents per hour; two months later, they were back at work after getting a boost of twelve cents. A *Daily Tar Heel* story in January 1952 said construction on the new buildings had been affected by shortages in steel and limestone as well as those strikes in 1951. It was a busy period of University expansion; also under construction was University Hospital, due to open in May, with a dental wing and nurse dormitories to follow in September. The north wing of the School of Medicine was to be open in one year. A new addition to the library was also under construction, and plans were about to commence on an expansion of the Venable Hall chemistry building.

Helping to get this new complex funded and built was the first major accomplishment of the Business Foundation. Dr. Rollie Tillman Jr., who served as director of the MBA Program and later the founding director of the Frank Hawkins Kenan Institute of Private Enterprise, frequently delivered talks on the evolution of business education at Chapel Hill and routinely applauded the work of the Business Foundation in key junctures.

"There is no way to calculate the impact of that foundation on scholarship funds, faculty salary supplements, research staffing, technology enhancements, all aspects of the school," Tillman said. "As a result of their leadership, and just plain clout, the Business School got a new home."

While construction continued, the University welcomed a dean and initiated several important new programs, one of the first being to rename the operation to the School of Business Administration. Its new dean was Thomas Henry Carroll (no relation to Dudley Carroll), who took over in September 1950 and came from a similar position at Syracuse University. Carroll was California born and educated (Cal-Berkeley 1934) and was assistant dean at Harvard prior to World War II service, and his first exposure to Chapel Hill was a war-time visit as a Navy officer to the Navy Pre-Flight Training Program stationed on the UNC campus. Dr. John Woosley, head of the search committee, said Carroll was a man "with a dynamic personality and a genial and charming manner."

The Syracuse student newspaper, *The Daily Orange*, lamented his departure: "It was Dean Carroll who took over the position four years ago at the age of thirty-one and transformed the college from one of the weakest to one of the strongest in the country. And business administration is still growing, thanks to the dynamic leadership of the lanky dean. Carroll perfectly typifies the progressive spirit of the young administrators found in a university which is moving forward. His decision to leave hurts."

Carroll was quick to launch important new initiatives in the School of Business Administration. With Professor Gerald Barrett taking the leadership reins, a one-year Master of Business Administration program was launched in January 1952. The first graduate was Lynn Crawley; Taketo "Mike" Furuhata was the first international graduate in 1955, and Elizabeth Moore was the first woman in 1957.

"The economic, political and social forces of our time create ever increasing demands upon all business executives for mature and far-sighted policy decisions," Carroll said upon the program's launch. The master's curriculum, Carroll noted, would "target those with degrees in liberal arts or engineering and those who majored in business but want additional education as preparation for increased administrative responsibility."

A new initiative known as the Executive Program was launched in October 1953 upon the school's moving into its new buildings. It was directed by Dr. Willard J. Graham, a professor of accounting who came to Chapel Hill a year earlier from the University of Chicago, where he directed a similar program for ten years. "We stole a great professor away from the University of Chicago," Tillman used to say in his student orientation talks.

Over a period of six months, twenty-five North Carolina business executives would assemble in Chapel Hill on twelve alternate weekends for an intensive course of classroom study and discussion, after which spend a full week in residence study.

"This program is not a series of weekend conferences," Graham said. "It is a tough, work-and-study program that will demand about 250 hours of homework—such as reading, studying, solving cases and problems and writing reports—in addition to about 135 hours in class."

"They called it 'spaced learning,'" Tillman said during a 1990s talk, "and we still employ it in Executive Education. People come for a week and then they go home for a month and they come back and forth and apply what they've learned. That was an important day in our development because it began to bring more and more prospects for the hiring of our students. There was a wonderful synergy between Executive Education and the placement of students. Businessmen came to Chapel Hill and they began to trust the kind of education that our students were getting."

The tuition of $1,000 would be paid by the businessman's employer, and when in Chapel Hill they would stay in The Carolina Inn. "Special arrangements have been made to serve meals in a private dining room (even on football weekends!)," noted a *Daily Tar Heel* missive.

Executive Education would be an important part of the school's ability to augment its revenue stream over the coming decades. Professor Robert Headen (MBA 1960) joined the faculty in 1967, and his skills at combining financial analysis with marketing strategy planning resulted in his being a major contributor to the school's Executive Education programs, which in the 1970s were housed in the basement of Carroll Hall, with faculty offices and classrooms on the upper floors. As he headed downstairs to teach in a management program, he liked to point out to junior colleagues that his executive courses generated income for the school to be able to give junior colleagues summer research support—and pay for everything else that was "overhead."

Carroll served as dean for just three years. The thirty-nine-year-old, one of the youngest deans in American business education, resigned in November 1953 to become vice president of the Ford Foundation in New York City, effective the following summer. He stayed in that position for six years before becoming president at George Washington University in the nation's capital. A *New York Times* notice of his death from a heart attack in 1964 at the young age of fifty spoke of the type of leader and educator Carolina had employed in an earlier time: "He was considered a new type of university president in this city—a young and attractive intellectual with the aplomb of a diplomat, a broad academic and administrative background and thorough fundraising and financial experience."

One assumes that Carroll looked fondly on his short stint in Chapel Hill in 1957 when the Ford Foundation announced a $60,000 grant for a five-year research program at UNC. The funds were to be used for research leaves-of-absence for faculty in lieu of summer-school teaching, operation of faculty research seminars and employment of clerical assistants and provision of computing assistance.

Arch Richard Dooley, a faculty member since 1950 and assistant dean for two years, was elevated in July 1954 to the deanship, but his appointment would not start until September 1955 as he was already committed to a year as a visiting professor at Harvard Business School. Longtime UNC Professor Richard J.M. Hobbs was named interim dean for fifteen months.

Dooley was a native of Oklahoma City with an undergraduate degree from Yale and an MBA from Harvard, and apparently he enjoyed his year back in Cambridge and was made a sweet enough offer to remain there and decline the Carolina deanship. It turned out to be a long-term move for Dooley, who spent thirty-seven years on the Harvard faculty.

Hobbs had been at Chapel Hill since 1929, his background implying past connections with Dudley Carroll that likely brought him to Carolina. He held degrees from Guilford College, Haverford College and Columbia University Law School and had practiced in Greensboro before joining the UNC faculty. He was active in city and county government as a longtime member of the Chapel Hill Board of Aldermen and Orange County Board of Commissioners.

****

LOCATION.

DAVIE KER JAMES SWAIN CALDWELL SPENCER ALDERMAN BATTLE WHITEHEAD STOCKARD McNIDER CHAPMAN VENABLE PHILLIPS HARRIS KIMBROUGH
EAST FRANKLIN STREET
UNIVERSITY
-of- NORTH
CAROLINA
-at CHAPEL HILL-
CARMICHAEL WILSON MOREHEAD GRAY HENDERSON POLK JOHNSON ASHE GRAHAM MASON WILLIAMS GREEN AYCOCK PERSON FRIDAY HILL PATTERSON

LOCATION.

Kenan-Flagler has had five homes on the University of North Carolina campus, shown at left in a 1963 map published in the "Carolina Alumni Review." The school started in two rooms in Alumni Hall (above), then moved to Saunders Hall (above right, now known as Carolina Hall) in 1922 and then to Bingham Hall in 1929.

LOCATION.

Carroll Hall (above) stood at the head of a three-building court that opened in 1953 flanked by Hanes and Gardner Halls. The school spent forty-four years headquartered in those buildings before moving to South Campus and establishing a home in the McColl Building in 1997.

McCOLL
Carolina
FOR ALL that's now
FOR ALL that's new
WHAT ARE you FOR?
#UNCFORALL

Far East To Carolina

Mike Furuhata

Understanding American English was difficult enough for a couple of young Japanese college students. Add a *Southern* accent to the mix and it was frustrating indeed to Taketo Furuhata and Haruna Kurata, soon to be graduates of Keio University in Tokyo, when they interviewed for scholarships in 1952 to attend grad school in the United States.

"We repeated 'I beg your pardon' and 'Please repeat your question' over and over," Furuhata remembers of their conversation with Roy Morgan, an American attorney from Virginia. Morgan was living in Tokyo and represented some U.S. business interests who were offering to bring two Japanese students to the U.S. for graduate studies. "We left his office with big disappointment because we could not communicate with him fully."

Fortunately, both young men struck a chord with Morgan and several weeks later they learned they had in fact been selected for one-year scholarships. Kurata was placed at Wayne State in Detroit and Furuhata at Chapel Hill, where he would adopt the American name of "Mike." He was told that at least part of the funding for his scholarship came from Ben Cone, a 1920 UNC graduate and member of the noted Cone family of Greensboro textile heritage, and Ralph Price, whose father Julian was the long-time president of Jefferson Standard Life Insurance Co.

"It took fifty days to get from Japan to Chapel Hill," Furuhata says. "I took a cargo boat from Yokohama to Brooklyn via San Francisco and Long Beach and the Panama Canal, which took forty days. That was the cheapest way to go to North Carolina."

Upon arriving at Carolina, Furuhata told Roy Armstrong, a foreign student advisor, that he

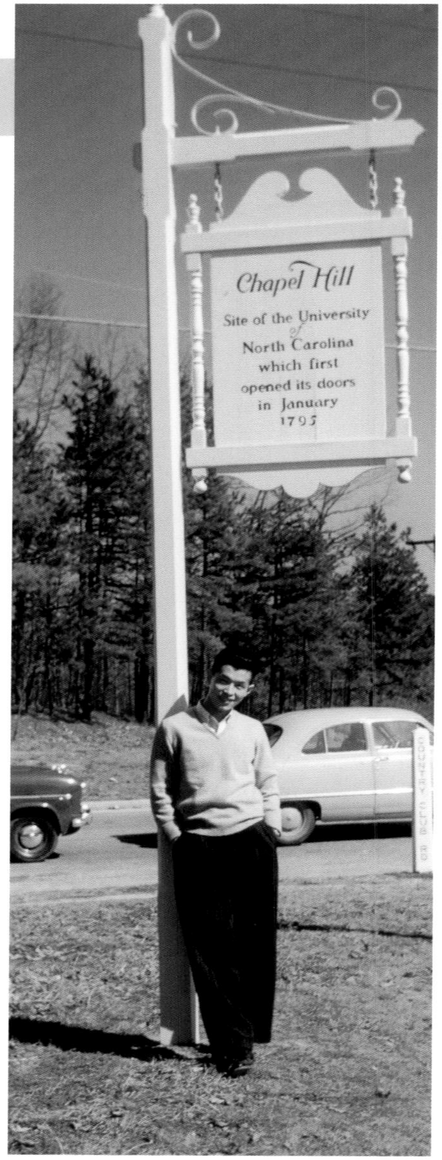

Mike Furuhata poses under a street sign (above) during his Chapel Hill experience, which included academics and attending athletic contests.

wanted to pursue a master in political science. Armstrong reviewed his transcript and said none of his credits would transfer as prerequisites for political science, and his degree would take four and a half years. Instead, Armstrong advised him to enroll in the new MBA Program, which he did in the spring of 1953. He received a fellowship for his second year, receiving room and board, and augmented his bank account by working at Sears Roebuck in Greensboro. Mike has fond memories of the friends he made, one of them Erwin Danziger of the family that owned and operated the Rams Head Rathskeller.

"In my days, 'business school' was not in existence in Japan," Furuhata says.

"Almost every class I attended at UNC was new and stimulating. My experiences, studies and 'Southern' English at UNC were not only useful but also indispensable during my entire company life."

Furuhata graduated in 1955 and became the first international MBA graduate at Kenan-Flagler. He went on to a long and successful career with ITOCHU International, a conglomerate with interests in textiles, machinery, metals and minerals and spent eight years in the States at a company division in

Chicago and then at headquarters in New York. He retired after forty years and then had a successful run in the telecommunications industry in the 1990s, rising to president of International Digital Communications.

Along the way, Furuhata met IBM executive and Kenan-Flagler Dean Paul Rizzo and accepted Rizzo's invitation to serve on the school's International Board of Visitors. He also passed the Kenan-Flagler baton to another Japanese executive.

Koichiro "Kane" Nakamura worked for IDC under Furuhata and had heard him speak of his American and Kenan-Flagler experiences and in 2005, when he decided an MBA would further his career, applied to Kenan-Flagler and was accepted. He attended from 2006-08 and got his MBA in 2008 and since then has worked in Japan and China and in the spring of 2018 learned he was moving to California—all the closer to Chapel Hill.

"I promised myself I would come back and raise my kids in the U.S. and hopefully give something back to the community," he said at the 2018 Alumni Weekend. "Chapel Hill is home, very much home."

Kane has moved twenty-seven times since he was born—bouncing from Tokyo to Japan to Shanghai to Chicago to California. Chapel Hill has a special place in his heart.

"It feels like utopia," he says. "People are so nice and friendly. People ask me when I share my experiences here, 'What is the downside of Chapel Hill?' The only thing is that since it's utopia, it's hard to get back to the real world."

Faculty Elevated Under Lee

Chancellor Robert House's selection for the new dean's post turned out to be a key juncture in the development of business education in Chapel Hill with the appointment in September 1956 of Maurice W. Lee, who had most recently led the School of Economics and Business at the State College of Washington in Pullman, where he had been since 1947. Lee was a native of Chicago and had a PhD from the University of Chicago. He would stay in his job for twenty years, and his six-foot-four frame and closely-cropped white hair were indelibly etched into the memories of thousands of mid-1900s UNC business students.

Lee worked hard to recruit outstanding faculty to Carolina and launched a course called BA199, a management simulation course. It put senior business majors in charge of their own company and forced them to make policy, investment and budget decisions as the course evolved through the semester. He is "widely acknowledged as a leader of thought on collegiate business education and has been primarily responsible for the preparation of the statement of standards governing undergraduate collegiate education for business in this country," noted a 1957 *Daily Tar Heel* story.

"Dean Lee was a tall, stately gentleman whose imposing stature and reputation served him and the school well," says Dr. John P. "Jack" Evans, Professor Emeritus of Operations whose half a century at Kenan-Flagler in multiple roles began in 1970 as an associate professor. "Dean Lee was an excellent author and expositor on economic policy in the classroom and was particularly popular with those who attended the Executive Program. I still encounter alumni who remember fondly taking his classes as either undergraduates or MBA students.

"Over his twenty years as dean, he hired many faculty, consistent with the objective of acquiring people who would be successful at both teaching and scholarship. By the time I joined the faculty, we already had such senior faculty as Harold Langenderfer, Rollie Tillman, DeWitt Dearborn, Dick Levin and Jack Behrman. These were people who played a significant role in the school's aspirations and determination to build a top-notch MBA program. Other key senior faculty members included Avery Cohan, Henry Latané, Richard McEnally, Cliff Kreps and Curt McLaughlin who, in addition to other teaching responsibilities, helped to strengthen the doctoral program."

Lee's economic views and forecasts were regularly quoted close to home in *The Daily Tar Heel* and, from a distance, in *The New York Times*. His *Economic Commentary* newsletter was published three times a year from 1976 for nearly a decade. Lee presided over the school's first endowment drive, known as The Program for the Seventies, and the expansion of Carroll Hall in 1971 with an adjunct building behind and to the west of the original building—less than twenty years old but already bursting at the seams. Lee had hired Roy Holsten, Carolina class of 1950, to serve as associate dean for external relations. Holsten played a significant role in developing the relationships that enabled The Program for the Seventies to be successful.

The Carroll Hall addition was projected to cost $1.6 million when announced in 1969 and was designed by the Columbia-based architectural firm of Lyles, Bissett, Carlisle and Wolff, which was developing a deep portfolio of collegiate buildings and had recently designed and built the new basketball arena for the University of South Carolina. The contemporary looking structure encompassed 56,000 square feet and dwarfed the original 32,000 square foot building, literally engulfing the original auditorium with a wrap-around design. The brick and limestone were planned to match the traditional materials of the original neo-Georgian buildings along Polk Place, but the modern lines and generous use of glass gave the addition a contrasting look to the original Carroll Hall (which today is the home of the UNC School of Media and Journalism).

"Maurice Lee was a man whose very being emanated integrity, authority and order," said economics professor David McFarland upon Lee's death in 1985. "He was endowed with a ten-man share of what used to be called 'presence' and is now known as the 'right stuff.'"

The mid-1970s saw the culmination of a multi-year effort from faculty members in the Department of Economics to gain more autonomy and resources within the School of Business Administration. Chancellor Ferebee Taylor launched a study in 1973 on the proper fit for the economics program and a year later announced that economics would morph out of business administration and become a department in the College of Arts & Sciences, effective July 1974. When Lee, an economics PhD, retired from the deanship two years later, he would continue to teach in both economics and business administration.

Carolina's School of Business Administration in the 1960s reflected the white-male orientation of its overall student body. The school offered an undergraduate degree in business administration, a full-time MBA, PhD program and a modest Executive Education program (which would be renamed to Executive Development in the 2000s). The 1968 MBA class was the first to graduate in the newly created two-year program. The faculty was all white, male and American, and ninety percent of undergraduates were white males from the state of North Carolina. There was only one woman on the faculty by 1976 while half the enrolling freshmen at Carolina were women. The MBA Program had grown to two sections by the mid-1970s.

"During the sixties and early seventies, partly influenced by views of the Vietnam War, the major in business administration experienced somewhat mixed views," Evans says. "You were not seeing a lot of the pressure from parents that is evident today of pushing young people with the line, 'I don't care *what* you major in, but major in something that will help you get a job.' Our enrollments in the early seventies were fine, but our numbers were nothing spectacular. That was to change dramatically in the late seventies."

Dean Lee and his associates made an important step in 1973 to help the school become more diverse by joining The Consortium for Graduate Study in Management, a cooperative network of universities established in 1966 by Washington University's Professor Sterling Schoen. His mission was to give African-American men the business skills they need to secure positions in American corporations. Washington University, Indiana and Wisconsin were the charter members, followed two years later by Rochester and the University of Southern California. The Consortium expanded its membership in 1970 to include women, Hispanic Americans and Native Americans.

UNC was the first Southern institution and sixth overall to join. Many years later in 2017, Doug Shackelford was named its twentieth chair of the board of trustees.

"This should have important economic and cultural benefits for the region and means that the School of Business Administration will have a major role in hastening the entry of minorities into managerial positions in both government and industry," said Associate Dean Claude George.

A story in *The Daily Tar Heel* in late November 1973 reported that "blacks, American Indian and Spanish-American students are eligible for graduate fellowships

Maurice Lee, Kenan-Flagler dean for two decades starting in 1956.

Another Colorful Character

Dr. Henry Latané

HENRY AND FELICITÉ LATANÉ PLAZA
IN RECOGNITION OF THEIR SUPPORT FOR
THE FACULTY, STUDENTS, AND STAFF OF THE
KENAN-FLAGLER BUSINESS SCHOOL

Doctoral candidates from the 1960s and '70s fondly remember Professor Henry Latané who brought his dog Fidel to Carroll Hall every day, ruminated on the gyrations of the stock market and developed cutting-edge research on how earnings affect stock prices.

"He was one of the giants who helped build this place," says finance professor David Ravenscraft.

"He was not quite Nobel Prize material, but close," says Dr. Richard Rendleman, who studied under Latané and then was on the faculty full-time at Kenan-Flagler from 1983-2008. "I think he always felt like he should have been Nobel Prize, but he was that level of scholar and it was a tremendous experience to be able to work with him."

Born in Buchanan, Va., Latané (pronounced *latt-an-AY*) earned a bachelor of arts degree from the University of Richmond in 1928 before matriculating to Harvard and earning his MBA in 1930 and going straight to New York, later wryly saying that he was the "last man hired on Wall Street before the Depression." Despite the tough economic times to begin his career, Latané became one of Wall Street's premier financial analysts during the 1930s and '40s, working for Bankers Trust Co. from 1930-40 and Lionel D. Edie and Co. from 1940-51. He moved to Chapel Hill in 1951 to develop his work on portfolio theory and achieve his PhD in economics, which he did in 1958. In 1960, he held a joint appointment to the Business School as Meade H. Willis Professor of Investment Banking as well as professor in the Department of Economics.

Latané developed a stock-picking methodology he called "SUE"—standardized unexpected earnings. Each quarter for a handful of companies, he would use a statistical progression to predict earnings.

"If the next quarter's earnings

were substantially higher than predicted, then he would buy the stock, and if they were substantially lower, he might short or sell the stock that was already in his portfolio," says Rendleman, a PhD candidate at the time who helped evolve the methodology. "Back in the eighties, we were the only people doing this. *The Wall Street Journal* quoted us frequently. Today it's commonplace to see earnings surprises, but no one else was looking at them at the time."

Latané encouraged Rendleman to work on option markets, which were brand new at the time, and Rendleman published research from 1979 through the 1990s in various financial journals that encompassed implied volatility, portfolio insurance, interest rates swaps and other subjects. Some were written in conjunction with Latané and Charles Jones of N.C. State University.

"We ended up while I was a PhD student publishing a paper on options that even to this day gets widely quoted," Rendleman says.

Latané retired in 1980 and died in 1984. The Henry & Felicité Latané Plaza outside McColl Building was dedicated in June 1998, and the annual PhD banquet is named after him. ❖

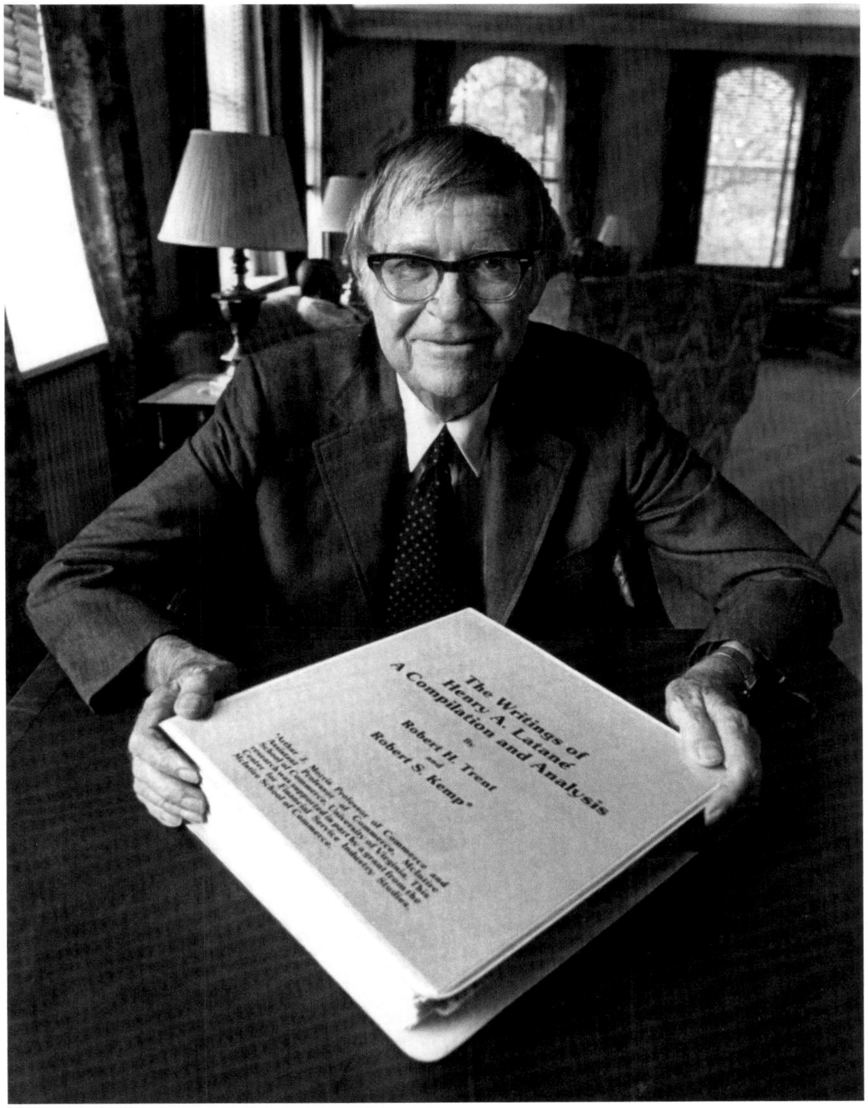

The legacy of Professor Henry Latané (above) is preserved today in front of the McColl Building with a plaza named in honor of Latané and his wife Felicité.

The Carroll Hall addition was positioned on the west (or rear side) of the original building and opened in 1971, more than doubling the size of the School of Business Administration.

given by the UNC School of Business Administration." The fellowships, funded by 135 corporations across the nation, included tuition and $2,000 living expenses for the first year and a $1,000 allowance for the second year. Thirteen fellows were enrolled at Carolina that year. North Carolina firms that supported The Consortium included Akzona Inc., of Asheville, Burlington Industries Inc. of Greensboro, and R.J. Reynolds Industries of Winston-Salem.

"That was an important and significant period for our school," remembers Dr. Jay E. Klompmaker, who spent three decades on the faculty beginning in 1972 as a professor of marketing. "The number and quality of our minority students went *whoosh*, just like that."

Dr. Harvey M. Wagner, a forty-five-year-old professor of management at Yale University, was named by Chancellor Taylor to succeed Lee in July 1976. Wagner had earned national recognition in the fields of operations research and mathematical economics. He was educated at Stanford (undergrad and graduate degrees in statistics) and at the Massachusetts Institute of Technology (PhD in economics), and he taught at Stanford before moving across the country to New Haven.

Wagner's tenure as dean would last only two years as he stepped down in June 1978 to concentrate on teaching, research and consulting, but he made a career-long impact on Kenan-Flagler by remaining on the faculty and involved in the school through his death in 2017 at the age of eighty-five. He had a longstanding consulting relationship with McKinsey & Company, and his book, *Principles of Operations Research with Applications to Managerial Decisions*, became a classic text which helped tens of thousands of graduate students learn concepts related to operations research. Wagner continued to offer his doctoral seminar every year as well as courses in spreadsheet modeling, and his latest research into his eighties involved machine learning and artificial intelligence in operations.

****

Post-1970s Sees Boom in Enrollment

Jack Evans in 1978 was a professor and associate dean for academic programs and was appointed interim dean and then given the post full-time one year later. He held the deanship for nearly a decade until 1987 and would lead the school through significant growth in the 1980s.

"All of a sudden we were flooded with undergraduate majors," Evans says. "We reached a point around 1979-80 where something like one of five under-grad majors was a business major. That totally threw our student-faculty ratio way out of whack. We were teaching business-required courses in sections of three hundred. That was a problem."

Evans did the math and figured the school needed thirty-five more faculty positions to bring the school's student-faculty ratio to the level that existed in the College of Arts & Sciences. He knew from a practical standpoint that was not going to happen. So the solution was to reduce the number of business majors.

"At the peak, I do remember us having nearly 1,400 business majors in their junior, senior and hangover fifth years," he says. "Our objective was to reduce that to a range of seven hundred to seven-fifty new majors entering each fall, which we did over three years. We introduced a grade-point threshold that sophomores had to have to move into a business major. At first, that wasn't popular with some other departments. They said, 'You're going to skim the cream off the top and leave the dregs for us.' But we felt obligated to give business majors a quality education, and teaching sections with three hundred people was not it."

Evans also shepherded the school through the advent or expansion of three key initiatives—creating a Master of Accounting program in 1985 with the first eight graduates emerging in 1986, offering an Executive MBA Evening Program in 1986 and affirming that Executive Education was an important part of the school's mission and should therefore be a factor in how the school hired faculty. The latter two were particularly noteworthy as they expanded the school's reach more deeply into the established business community; they provided more opportunities for working executives to study for an MBA and to give business what it wanted in terms of advancing executives' careers with salient education.

"Each of these issues made for some intense, sometimes awkward, faculty discussions," Evans remembers. "Some thought a Master of Accounting would dilute the MBA Program. Some worried an Evening MBA program would be a watered-down version of the full-time program with less-qualified faculty. But other schools around the country were going in these directions, and the business community perceived Executive Education as important to them. We hammered each issue out and each became a successful part of the school. We might not have today the $20-plus million business we have in Executive Education if we had not committed to the notion of mid-career, professional development as being part of our mission."

One of the early proponents of establishing the Master of Accounting program was Thomas W. Hudson Jr. (BSBA '46). Hudson and his wife Mary endowed the leading fellowship awarded in the MAC Program. Later in conjunction with the accounting firm Deloitte, they also endowed the Thomas W. Hudson Jr./Deloitte & Touche Distinguished Professorship. And in 2004, the Hudsons established the Thomas W. Hudson Jr. MBA Fellowship, awarded annually to two candidates based on outstanding leadership, academic performance and career potential.

The Master of Accounting Program turned thirty years old in 2015 and soon after in October 2016 graduated its first class of twelve students from its online MAC program. Two hundred and fifty students were enrolled in early 2019 in the online format, which attracts a variety of students—

recent graduates to working professionals to current and former military.

"You find our alumni at all of the Big Four accounting firms, as well as at middle-market firms, global corporations, public-sector entities, startups and nonprofit organizations," says Jana Raedy, Associate Dean of the MAC Program and Associate Professor and Ernst & Young Scholar in Accounting. "Carolina accounting graduates have a profound influence on the accounting profession, both nationally and internationally."

The mid-1980s also saw the inception and creation of the Frank Hawkins Kenan Institute of Private Enterprise. Kenan, a 1935 school graduate and Chapel Hill businessman with interests in oil and gas, transportation and commercial real estate, had taken over the management of the Kenan family's interests in the William R. Kenan Jr. Charitable Trust upon Mr. Kenan's death in 1965. Over time he moved the Trust's management from New York to Chapel Hill, and with the encouragement of UNC President William Friday, the University arranged for an office building to house the Trust to be located on a hill on South Campus. The Kenan Center was announced in 1983 and opened in 1986.

Kenan was a sharp businessman who believed in the tenets of free enterprise. "I believe all the freedoms that we enjoy are related to free enterprise," he said. "If you neglect that, we'll lose the others."

"Father said that free enterprise created the family fortune in the first place," says his son, Thomas S. Kenan III, a 1959 UNC graduate in economics. "He thought we should take some of that money from the Trust and build something for free enterprise."

Kenan sensed that the academic community in general failed to appreciate and respect the role of business and talked at length with Friday about a means to link education, business and government in one stable platform. Over the years, Kenan got to meet a number of professors from around the country who came to Chapel Hill for convocations of the Kenan Professorships.

"I found that few of them knew about business or the effects of business on education," Kenan said.

The Kenan Institute of Private Enterprise opened in 1985 and a year later moved to the new Kenan Center.

"You look at Mr. Duke, Mr. Ford, Mr. Rockefeller, Mr. Hill, Mr. Morehead," Kenan noted. "Look at Harvard University, Cornell, all those universities. If it wasn't for private philanthropy, they wouldn't be here. The system allowed those people to accumulate wealth, create industries and jobs. It's the greatest system in the world. I think it's not understood very well by politicians and academicians. "

By this time, the school had been under the direction of Evans for nearly a decade. Deans were given five-year appointments and by 1986, Evans had served eight years, counting one as interim dean after Wagner's departure. With a significant fund-raising campaign on the horizon for both the University and the School of Business Administration, Evans thought it best that a new dean step in.

"I thought it was important for the school to have the same dean through any fundraising effort, and I wasn't sure it was a good thing for either me or the school for me to be thinking about fifteen years as dean," says Evans, who stepped down in the summer of 1987 and returned to the school's faculty as an operations professor.

Chancellor Christopher Fordham appointed Dr. Bill Little, a long-time chemistry professor and later a University administrator, to head the search committee that convened in the summer of 1986.

"This selection will do much to set the course for the school during a crucial period of its history and the history of the University," Fordham wrote the committee, adding that the new dean "should be prepared to bring it into the top dozen schools in business administration in the United States."

****

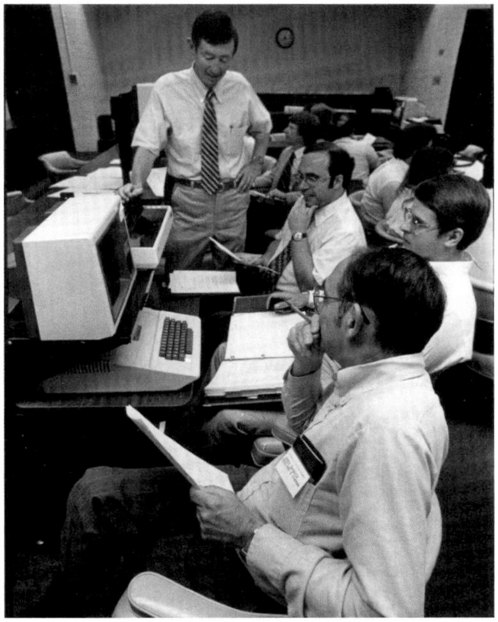

Among the giant shoulders that Kenan-Flagler grew upon during the 1970s and '80s were faculty members the likes of (clockwise from top left) Jay Klompmaker, Harold Langenderfer, John Pringle and Gerald Barrett.

Four Times A Dean

Jack Evans

Doug Shackelford and Jack Evans are both big baseball fans, Evans pulling for the St. Louis Cardinals and Shackelford the Atlanta Braves.

"I've reminded Jack that Joe DiMaggio was always introduced as the 'greatest living baseball player,'" says Shackelford, Kenan-Flagler dean since 2014. "I've told Jack that's how I'll always introduce him. I think that he's the greatest living Kenan-Flagler professor."

Evans joined the Kenan-Flagler faculty in 1970 as an operations management professor after growing up in Indiana and matriculating at Cornell. His half-century of teaching, mentoring, research and leadership is unrivaled, serving eight years as dean from 1978-87 and then stepping in three more times as interim dean—in 1997, 2003 and 2013.

"I'm not sure anyone at UNC or for that matter any campus has ***ever*** had four different times in the dean's office," Shackelford says. "I've kidded Jack that he's not done—that he needs to be ready to come out of the bullpen when I step down."

Evans' stint as dean from 1978-87 was marked by launching what became the Executive MBA Evening and Master of Accounting Programs and expanding Executive Development to include custom programs. Evans also served as president of the Association to Advance Collegiate Schools of Business and later led its overhaul of the accreditation process for business schools.

It took a special man to have a successful run as dean, then work under six subsequent deans and pinch-hit three times—and live to tell about it.

"Jack is just a consummate gentleman and has a great sense of humor," says Jean Elia, a colleague of Evans' over a quarter of century on the Kenan-Flagler staff. "And he's so smart. Jack had the broader University perspective as well as the school perspective. There is nothing polarizing about Jack, so you would never find a cohort faculty that said, 'That's just a terrible idea.' Everybody saw it as, 'What? Of course. Why not?' The way in which he led was one of engagement and collegiality and so that made it really easy."

Shackelford agrees.

"He embodies much of our collegial culture—perhaps it attracted him here or perhaps our culture was molded by him or maybe some of both."

Evans' long history at the University includes fifteen years of service as its faculty athletic representative, two terms as president of the Atlantic Coast Conference and an appointment as interim vice chancellor for finance and administration for UNC.

"Jack was seldom the first person to speak on an issue, but he was always the person the other faculty representatives and athletic directors wanted to hear from," says Dick Baddour, Carolina's athletic director from 1997-2011. "Every time a new person would join the group, he or she would naturally gravitate to Jack to seek his opinion, reasoning or direction. Jack is one of the most respected individuals I have ever known and it was that respect that endeared him to others. He gained that respect through thoughtful analysis, fact-based decision making and sensitivity to all sides of an issue."

Jack Evans juggled eras and personalities like no one else at Kenan-Flagler over nearly half a century as a faculty member, dean and interim dean; here he's chatting with Frank Kenan during the school's crucial 1980s expansion era.

Evans was awarded the General Alumni Association's Distinguished Service Medal in 2011, and the citation read in part: "Jack is a stalwart Midwesterner with an extraordinary work ethic. He approaches every task he's given with the utmost competence, diligence and thoroughness. He's not in it for personal glory."

When Shackelford ascended to the dean's post in 2014, Evans was at the ready for an assist after running the Kenan-Flagler shop for a year after Jim Dean left to become University provost in July 2013.

"He had a detailed list of the things that I needed to consider—both in the short-run and the long-run," Shackelford says. "It was really helpful and showed that he had not just been a caretaker as interim dean but was thinking carefully about what the next dean would need—whoever that might be."

Dave Hartzell earned his PhD at Kenan-Flagler in 1984 and returned to the faculty in 1988 to teach real estate and finance.

"When I first met Jack I said, 'I want to be like him when I grow up,'" Hartzell says. "And then when he hired me back, I said, 'I *still* want to be like him when I grow up.'"

Dick Levin

Creating MBAs

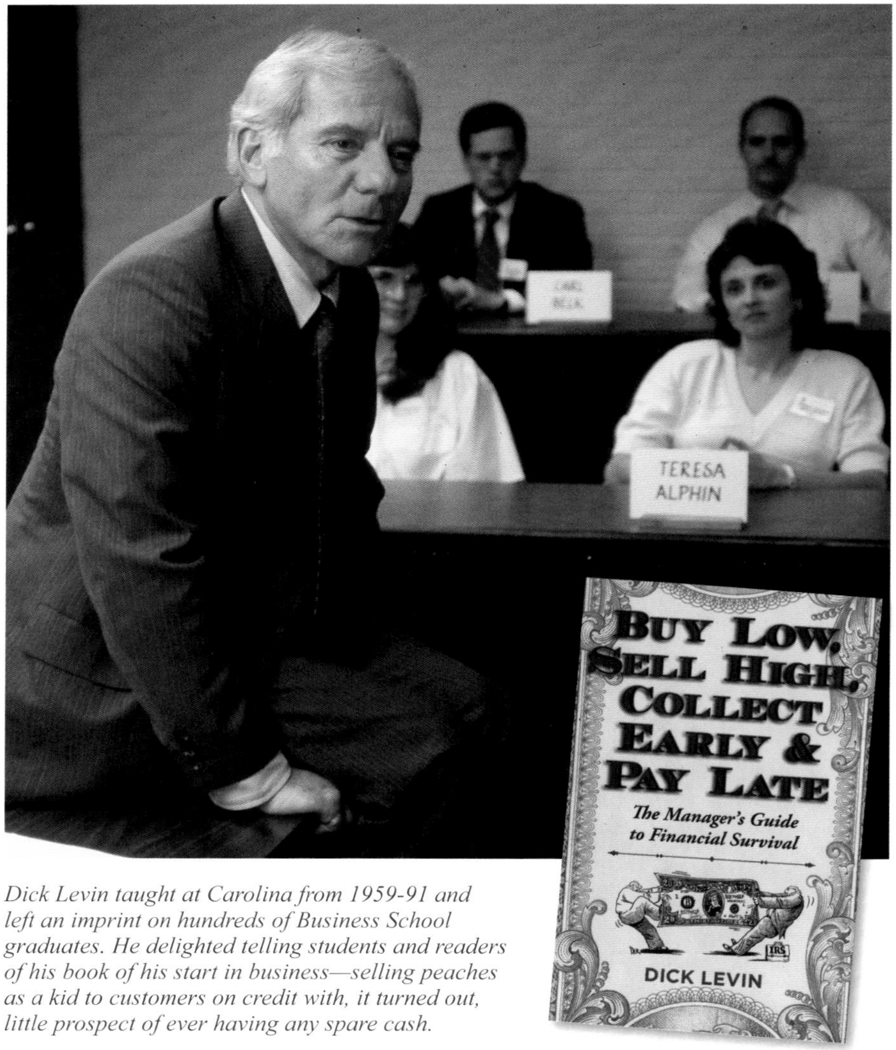

Dick Levin taught at Carolina from 1959-91 and left an imprint on hundreds of Business School graduates. He delighted telling students and readers of his book of his start in business—selling peaches as a kid to customers on credit with, it turned out, little prospect of ever having any spare cash.

For a little color and perspective on Dick Levin, one of Kenan-Flagler's most revered professors over more than three decades, one merely has to read his bio note in his 1983 book ***Buy Low, Sell High, Collect Early, Pay Late***.

"He's collected several dollars as an engineer, piano player, Air Force officer, teacher, writer, real estate investor and consultant," the note read. "And he paid out a few on planes, boats, apartment houses and oceanfront real estate. His favorite fixed asset is his Piper Twin Comanche (which ***really*** moves)."

Levin graduated from N.C. State University in 1951 and was awarded his PhD at Carolina in 1959. He joined the Business School faculty that year and continued teaching in Carroll Hall until his retirement in 1991. He was perhaps most remembered for his integrated management class and for driving a flashy Mercedes convertible with the vanity plate CR8MBAS.

Dave Hartzell was a young associate professor in the late 1980s and shared a suite in Carroll Hall with Levin, Jack Behrman, John Pringle and Jack Evans."I was so outmatched by these icons," he says.

Levin was across the hall and Hartzell recalls students lined up outside Levin's office to discuss their

"He would grade them over the weekend and hand them back on Monday, and it was brutal."

Dave Hartzell

grades in his integrated management class. They were graded on a scale of one to ten on the one-page papers that analyzed a case.

"He would grade them over the weekend and hand them back on Monday, and it was brutal," Hartzell says. "These were MBA students who were high-achievers, people who had never gotten threes and fours on a one-to-ten scale in their lives. He gave them the opportunity to debate their grades. If he missed something and they made a good case, he'd give them a point. But if he disagreed, he took a point off. The percentage of people who got nicked one point was probably pretty high. And they would walk out with their tails between their legs."

Levin got his first lesson in business as a kid growing in rural Williamston, N.C., and spending a month selling peaches to cash-poor migrant farmers who promised they would fork over the cash when they got paid in August. He was already counting that $800 profit when his father, a traveling salesman, was aghast that he had not actually *collected* a penny of it—and, of course, never would. A few years later, he worked for a second-hand furniture dealer who told him, "Kid, just remember, 'Buy low, sell high, collect early and pay late.'" He later used that phrase as the title for his book with the added subtitle, "The Manager's Guide to Financial Survival."

During his undergraduate and graduate years, Levin turned his piano playing skills into the popular band, "Dick Levin and his Orchestra," traveling throughout the South to play at inaugurals, socials and university dances. One year the band made sixteen performances from Alabama to Maryland over the Christmas break.

He wielded pithy one-liners:

"Stand next to smart people; they help you avoid dumb mistakes."

"Behind every successful CEO is someone coming along with a broom to sweep up."

"For good-looking white Protestant males of average intelligence with a low need to take risks and high need for structured support systems,

banking is a terrific fraternity."

Levin was inducted into the University's oldest and most prestigious society, The Order of the Golden Fleece, in 1973. He died in 2016 at the age of eighty-six.

Snapshots | WOMEN BREAKING BARRIERS

Women at Kenan-Flagler have come a long way since learning new business machines in the 1950s (opposite page, middle-right photo). Today Carolina Women in Business is a student-run organization providing the women of Kenan-Flagler with opportunities for career and community development and networking in preparation for their post-MBA journeys. The group's board of directors from 2018 is shown above, with the lone male being the group's VP of Allies. Two members of the MBA Class of 2019 and key officers with CWIB are pictured far left: Charlotte Burnett, the CWIB president in 2018, and Colleen Parra, the head of planning for the CWIB conference in October 2018.

The Man Behind McColl Building

Bill Moore was delighted to have Hugh McColl Jr., the recently retired banker who'd overseen the growth of Charlotte-based NationsBank and its 1998 takeover of Bank of America, as a guest lecturer in his investment banking class at Kenan-Flagler in the early 2000s.

"Bill, what would you like me to talk about?" McColl asked upon arrival in Chapel Hill at the building bearing his name.

"Leadership," Moore answered.

Whereupon McColl ditched his planned address and launched into a treatise on his days in the Marines after his graduation from Chapel Hill (BSBA 1957) and a four-decade career making roughly a thousand acquisitions of banks from Florida to San Francisco.

"I started by talking about Jesus Christ walking by the Sea of Galilee and saying to these two fishermen, 'Put down your nets and follow me,

Hugh McColl Jr.

Hugh McColl as seen in the 1955 "Yackey-Yack" yearbook as president of Beta Theta Pi fraternity.

and I'll make you fishers of men,'" McColl says of what became an annual talk to Moore's class. "Flash forward 1918 years or thereabouts and you're in France in World War I and lying in a wheat field and you're a Marine. You're being machine-gunned by the Germans in Belleau Wood and you're out of ammunition, and sergeant Dan Daly stands up and says, 'Come on you sons of bitches, you want to live forever, follow me!' They charge the Germans with nothing but bayonets and rout them and win the day.

"And so the questions is, 'Why did one man promise everlasting life and people followed him, and another man promised glorious death and they followed *him*?"

McColl then spent the next hour telling the students about the art of taking people where they can't go by themselves, of building a team, of caring about his subordinates. He told them as he told the Kenan-Flagler graduating class during commencement exercises in 1991, "You do not *manage* people. You lead and inspire people."

McColl asked at the end if there were any questions. A young man stood up and said he'd read books on leadership, taken classes on leadership and been involved in athletic

While his grandfather cut the ribbon to the new McColl Building in 1997 alongside Federal Reserve chief Alan Greenspan (above), young John McColl Jr. was in the audience taking photos. Twenty years later, John would enter Kenan-Flagler to pursue his MBA.

leadership through his participation on a Carolina varsity team.

"And I learned more about leadership in forty-five minutes today than all of those things combined," he said. "Thank you."

"Hugh's sessions were an annual highlight of the investment banking class," Moore says of a decade's worth of visits from McColl. "It was very inspiring to hear a truly great man like Hugh talk about leadership."

McColl grew up in Bennettsville, S.C., the son of a 1927 UNC graduate of what was then known as the Department of Commerce. Hugh Sr. and his brother owned banks and ran a cotton farm and mill, so Hugh Jr. grew up around finance and learned as a fourteen-year-old to help with his father's accounting ledgers. He was a C student at Carolina—"If we'd had the numerical system at the time, it would have been 1.99999," he says with a rueful smile—but adds his classes in accounting, finance and business law stood him well in 1959 when he entered the banking business with American Commercial Bank in Charlotte.

"I always had a knack for numbers and arithmetic going back to my

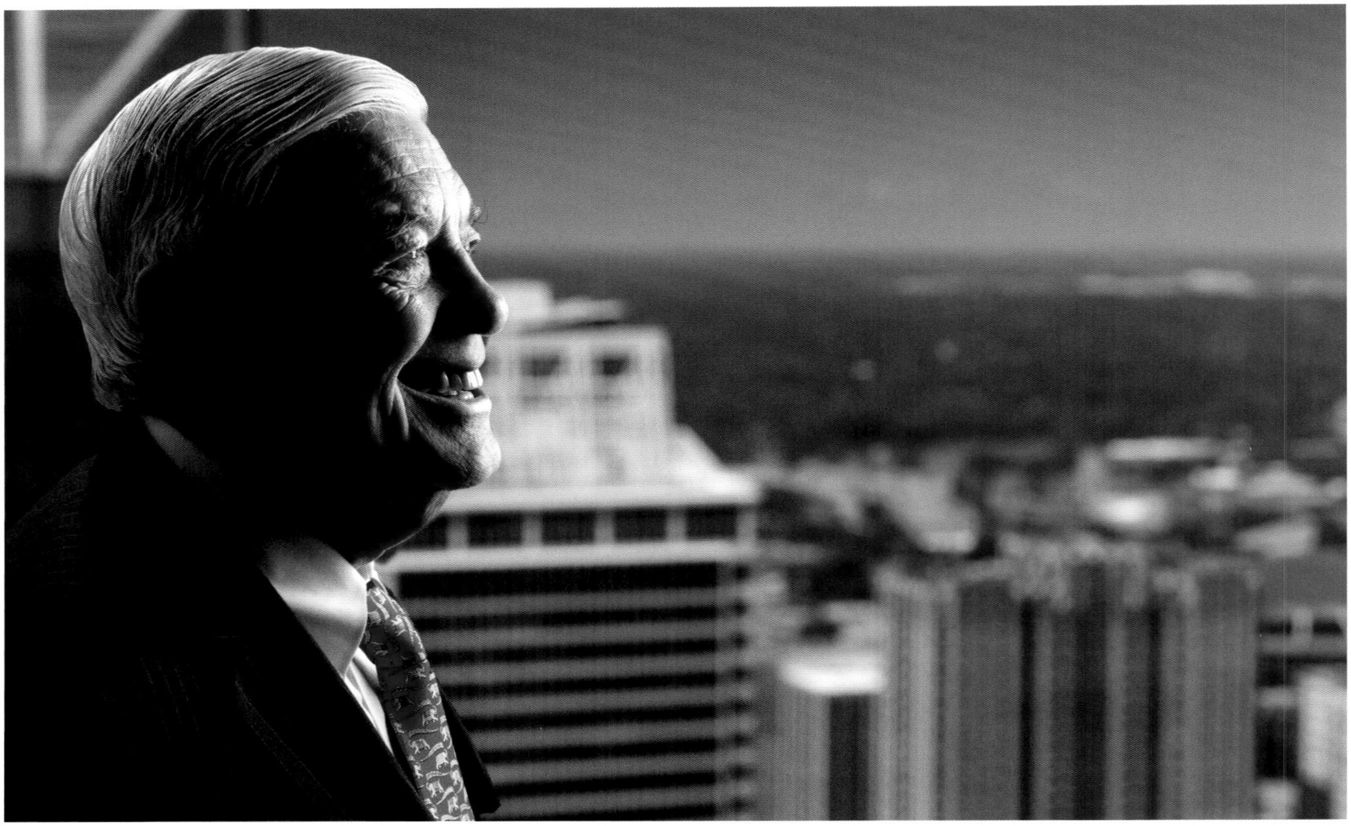

Hugh McColl posed for this portrait in his office atop the Bank of America headquarters in Charlotte in 2016.

fascination with baseball as a boy," says McColl, who turned eighty-three in June 2018 and remains active in investment banking and philanthropy. "You were always figuring batting averages, you're doing arithmetic to the third decimal. You learn that one-for-seven is a .143 batting average, that two-for-seven is .286."

He pauses and taps his head. "Those numbers become ingrained up here. When you're in negotiations, you always have a lot of numbers. The relationships of the numbers were always clear to me. I always knew exactly what the relationship equaled. It helped me in figuring what could or couldn't be done. People were amazed how quickly I could do arithmetic. It's all baseball."

He also learned probabilities and reading people's eyes and body language from boyhood as an avid poker player. One of his best friends in Bennettsville was crippled and confined to a wheelchair, so card games were one the few activities the boys could play together. McColl's skills evolved through college and the Marines, where he won $45,000 playing poker over a month's time on a Marine aircraft carrier stationed off

"The Marines were my grad school. That's where I really learned that everybody pulled their pants on the same way. If you wanted to get something done, you had to do it together."

Hugh McColl Jr. (BSBA '57)

---

the coast of Morocco.

"That was exactly ten times my starting salary at the bank that September," he says. "I played poker for years until I quit after a big game at the bank. I won money from a boy who couldn't afford to lose it. I tried to give it back to him, but he sulked and wouldn't take it. I decided it was one thing to win it from a Naval pilot on an aircraft carrier, it was another thing to win it from someone you work with."

McColl's experiences as president of the Beta Theta Pi fraternity and on the Tar Heel lacrosse team at Chapel Hill and two years in the military taught him the value of teamwork.

"The Marines were my grad school," he says. "That's where I really learned that everybody pulled their pants on the same way. If you wanted to get something done, you had to do it together. You don't ask a man to do something you won't do or haven't done yourself. Troops see before the officers. You learned you lead from in front. You don't *order* them up a hill, you *lead* them up the hill. The Marines teach a lot of great values, mostly that the person next to you is your teammate. I kept that throughout the history of our company. If we bought your company and you came to work for us, we accepted you immediately as a member of our team. You could only prove that we shouldn't."

McColl became president of NCNB in 1974 and CEO in 1983. He and his predecessor, Tom Storrs, knew that in order for the bank to grow, it had to burst through the shackles of Depression-era banking laws that restricted banks to doing business within their own borders. Over time in the eighties and nineties, laws were passed first among Southern states and later on a national basis allowing banks to buy institutions elsewhere.

"We changed the entire banking industry in the United States," McColl says. "That's as modest as I know how to put it. But I stress that *we* did it—we had a great legal team and some great minds. We wanted to survive, and we were not going to survive if we had to depend on a living in North Carolina."

McColl retired from Bank of America in 2001 and started a private equity firm called McColl Partners. Once his team met with a group of potential clients who wanted to shop their company to suitors in the software space. The CEO at the end of the meeting thanked McColl for his firm's time and presentation but said he didn't think McColl Partners had quite the clout to give his firm access to a company such as Microsoft to the degree that Goldman Sachs or Morgan Stanley might.

Whereupon McColl pulled out his cell phone and tapped out a text message. Within a couple of minutes, the phone rang.

"Hey, Billy," said McColl, who interrupted the meeting for a quick chat with Bill Gates. Needless to say, Hugh McColl got the assignment.

The Rizzo and Fulton Rocket Shot

The Business School in Chapel Hill was healthy and well respected on a regional level, but over the next decade it would be catapulted into a new realm by a pair of leaders cut from a different bolt of cloth—a pair of native sons who came to the deanship not from another position in academia but from the business world itself—Paul Rizzo from 1987-92 and Paul Fulton from 1994-97 (with interim dean Carl Zeithaml in between). Both were Carolina business graduates (Rizzo in 1950 and Fulton in 1957).

Rizzo grew up on a farm in upstate New York and had been recruited by Cornell coach Carl Snavely to play football there. But when Snavely moved to UNC in 1945, he talked Rizzo into following him south. Rizzo came to Chapel Hill with two pairs of overalls, two flannel shirts, a shaving kit and a toothbrush and became a well-liked and respected blocking back on the famed Charlie "Choo Choo" Justice era teams of the late 1940s. Rizzo joined IBM in 1958 as a financial manager and became vice president and corporate controller in 1965 and senior VP and chief financial officer in 1971. During the 1970s as the executive in charge of product development, he made the pivotal decision to produce computers for the mass market, which led to the development of the IBM personal computer.

As vice chairman in the mid-1980s, Rizzo was facing the mandatory retirement age of sixty for senior officers and in 1987 was contemplating his next move. He had retained ties with the School of Business Administration by virtue of serving on the board of the Kenan Institute of Private Enterprise, so he was likely aware of the opening. One story goes that Rizzo by coincidence was on a flight to Japan with then-UNC trustee and 1951 graduate Richard Jenrette, who told him the school was looking for a dean and that Rizzo would be perfect for the job. William M. Moore Jr., (BSBA 1967) who had launched the investment bank Trident Financial Corporation in 1975, also knew Rizzo and encouraged him to take the job.

Rizzo accepted the appointment early in the spring of 1987 and word quickly circulated among the business community before the news went public. Typical of the reaction was that from William Burns, then CEO and chairman of Durham's Central Carolina Bank (later to merge with SunTrust): "There's no question that he will bring a dimension to the School of Business that would have been impossible to achieve through a regular professor," he wrote to Frank Kenan.

Rizzo became dean on Sept. 1, 1987, and said one of his goals was for the school to become in five years "the most globalized school in the country." He encouraged all of the eighty-two faculty members to teach or do research overseas.

"Paul has freed the faculty to move a little faster and dream a little bigger," said Dr. Mike Miles, then chairman of the MBA Program.

Dr. David J. Hartzell worked on his PhD in Chapel Hill from 1981-84, went to Wall Street and returned in 1988 as a faculty member.

"At the time, we knew we had a good school but there were no rankings," remembers Hartzell, today the Steven D. Bell and Leonard W. Wood Distinguished Professor in Real Estate. "We were a regional school and we had two guys, Dick Levin and Jack Behrman, who were the broad shoulders that all of us stand on right now. You add Jay Klompmaker, Jack Evans, Mike Miles, John Pringle, Dick Blackburn—those guys worked really hard to create the stuff that's in place now."

One professor who certainly took Rizzo's international mandate to heart was Doug Elvers, who in 2019 had completed fifty-one years on the faculty in a myriad of roles, including associate dean of the Undergraduate Business

Program, area chair of operations, associate director of the full-time MBA Program and associate dean for administration. As the Berlin Wall fell in Germany in 1989, Elvers recognized something lacking in the Carolina curriculum. "We were not teaching enough about what was going on in Europe and elsewhere," he says.

From 1990 to 2004, Elvers taught forty-eight courses outside the U.S. in conjunction with the UNC Summer School and endorsed by the UNC Kenan-Flagler faculty. He took students to England, Germany and Belgium, and taught as a visiting professor in Nigeria, Germany, South Africa, England, Venezuela and Austria.

"By teaching in these different environments, I picked up different viewpoints," says Elvers.

Paul Rizzo pauses on the steps in front of Carroll Hall upon his return to Chapel Hill in 1987 from a career with IBM.

Rizzo's arrival as the dean happened to coincide with the launching of the first high-profile ranking program from a national magazine that further launched the UNC School of Business Administration on an upward trajectory. Carolina had long enjoyed a favorable reputation and was tabbed "best in the Southeast" in a 1960 study that appraised business schools across the country. Allan Carter, dean of the graduate school at Duke University (which did not have a business school at the time), was a member of research team and wrote in the report "without hesitation that Chapel Hill's business school is the best I saw." A survey of business school deans nationwide was published by *MBA Magazine* in 1977 and ranked Carolina's MBA program first in the Southeast and fourth "most improved" nationally.

But it was *BusinessWeek* starting its MBA program rankings in 1988 and listing UNC as No. 8 that gave the school a degree of swagger it had never enjoyed. *U.S. News & World Report* began ranking schools in 1990, and *BusinessWeek* added undergraduate business program rankings in 2006. (Bloomberg bought *BusinessWeek* in 2009 and it's now known as *Bloomberg BusinessWeek.)*

"All of a sudden it was like, wow, this is what we've

tried to do and nobody ever really measured it before," Hartzell says. "That sort of put us on the map. At the same time, Paul Rizzo changed this place from kind of a regional school and kind of a relaxed environment to a much more professional business environment. People started wearing ties to class. He was an IBM-guy and always wore a white shirt, tie and dark pants."

Dr. David Ravenscraft joined the faculty in 1987 and was impressed by the quality of teaching and the convivial relationship between professors and students and soon was joining the tradition of professors walking from Carroll Hall with MBA students for lunch at Spanky's and the Ram's Head Rathskeller, aka "The Rat."

"There was a real dedication to our students," says Ravenscraft, today the Fulton Global Business Distinguished Professor of Finance. "And when I came here I thought that was just one of the best kept secrets, and it's too bad that people don't know about that."

Then came the *BusinessWeek* rankings that included an overall ranking and separate categories taken from two surveys—one of corporate recruiters and a second of recent graduates. Carolina was ranked No. 2 in the graduate list with the note "most admired faculty by grads; ambitious new dean hails from IBM; a bargain at the price." Indeed, Carolina's annual tuition of $4,916 was roughly half of seventh-ranked Virginia's $9,288 and a third of the top-ranked school, Northwestern's Kellogg School of Business at $14,124.

"Every other survey would talk to deans and maybe recruiters and look at some statistics, but *BusinessWeek* surveyed the students for the first time," Ravenscraft says. "They were the first one to ever do that. And it was revolutionary in a way. But our best-kept secret was featured in that survey. It was certainly a break that someone surveyed the students and played to one of our big strengths—it made a huge difference."

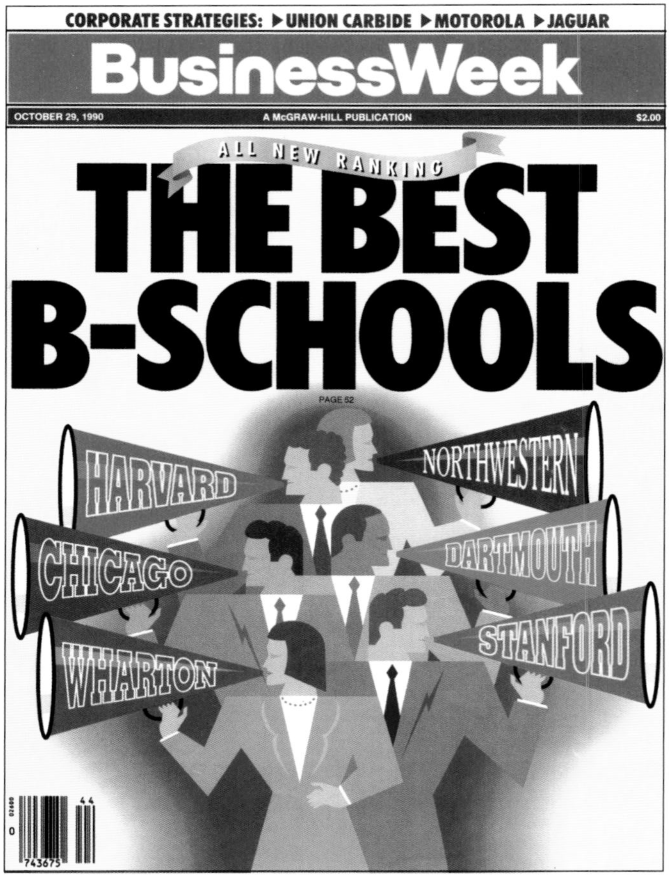

Paul Hardin, who took over for Fordham as chancellor on July 1, 1988, quickly came to appreciate what the school was accomplishing on a comparatively limited budget. Hardin pointed out Carolina's business school budget was $8.5 million while neighboring Duke's business school was $13 million—and Duke didn't have an undergraduate program.

"If we can accomplish that with our limited resources, imagine what we can accomplish with just a little help," Hardin wrote to Frank Kenan in reference to the *BusinessWeek* rankings.

Cover Story

HOW THE SCHOOLS STACK UP: BUSINESS WEEK RATES THE TOP 20

Who has the best graduate business school in the U.S.? The deans say Stanford. The chief executives point to Harvard. BUSINESS WEEK's poll of corporate recruiters and graduates gives Northwestern University's J.L. Kellogg Graduate School of Management the nod.

BW randomly polled about 3,000 1988 graduates of 23 schools that often make the top-20 lists. We received 1,245 replies to the 35-question survey, a response rate of about 42% of those sampled and about 15% of all the full-time MBA graduates of those schools in 1988. The graduates assessed the quality of the teaching, curriculum, environment, and job placement efforts on a scale of 1 to 10, and the schools were awarded an average total score.

The poll of corporate recruiters—similar to a 1985 poll by consultants Brecker & Merryman Inc.—was mailed to 265 companies that have recently recruited at a third of these leading 23 schools. BW received 112 responses, a 42% rate. A school given top preference by a company received a score of five, while a school ranked fifth was awarded a score of one. Recruiters also named the best schools in such areas as marketing and finance. Financial companies represented 25% of the responding sample; consumer products, 21%; services, 12%; high tech, 11%; and manufacturing and consulting, 9% each. The final ranking is a composite of the

BW rank	School	Corporate poll rank	Graduates' poll rank	Highlights	1988* graduates	Annual tuition	Applicants accepted
1	NORTHWESTERN (Kellogg)	1	5	Recruiters rate it tops in marketing and in dead heat with Harvard in general management	505	$14,124	20%
2	HARVARD	3	6	Grads say it's the most competitive, with the best connections; case-study approach	789	14,250	14
3	DARTMOUTH (Amos Tuck)	15	1	Small classes and emphasis on teamwork make it the friendliest campus	161	14,000	19
4	WHARTON	2	13	Recruiters rank it best in finance; grads grouse about quality of teaching	743	14,767	21
5	CORNELL (Johnson)	11	3	Known as strong in finance; earns new honors in operations management and marketing	194	13,800	27
6	MICHIGAN	5	12	Blends analytical with practical; highest percentage of minority students (25%)	414	12,850	33
7	VIRGINIA (Darden)	14	4	Toughest workload; grads liken "excessive" demands to frat hazing; Harvard-like regimen	212	9,288	25
8	NORTH CAROLINA	19	2	Most admired faculty by grads; ambitious new dean hails from IBM; a bargain at the price	145	4,916	27
9	STANFORD	7	8	Seeks "balanced excellence" in teaching and research; high-tech firms like it	306	14,094	8
10	DUKE	10	7	Aggressive dean moved school into top 10; a leader in information technology			
13	CARNEGIE-MELLON	12	9	Known for its quantitative approach; grads rank workload as second toughest	139	13,566	25
14	COLUMBIA	6	19	Grads call it intensely competitive and rate it dead last in forging friendships; lures top-flight lecturers	725	14,000	30**
15	MIT (Sloan)	17	10	Recruiters rate it best in operations management; top percentage of foreign students (35%)	185	14,500	22
16	UCLA	8	16	A leader in financial theory; grads say profs stress research over teaching	391	6,527	19
17	CALIFORNIA (Berkeley)	16	14	Relatively high proportion of minorities, women; a leader in organization theory	235	6,037	22
18	NYU (Stern)	13	22	Was your MBA worth its cost? Grads were least satisfied here; flush with cash, may be on the rise	603	13,154	29
19	YALE	22	15	New dean plans overhaul; grads rate it tops at fostering teamwork, worst at placement	187	13,500	20**
20	ROCHESTER (Simon)	23	17	Grads praise topical material and research; renown in economics and finance	156	12,400	40

DATA: BW (research by Celeste Whittaker, Judi Crowe) * Full-time program only **BW estima

78 BUSINESS WEEK/NOVEMBER 28, 1988 COVER STORY

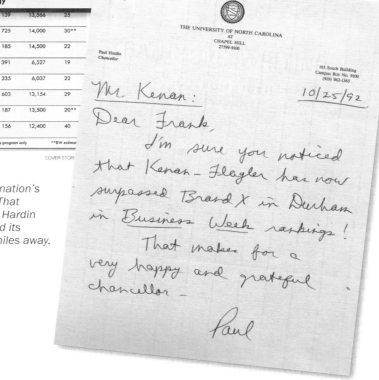

"BusinessWeek" magazine launched its rankings of the nation's top business schools in 1988 and listed UNC at No. 8. "That put us on the map," said one professor. Chancellor Paul Hardin was pleased four years later when the school maintained its prominence and in fact outranked a certain rival eight miles away.

THE UNIVERSITY OF NORTH CAROLINA
AT
CHAPEL HILL
27599-9100

Paul Hardin
Chancellor

103 South Building
Campus Box No. 9100
(919) 962-1365

Mr. Kenan: 10/25/92

Dear Frank,

I'm sure you noticed that Kenan-Flagler has now surpassed Brand X in Durham in Business Week rankings!

That makes for a very happy and grateful chancellor -

Paul

The school was now thirty-five years into its Carroll Hall facility and fifteen into its early 1970s expansion, and it needed a new home to keep up with its quickly evolving reputation.

The Kenan Center was up and running in 1986 on its hill on South Campus, and at one point there was a plan to build two adjacent buildings, one to house the General Alumni Association and the other for conferences and continuing education. The GAA had long since outgrown its headquarters in the Whitehead Building at the corner of Columbia Street and McCauley Street, and its building would stand to the front and east side of the Kenan Center, closer to the site of the Dean Smith Center, which opened in 1986, and the conference center would be to the west side. But Frank Kenan told Fordham there would not be enough room on and around the hill for parking for a conference center, which is when that concept was scrapped and resurrected on the site off Hwy. 54 east of campus—the structure that became the Friday Center and opened in 1991. GAA Executive Director Doug Dibbert was told his building would move to the west side of the Kenan Center, and an article in the summer 1986 issue of the *Carolina Alumni Review* pictured the building on that site.

"We had construction documents for a 45,000-square-foot, $7 million building and were ready to turn dirt," Dibbert says. "Then one day, the University said, 'Never mind, we might want to build a business school there one day.'"

"It became clear that Mr. Kenan had greater ambitions for top of that hill," says Tom Lambeth, at the time the chair of the Alumni Association.

So the GAA acquired the current site for the George Watts Hill Alumni Center adjacent to Kenan Stadium, and it was left for Friday, Fordham and Kenan to work out the details of if and when the Business School would move.

"Bill Friday told Father, 'I saved that hill for you,'" Tom Kenan says. "Every dean and department head on campus wanted that hill."

"If ever there was a case where you were blessed to have something happen that originally upset you, this was it," Lambeth says. "The Alumni Center wound up in a much better place and the Business School fit nicely on the hill with the Kenan Center."

Frank Kenan stepped forward to continue the family's legacy of support to the University. Hardin announced on April 26, 1991, that the Kenan Trust was giving $10 million toward a new facility to be located on the hill alongside the Kenan Center. And the name of the school would be changed to Kenan-Flagler Business School—in honor of Mary Lily Kenan and her husband, Henry Morrison Flagler.

"I can think of nothing that we can do that would be a greater memorial to Mary Lily Kenan and Henry Flagler than to have one of the ten best business schools in the country be named for them," Kenan said.

"The Kenan name had been so important to the University for many, many years," Tom Kenan adds years later. "Mary Lily Flagler established the Kenan Professorships in 1917 to honor her father and his two brothers, who had all gone to Carolina. It was the largest private gift to a university in the country. Bill Friday told Father that the University would never have reached its level of greatness without those professorships. And of course, her money came from Henry Flagler.

"Father said, 'Why not put *both* names on the business school?'"

Hardin admitted that when Kenan made the proposal he had to do some research on the legacy of Flagler, a pioneer in the oil business and the primary developer of the East Coast of Florida.

"I think it's highly appropriate for the Flagler name to be memorialized on our campus," he told Kenan. "My own convictions in that regard were strengthened as I read a biography of Henry Flagler and came to realize how important his contributions were to the economic development of our country, particularly the state of Florida."

Hardin measured the gift as now putting at $40 million the Kenan family's total contributions to Carolina—from the Kenan Professorships to Kenan Stadium to chemistry facilities and a host of other programs and initiatives.

"The greatest gift that the Kenan Trust can make to the University, the state of North Carolina and, in fact, the region, is to ensure the quality of the Business School at the University of North Carolina," Frank Kenan said. "The school trains business leaders and is absolutely essential to the continued growth in our economy and improvement in the standard of living of our people."

Paul Fulton brought business acumen and plenty of connections to his role as dean in 1994; here he's chatting with Governor Jim Hunt at a school function.

Not surprisingly, the strictures of an academic and university environment tried the patience of a businessman, and Rizzo was not interested in another term as dean, leaving Kenan-Flagler in August 1992 and joining Robert C. Eubanks Jr. in launching Franklin Street Partners. Rizzo died in February 2017 at the age of eighty-nine.

The template of *executive-cum-academic* worked, though, and toward the end of his tenure Rizzo suggested to old friend Paul Fulton that he apply for the post. Fulton had been president of Sara Lee Corporation based in Chicago since 1988, but he had long-running ties to the state and to UNC. Fulton lived in Winston-Salem for many years working for Sara Lee subsidiary Hanes Hosiery before moving to Chicago. In the early 1990s, he was on the executive committee of the Bicentennial Campaign for Carolina and was a Board of Visitors member for the University as well as Kenan-Flagler Business School. Fulton visited Chapel Hill for an informal interview, but a news report leaked and got back to Chicago, and his boss talked him out of leaving.

The search committee looked at a number of candidates but circled back to Fulton, who by the second knock was ready to answer the call. He accepted the job in mid-1992 with the plan of retiring from Sara Lee at the end of 1993 and moving to Chapel Hill. Dr. Carl Zeithaml, the associate dean for academic affairs and a faculty member since 1986, was appointed interim dean.

Fulton started on Jan. 1, 1994 and worked through the fall of 1997—"About a hundred years," he says with a laugh. "No, seriously, I wouldn't trade it for anything. It was a wonderful experience. But it didn't feel like it every day. Academia and business are two different worlds. Both Rizzo and I found that out."

Fulton's priorities were to build on the development and fundraising acumen of Rizzo, oversee the new building and find additional space for Executive Education. He recognized that the school was underfunded when compared to its peer group.

"Paul Rizzo had that persona and reputation to put us on the map from the day he stepped foot on campus,"

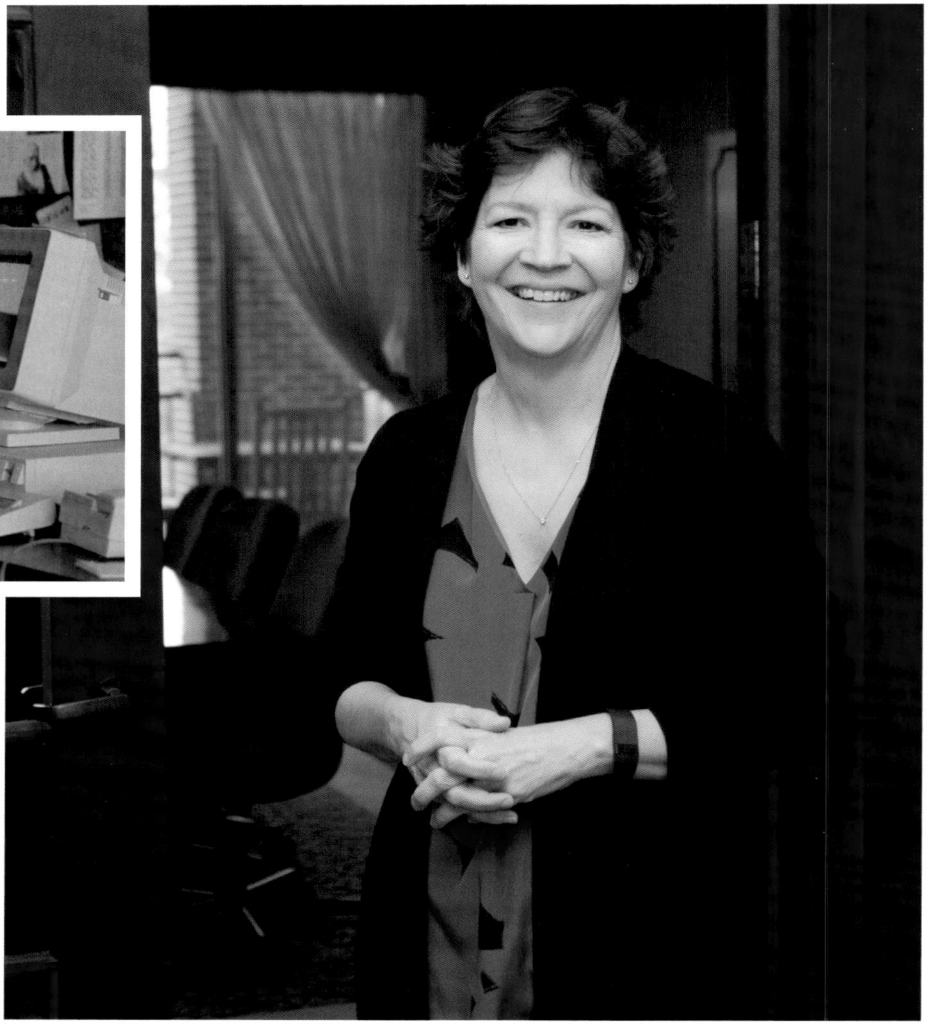

Jennifer Conrad joined the Kenan-Flagler faculty in 1985 and today is the Dalton McMichael Distinguished Professor of Finance. Over three-plus decades, she's proud of the school's emphasis on teaching: "We've never taken our eye off the ball in terms of teaching. So the culture that they had put in place around that engagement with students, certainly starting well before I got here, is still there. It's a remarkable accomplishment given the other changes in the school."

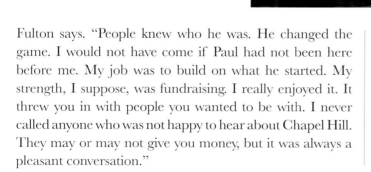

Fulton says. "People knew who he was. He changed the game. I would not have come if Paul had not been here before me. My job was to build on what he started. My strength, I suppose, was fundraising. I really enjoyed it. It threw you in with people you wanted to be with. I never called anyone who was not happy to hear about Chapel Hill. They may or may not give you money, but it was always a pleasant conversation."

Fulton apparently had a pretty good batting average.

"We used to joke if you see Paul Fulton coming, hide and don't answer his phone calls because it's going to cost you money," says Jay Klompmaker, who was an active supporter of the Carolina athletics program and served as an officer of The Rams Club. "Paul wouldn't let you go until you gave. I'll never forget, I went to the ACC Tournament one time and I looked and Paul was sitting right in front of

> *"Paul took all the blame in the press and we got all the benefit, a huge benefit that extended to other professional schools at UNC who followed suit."*
>
> Professor David Ravenscraft

me. I turned to my grandson and said, 'Just watch—this game is going to cost me money.'

"Seriously, though, he was the best fundraiser this school's ever had."

The MBA Program in the mid-1990s when still in Carroll Hall had three sections of approximately sixty-five students, or a total of 195 in one graduating class. Since it was a two-year program, two classes were enrolled and paying tuition—just under four hundred students.

"That was one of the smaller MBA programs when you looked across the playing field," Jack Evans says. "There was a feeling that we needed to grow the MBA program, and with moving to McColl and a larger facility, the plan was to add a fourth section. That would take us to a program with about 550 students."

That would cost money, as it would require hiring thirteen or fourteen new faculty members and support staff as well—not to mention the infrastructure to house them all.

"In-state tuition was locked in at $3,000," Fulton says. "You could never have a great business school on that tuition."

Fulton had a gutsy and aggressive strategy to address the issue, and it would forever change the way the school operated and affect its long-term financial health. Fulton added the fourth section to the MBA Program and negotiated a deal with key members of the State Legislature to allow Kenan-Flagler itself and not the University as a whole to keep the additional tuition.

"It was the greatest thing—financially speaking—that's ever happened to the school," says Doug Shackelford, a Kenan-Flagler graduate and since 2014 the school's dean. "It's worth some $27 million a year to our bottom line right now. If Paul had not broken every rule in the book, everything you see wouldn't be here. He got us funding and suddenly we could start to get on the map. We raised tuition and got market tuition.

"He got us financially on a path where we could build a great school."

Ravenscraft elaborated on that point in remarks at Fulton's eightieth birthday party in 2014.

"Amidst some incredible public outcry and the opposition of some very senior UNC administrators, Paul got the legislature to approve a tuition differential for the MBA Program that went to the Business School," he said. "Paul took all the blame in the press and we got all the benefit, a huge benefit that extended to other professional schools at UNC who followed suit."

"Paul had the vision and the fortitude to begin lobbying for us retaining all the tuition associated with that fourth section," Evans says. "And that was kind of the genesis of 'school-based tuition' as it's known in the University now because all the professional schools are doing it at some level."

Fulton admits the new accounting resulted in "a lot of unhappy people. I had stirred the pot a little too much. I had breakfast with (UNC System President) Molly Broad and told her I always practiced that I'd rather ask for forgiveness than permission. She said that was an issue that needed to be opened."

****

Paul Rizzo & Paul Fulton

A Tale Of Two Pauls

From the PC to pantyhose, two Kenan-Flagler deans from the 1980s through the mid-1990s brought serious chops borne of cutting-edge innovation in the business world to their academic posts.

Paul Rizzo was on the front line of management at IBM in the late 1970s and into the eighties when Big Blue made the transition from emphasizing expensive mainframe computers to mass producing smaller units that could sit on an individual's desk.

And Paul Fulton led the team with idea while at Hanes Hosiery in the late 1960s to take pantyhose from the private labels and counters of department stores to the aisles of drugstores and grocery markets, packaging them in plastic egg-shaped cartons and covering the nation with commercials and print ads hooked on the jingle, "Nothing beats a great pair of L'eggs."

Both Carolina business graduates (Rizzo 1951 and Fulton 1957), they returned to Chapel Hill after distinguished careers to lead Kenan-Flagler into a new realm of relevance among national business schools. Rizzo took the reins from 1987-92 and Fulton from 1994-97.

"That was a glorious time to be here," says Doug Shackelford, the Kenan-Flagler dean appointed in 2014. "We had the greatest guys in the world in charge of the place. There was no stopping them. We were chugging along on a steady pace. Then all of a sudden, it was a rocket shot. The guy in the corner office was going to get what he wanted."

Legion are the stories of two Type-A personalities accustomed to the take-charge world of business trying to assimilate into the nuances and relatively languid pace of academia and a public institution. Rizzo was told on his first day in Carroll Hall that he needed to go to another building to sign some paperwork in order to get paid; he flipped that away as a waste of his time. He actually resigned in the first week when Chancellor Chris Fordham answered a question with, "That's not the way we do things here," but they quickly found middle ground and Rizzo was back on the job.

Shackelford remembers a faculty meeting several years later when Fulton made a decision and told the group he planned to act.

"Someone said, 'I think we need to talk about it,'" Shackelford remembers. "Paul said, 'You can talk all you want, but this is what I'm going to do.' And he walked out of the room."

Rizzo played football at Carolina during the post World War II "Justice Era" and joined IBM in 1958. He quickly rose through the ranks and became vice president and corporate controller in 1965 and senior VP and chief financial officer in 1971. He was named to the IBM Board of Directors two years later when he was named a senior vice president, and he oversaw IBM's data processing product group as well as the corporate finance unit.

Rizzo was on a committee that gave the go-ahead for the production of the 4300 computer line, a lower-cost mainframe computer that could be mass marketed. "He was the guy who created the mentality which enabled them to go from the 4300 to the PC. He basically changed them from a custom shop to a mass-production shop," *Business North Carolina* magazine said.

Paul Rizzo (opposite) as vice chairman of IBM, Paul Fulton (above) as president of Sara Lee Corporation.

Nicholas Donofrio was secretary to the IBM Corporate Management Board in the mid-1980s when he first met Rizzo.

"Paul was the quintessential IBMer circa 1950-80, but he was anything but stereotypical," he told *THINK* magazine. "He was never afraid to ask the hard question, to think the unthinkable and do the improbable. Paul gave his unflagging

Paul Fulton was vice president of marketing at Hanes in 1971 when the company launched its revolutionary line of pantyhose packaged in a plastic egg-shaped container. Years later he was feted at a party for his eightieth birthday by his friends at Kenan-Flagler (opposite).

support of IBM's S/360 midrange systems, and he showed amazing patience to understand detail and communicate it in digestible pieces to his colleagues. He was always willing to let someone else be up front—as he was in the back making things happen."

Rizzo said he learned how to oversee IBM's vast development organization "by hitting the road—you can't learn a lot sitting in a meeting. You get out and talk to people—in the branch offices, in the plants, in the laboratories. If you really want to find out what's going on, find out from the troops."

As soon as Rizzo finished his five-year term as dean in 1992, he returned to IBM to help stabilize a company in the throes of near collapse. He stayed more than a year to recruit and advise new CEO Lou Gerstner. Then he settled in Chapel Hill and was one of the founders of Franklin Street Partners, an investment and money management firm. Rizzo died in February 2017 at the age of eighty-nine.

"Paul was the guy who called me about becoming dean when he left," said Fulton, who stepped in at the beginning of 1994. "I wouldn't have come if Paul had not been here before me. He stepped foot on campus and immediately things changed.

People knew who he was. He put the school on a different path."

Fulton is a native of Winston-Salem and was six years behind Rizzo at Carolina, and after two years in the Navy, he went to work as a trainee at Hanes Hosiery in 1959. He had advanced to vice president of marketing when the company, through its agency Dancer-Fitzgerald-Sample and noted package designer Roger Ferriter, introduced the L'eggs product in 1971. Within months, L'eggs was the top-selling brand in the hosiery market, and Hanes recorded $120 million in L'eggs sales in 1972 alone.

"The brand just exploded," Fulton remembers. "The market was still 50-50 stockings and pantyhose at the time. Pantyhose took off from there."

Fulton was named president of L'eggs Products in 1972 and later promoted to executive vice president of Hanes Corporation with responsibility for L'eggs Products and Hanes Hosiery. Hanes Corporation was acquired by Sara Lee Corporation in 1979 and Fulton was elected president of the Hanes Group and senior vice president of Sara Lee Corporation in 1981. In 1987, he was elected executive vice president and a member of the board. He served as president of Sara Lee Corporation from July 1, 1988 through June 30, 1993. He started as the dean at Kenan-Flagler at the beginning of 1994 and served until July 1997.

Fulton was a bundle of energy and a tireless fund-raiser. He befriended one lady well into her eighties who liked risqué jokes and called her often with a good one, the lady eventually giving generously to the school. He connected to the "little guys" as well, once striking up a conversation with a meat carver in a buffet line at the Carolina Club and arranging to get the man and his son tickets to the ACC Tournament.

UNC
KENAN-FLAGLER BUSINESS SCHOOL
Paul Fulton
With gratitude for your vision, leadership, and extraordinary support
2014

"Except for a very few people like Bill Friday, Frank Kenan, and coaches Dean Smith and Roy Williams, Paul has had more impact on UNC and particularly Kenan-Flagler than anyone," says David Ravenscraft, who admits he's biased since he holds the named professorship in Fulton's honor.

"One of Paul's favorite sayings was all the faculty want to be a cost center, what we need is ***revenue*** centers. Paul provided them for us. Paul added a fourth section to the MBA Program under the condition that the Business School keep the tuition. This is in addition to the $30 million he added to the endowment while he was dean and the large cash flow from the enhanced Executive Development programs made possible with the Rizzo Center."

School Gets New Home in McColl

Paul Fulton never took office in the sparkling dean's suite on the fourth floor of the school's new headquarters on South Campus. He left in July 1997 to become chairman and CEO of Bassett Furniture Industries. But it was his initiative that got the name of Hugh McColl, a 1957 UNC business graduate, on the building. Fulton served on the board of directors of NationsBank and thought that naming the building for McColl, the bank's president and CEO, would be an appropriate gesture. Construction of the building was well underway in 1996 when he phoned McColl's close friend and fellow banking pioneer Hootie Johnson with the idea of NationsBank making a naming-rights donation to Kenan-Flagler. McColl and Johnson were both native South Carolinians who had merged their respective banks into the behemoth that had become NationsBank (and would later become Bank of America).

"Hootie was really close to Hugh and he liked the idea. He carried it from there," Fulton says.

NationsBank gave $10 million to have the building named for McColl, and it opened on Sept. 12, 1997, with Federal Reserve Chairman Alan Greenspan delivering the keynote address in a ceremony attended by some four thousand alumni, faculty, students and invited guests. The building opened for classes on Oct. 20 and cost $44 million—paid for in $16.5 million in public financing and $27.5 in private donations—and was spread out over 191,234 square feet. The new facility was outfitted with Dell computers, one million feet of audio, video, data and fiber-optic

"The most wired business school in America" opened for classes on Oct. 20, 1997, and hundreds of students, faculty, friends and alumni gathered for the ribbon-cutting and dedication ceremony. Soon after, ground was broken for the renovation for the DuBose Home at Meadowmont, with (L-R) Warren Baunach, Pete DuBose, Dan Drake, Mac DuBose, Charlie Loudermilk, Paul Rizzo, Michael Hooker, Paul Fulton, Tom Kenan and Jack Evans turning shovels.

The DuBose Home sits serenely amidst the trees and elegantly coiffed grounds just to the east of the main UNC campus. Today it's the centerpiece for the Paul J. Rizzo Center, one of the top enclaves for executive development and conferences in the United States.

cable and 2,800 internet connections. A student could even log-in to the internet from the dining hall.

"McColl is the most 'wired' business school in America," said Rollie Tillman, a 1954 graduate and later a professor of marketing and development official. "I was excited about moving into Carroll Hall in 1953, and I'm excited now."

Rizzo and Fulton both had hands in the conception and execution of an important new facility enhancement located off-campus and geared for Executive Education. The Carroll Hall space crunch in the 1980s affected the school's ability to bring out-of-town executives to Chapel Hill, and using off-campus hotel and meeting space was costly and cumbersome. Two rooms on the fourth floor of the new Kenan Center when it opened in 1986 were used for Executive Education, but having to ferry executives back and forth between The Carolina Inn prompted school officials to seriously think of creating an all-inclusive lodging and conference facility.

It would be quite fitting that Kenan-Flagler would come full circle in its expansion to a tract of land east of campus with direct connections over multiple generations to the Kenan family.

The family of Christopher Barbee was known as "the first family" of Chapel Hill as it owned more than two thousand acres of land, and in 1792 the family patriarch, known as "Old Kit," donated 221 acres on the crest of the hill in southern Orange County to University trustees to form the core of campus. One of Barbee's great granddaughters was Mary "Mollie" Hargrave, who married William R. Kenan Sr. (known as "Buck"), and their four children included Mary Lily and William R. Kenan Jr. (known as "Will"). The Barbee land was handed down several generations, then sold and finally acquired in 1931 by David St. Pierre DuBose, a 1921 UNC graduate who returned to Chapel Hill from Baltimore with the dream of creating a rural estate.

DuBose was married to Valinda Hill, the daughter of John Sprunt Hill, an early University benefactor who built and donated The Carolina Inn to his alma mater. DuBose built a handsome two-and-a-half story Georgian Revival house on the crest of the hill that originally was the site of the Barbee farmhouse. Valinda named it "Meadowmont" since it sat on a mountain surrounded by meadows.

Frank Kenan and his son Tom had spent many pleasant times over the years at Meadowmont as the Kenan and Hill families were related by marriage, and the youngsters of the extended families remembered riding horses and running through the pastures surrounding the home that opened in 1933. The DuBose family eventually sold much of its land for what became the Meadowmont mixed-use development and in 1988 donated twenty-eight acres of land and the family home to the University. The University took possession in 1994 following DuBose's death and wrestled with what to do with the land and house, which was in need of significant and costly renovations.

"Mr. DuBose wanted it to be the home for the UNC System president," Tom Kenan remembers. "Dick Spangler was president at the time and said, 'No way, I can't invite the legislature here, I won't get a dime if they saw this. That is not going to work.' So Father and Paul Rizzo said it would be a wonderful Executive Education center for the Business School. Whoever took it over was going to have to spend some money to do it right."

Fulton had stepped into the Kenan-Flagler deanship by the time DuBose died, and he came to the same idea in a conversation with Richard Jenrette, a UNC graduate, Wall Street titan and noted "collector" of historical mansions across the Eastern Seaboard and into the Virgin Islands.

"At the time, we were going to build an Executive Education center on land behind the McColl Building," Fulton says. "I mentioned that to Dick when I was visiting him in New York and he said, 'Have you seen the DuBose Home?' I said I had not. I got off the plane and went there

A sports bar, outdoor pool, state-of-the-art meeting facilities and the Steven Bell Hall are among the amenities putting the Rizzo Center atop the Executive Education pyramid. "I believe strongly in the goal and purpose of the Rizzo Center," says Bell (BA 1967). "It's functional, attractive and a good draw for the University."

and looked at it. I said, 'This is it.' We had to convince Chancellor Paul Hardin to give us use of it, then we had to raise the money to restore it."

The University announced in the fall of 1994 a $9 million gift from the Kenan Trust, with $8 million going to the Executive Education center and $1 million to establish a Center for Entrepreneurial Studies. Frank Kenan three years earlier had hoped the new Kenan-Flagler headquarters building being planned on land adjacent to the Kenan Center would be named for Rizzo in the same spirit that the University had named Carroll Hall for its eminent and original dean.

"I think Dean Carroll and Dean Rizzo have been as responsible as anybody in both creating and fostering the School of Business at the University of North Carolina," Kenan wrote in a 1992 letter to Paul Hardin.

Kenan was happy to change that focus, however, and donate to the new Executive Education center under the provision that it take the name of Rizzo, his old friend and fellow Tar Heel football letterman. (Kenan played in the 1930s, Rizzo a decade later.) The project would include re-storing the DuBose Home and building new lodging and classroom facilities. Members of the planning committee remember Kenan, who was in his eighties and not in the

best of health, perking up during one meeting when he heard an architect say that as a cost-savings measure, the roofs of the new buildings would be made of artificial slate in a color to match the natural slate on the DuBose House.

"Mr. Kenan asked, 'How much would it cost to use *real* slate?'" Bill Moore remembers. "The architects came back with some number well into six figures. Mr. Kenan had a check the next day for that amount."

Dave Stevens, senior associate dean for business and operations at Kenan-Flagler, attended the same meeting.

"Frank said, 'You know, someday I'm going to be looking down at this facility from up there, and I don't want to look at architectural shingles,'" Stevens says. "There shouldn't be anything second class, so we're going to put slate on the roof.

"That's why everything kind of looks like the house. We picked the brick to match the house. The dormers, the windows, the fireplaces, the chimneys—all are integrated with the home. The DuBose Home sits on a rise, on a knoll of the property, and everything else is just a little below it in elevation."

Kenan-Flagler broke ground for the Paul J. Rizzo Center in 1997—the year after Frank Kenan's death in June 1996—and it was dedicated on Sept. 22, 1999. The facility was comprised of the original DuBose House and two new buildings—McLean Hall, named in honor of the late James K. McLean Sr. (UNC '39) and his wife Sarah, and Loudermilk Hall, named for R. Charles Loudermilk Sr. (UNC '50).

Over two decades the facility has been expanded and today has 183 boutique hotel rooms, conference and meeting space, a sports bar and two restaurants and a variety of recreational amenities.

"Before the Rizzo Center, Executive Education was a three or four million-dollar entity, and now it's twenty-five," Stevens says. "I will put our facility up with any Executive Education center in the country. In our mind it's the best. I don't think anyone has anything close to it. That's not just ego. I would stand it up against anything."

****

The Meadow, The Mountain

The DuBose Home

To stand on the front porch of the DuBose Home at dusk, cocktail in hand, the hum of conversation and laughter all about and the sun filtering through the towering oak trees to the west is a sublime feeling. Old-timers say that before the foliage grew so thick, one could stand on that hilltop and gaze across the valley and meadows below all the way to the crest of what was called "New Hope Chapel" and where the University of North Carolina sprung up in the 1700s.

That's why Kenan-Flagler and UNC officials decided in the mid-1990s that the 1933 DuBose Home and the twenty-eight acres on which it sat would be perfect to house business executives from around the world attending the school's Executive Development program. The DuBose Home would be the historical anchor for receptions and meal functions, and around it would be hotel, meeting and conference facilities.

"I don't see there being any other use of the Meadowmont property," Chancellor Michael Hooker said in early 1996 when the idea took root. "It will substantially enhance the Kenan-Flagler Business School. Business schools can be broken into two categories—those with sophisticated executive education centers and those without. Those that do tend to be ranked at the top."

"Executive education is really the linchpin of a good business school," added Warren Baunach, associate dean for Executive Development, when the school broke ground in November 1997 on the $18 million Rizzo Conference Center. "It brings the business community to campus, which aids recruiting of our students. It takes faculty to corporations in the United States and abroad for consulting and research. It's really a great synergy."

Dr. John McNeely "Mac" DuBose was one year old when his family moved into the house in 1933—his father David St. Pierre, mother Valinda and siblings Pete and Faison. DuBose remembers as a boy playing in the woods, fishing for bass in the lake on the property and shooting quail. He also raised ducks and sold them to the grocery store at the bottom of the hill going up to campus, where Glen Lennox is today.

"I also tried to grow vegetables in a 'victory garden' after World War II, but all I could get to grow were onions and radishes," he says. "It was a wonderful place to grow up."

DuBose graduated from Carolina in 1955 and went to medical school at Johns Hopkins, then set up a surgery practice in Baltimore. As David and Valinda aged, they began selling off parts of what was once a 1,200-acre estate for what would become the Meadowmont community. All that was left when Valinda died in 1989 was the house

The view from the front (inset) and rear of the 1933 DuBose Home. Frank Kenan made sure that the new buildings of the Rizzo Center built in the 1990s had slate roofs to match the original home.

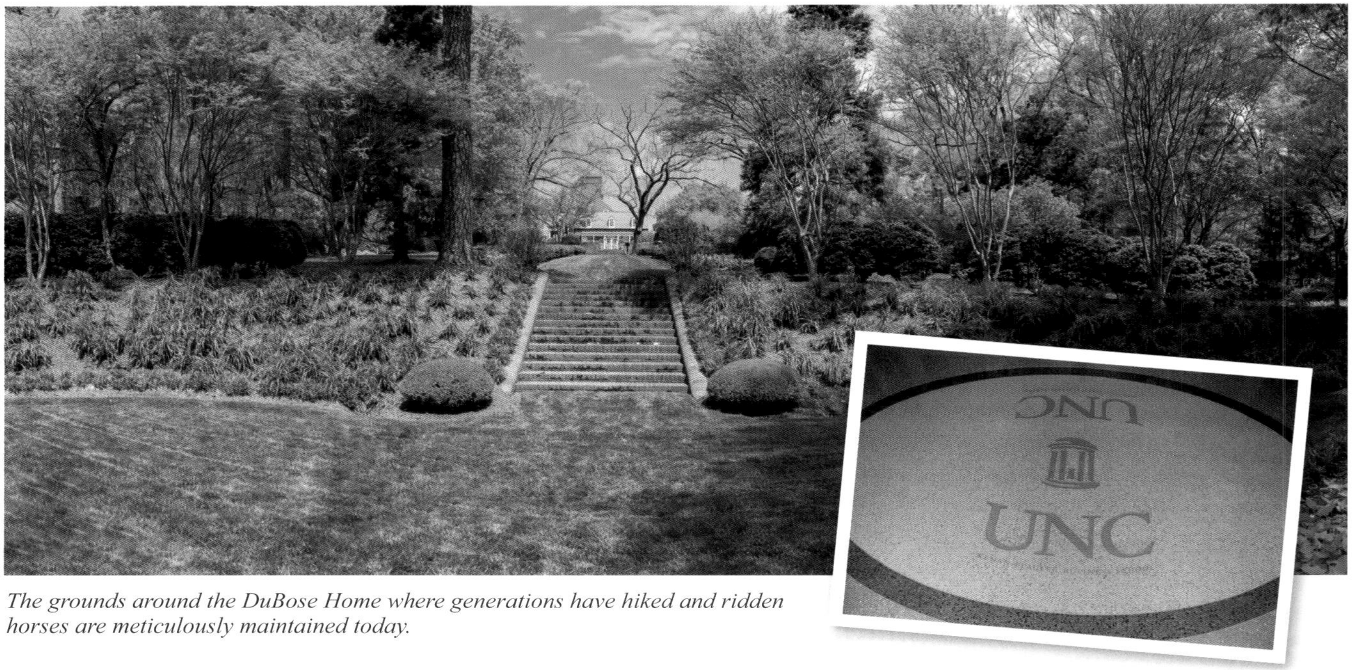

The grounds around the DuBose Home where generations have hiked and ridden horses are meticulously maintained today.

and twenty-eight acres.

"It was offered to my brother or my sister or myself," Mac said in July 2017. "We all declined because it was quite obvious it would take more to maintain it than either of the three of us could afford. With taxation the way it was, you might have a certain amount of material wealth, but you divide what's left after taxing it and it shrinks rapidly. You would have nothing left."

The DuBose family gave the property to the University, and it had five years from Valinda's death in 1989 to David's passing in 1994 to decide what to do with the house and land. Both Frank Kenan and Paul Fulton, the Kenan-Flagler dean in 1994, thought the site would be ideal for Executive Development.

It cost just under four million dollars to refurbish the house for commercial use, and there is an endowment fund left from the original DuBose family gift that supports a significant part of upkeep of the home and maintenance of the grounds. The house was reopened and dedicated on Sept. 22, 1999, and is on the National Register of Historic Places.

"It's a wonderful memorial to my parents," DuBose says. "This is a unique place, no other university has a facility like this. I'm very happy to share it, to know that it's going to be maintained."

Dave Stevens, senior associate dean of business and operations at Kenan-Flagler, remembers giving Dr. DuBose and his wife Lynne a tour of the house in 2000 when it first opened.

"He stopped upstairs and you could see his eyes well up," Stevens says. "He said, 'Dave you guys did it.' That meant a lot to me and to our staff. The DuBose Home and Rizzo Center are an important part of who we are and what we do."

Among the buildings at the Rizzo Center are McLean Hall, named in honor of the late James K. McLean Sr. (UNC '39) and his wife Sarah; and Steven D. Bell Hall, the wedge-shaped building at the top-right of the complex named for the 1967 Carolina graduate.

Tech Boom Keys New Horizons

Jack Evans stepped in as interim dean for the last four months of 1997 after Paul Fulton left and before the appointment of Dr. Robert S. Sullivan became effective. Sullivan had been director of the University of Texas at Austin's Innovation Creativity Capital Institute, and his arrival was lauded by Chancellor Michael Hooker as "a major coup." Hooker was most impressed in the search process by Sullivan's "ability to guide bold, ambitious technological initiatives that inspire students, faculty and the business community."

Sullivan began work in Chapel Hill on Jan. 1, 1998, and presided over the school until 2002, when he left to become the first dean at the newly formed Rady School of Management at the University of California, San Diego.

Under Sullivan's watch, the OneMBA Program was launched—an Executive MBA and equal partnership with five top business schools in four continents. David Ravenscraft, at the time associate dean of the Executive MBA Program, says the program was spawned out of a desire to address one of the school's weaknesses at the time.

"We recognized we were not as global as we would like, and to be a serious player, you've got to be global," he remembers. "We also recognized that what we *are* good at is teamwork. We're *really* good at teamwork."

Thus came the concept of partnering with other top business schools and offering a program that would take students around the world for study to learn from local professors and business people. Ravenscraft coordinated the planning and execution of the new venture, with the OneMBA program lasting twenty-one months and taking students from each of the partner schools and dispatching them to global residencies on four continents. A student might spend a week in the fall in Chapel Hill or Washington, D.C., a week in the spring in Mexico City, a week in the fall in an Asian city like Xiamen and then a week in the spring in a European city like Rotterdam.

The program operated successfully until "careful consideration of our organizational goals" from Dean Doug Shackelford prompted the July 2018 announcement that the class entering in the fall of 2018 would be the last cohort from Kenan-Flagler to go through the program.

Following Sullivan's departure, Chancellor James Moeser then turned to Carolina graduate Steve Jones (Morehead Scholar, 1974 BS economics, later Harvard MBA) to lead the school into its first decade of the new century. Jones had spent fifteen years in Australia, the last ten as CEO of Suncorp Metway Ltd., one of Australia's twenty-five largest companies, and as managing director of ANZ Banking Group N.Z. Ltd., one of New Zealand's top companies. Jones was also a management consultant at McKinsey & Company for six years before going to Australia.

He and his wife were trying to decide in early 2003 where to move their family that included four school-aged children upon their return to the United States, and two cities high on the list were Atlanta and Chapel Hill. Jones thought if they wound up in Chapel Hill that a part-time teaching gig at Kenan-Flagler would be fun. He was interviewed by a professor who mistakenly thought Jones was interviewing for the deanship.

"He looked at my resume and said, 'Well, maybe you should think about it,'" says Jones, who later joked that he became "the accidental dean" as a series of dominoes fell and he did, in fact, become dean effective August 1, 2003. That date would have been July 1, but Jones wanted to spend a month essentially as an unpaid observer around the school before officially taking the reins. For the third time in its last four dean appointments, the University was opting for a proven success in the business world rather than a career academician. Jones's extensive international

Jack Behrman

A Man Of The World

The Berlin Wall fell on Nov. 9, 1989, and one week later Ross Perot, the founder of Electronic Data Systems and eventual two-time Presidential candidate in the 1990s, was in Chapel Hill delivering the keynote address to the inaugural Kenan Conference on International Competitiveness. He built his talk around the measures he thought America must take to regain its edge in world markets.

"He challenged our students to *not* go to Wall Street, *not* go to Madison Avenue but get yourself over to Europe and watch those formerly state-run economies move to free market economies," remembers Jean Elia, who spent twenty-five years in administrative and leadership roles at Kenan-Flagler and the Kenan Institute. "And the next morning, Jack Behrman had students knocking on his door saying, 'How do we get there?'"

When it came to international issues, Behrman was ***the man*** at Kenan-Flagler.

Behrman, a 1943 Davidson graduate, earned his master of accounting in 1945 at Carolina. He taught in the Business School for more than twenty-seven years as a professor of international business, director of the full-time MBA Program, associate dean of faculty and Luther Hodges Distinguished Professor of Ethics.

Behrman worked in more than seventy-five countries over his career, and his crowning achievement at Kenan-Flagler was founding and directing the MBA Enterprise Corps immediately following the fall of the Berlin Wall. It started with sixteen top business schools in 1990 and grew to have more than fifty member schools.

The idea was to create a "Peace Corps for MBA students," with recent MBA graduates going on year-long consulting assignments to private and privatizing companies in countries that were moving out of planned economies. Hundreds of students served in more than thirty countries in central Europe, Russia, Africa, South America and Central and Southeast Asia. Behrman remained its chairman and CEO for fifteen years.

Ajit Dayal (MBA '83), CEO at the private equity firm QIEF Management, paid tribute to Behrman in 2013 by establishing through QIEF a program named The Jack Behrman "Pay It Forward" India Fellowship Award. Dayal credits Behrman among other Kenan-Flagler professors with instilling in him the obligation to pursue an ethical business career in an environment where many don't play by the same rules.

"Our goal in sponsoring this fellowship is to honor Professor Behrman by giving a student from India the opportunity to carry on the pursuit of peace and prosperity in the global economy and society," says Dayal.

Doug Shackelford added upon Behrman's death in August 2016: "When I visit alumni around the world, he is one of the professors they remember most fondly. I had the privilege of knowing Jack as a friend, and he gave me a sense of the treasure and legacy that each of us upholds as a member of this community."

perspective was a plus as well.

"It's a big deal when any school in the academy gets somebody as a dean who has not come up through the academic ranks, it's really rare," Jones says. "If you talk to a place that's never had one, they can't quite conceive of it. Rizzo and Fulton showed, 'This is a good thing.'"

Two of the first significant personnel moves Jones made were naming Doug Shackelford to senior associate dean for academic affairs and Dr. Valarie Zeithaml to associate dean of the full-time MBA Program. Shackelford was a veteran of the faculty in accounting and a respected tax scholar. Zeithaml was a professor of marketing and would later be appointed as the David S. Van Pelt Family Distinguished Professor of Marketing. Jones knew both from the application and interview process, and before he was hired, he told each of them that they would be important parts of his potential administration.

"If you're coming from outside, you have to have the best people inside take the most important leadership roles," Jones says. "You could see all the ingredients were there for a great business school."

Among the milestones of the next five years was the launching of real estate and private-equity funds within the school. The Kenan-Flagler Real Estate Funds were administered by long-time professor Dave Hartzell and since 2007 have provided students real-time experience in managing what had become through the spring of 2018 three funds with $8.1 million invested in over thirty-four deals. The Kenan-Flagler Private Equity Fund also was born in 2007 and was the first student-run private equity fund whose mission was to invest outside capital in an educational setting to deliver real returns for investors. The fund in 2019 oversees more than twenty investments across three active funds.

Jones also sensed a need for a more focused leadership training program and in 2005 created the STAR program, the name being an acronym for Student Teams Achieving Results, and the Leadership Initiative.

"Under Valarie's guidance, we chose 'leadership development' as the theme of what you get from a Kenan-Flagler education," Jones says. "If you want finance, go to Wharton. If you want tech, go to Stanford. If you want leadership development, you come here."

The STAR program put students and their faculty advisors in the role of consultants to real companies and continues today, with recent clients including such entities as NASCAR, Bayer Crop Service, ESPN, Lenovo, and Harrah's Cherokee Casino Resort. Students work in teams and each student at some point is put in a leadership position.

"You can learn the principles of leadership, but you only learn leadership through leadership experience and getting feedback and reflecting and coaching," Jones says. "Some things in the business world you can only learn by *doing*. STAR is about learning through experience and getting coaching and feedback."

Mindy Storrie, an Executive MBA graduate from Kenan-Flagler who had led the MBA Career Management Center, was the director of the Leadership Initiative at its inception and developed an integrated, experience-based program that assesses and develops MBAs' leadership skills. The focus began with MBA students and now extends to Undergraduate Business and Master of Accounting students.

"Most importantly, we are dedicated to ensuring our students have a range of opportunities to learn the theory and practice of leadership in significant and lasting ways," says Storrie.

"Teaching leadership principles is not enough," says Jones. "The formula for developing leadership skills also includes the trial-and-error application of those principles, followed by constructive feedback. Kenan-Flagler students apply what they've learned to solve real problems for real companies—where consequences matter."

Jones stepped down in 2008 after one term as dean and remains at Kenan-Flagler as a professor of organizational behavior. Looking back, he's most proud of the personnel components he helped put in place and the Leadership Initiative.

"I think that we—*we*—began to focus on leadership development, which has lasted and prospered," he says. "That's an enduring part of the work during my time."

Kenan-Flagler's global initiatives include a dual-degree MBA program with Tsinghua University's Department of Industrial Engineering, designed to meet the growing need in China for executives with both leadership skills and technical knowledge.This photo is the 2015 graduating class of the UNC Tsinghua program.

Dr. James W. Dean Jr. had been at Kenan-Flagler since 1997 as a professor of organizational behavior and had served multiple leadership roles, including associate dean for both the MBA and Executive Development programs and senior associate dean beginning in 2007. He was promoted to dean in July 2008 and took over in August.

Dean had earlier made a significant contribution to the school when, as associate dean of the MBA Program in 1999, he had the idea to synthesize the standards and culture he sensed at Kenan-Flagler into five "core values." It took more than six months of meetings, opinions and voting to arrive at *Excellence, Leadership, Integrity, Community* and *Teamwork*—five words that still resonate today through every fiber of the school.

"Two things that distinguish us from other schools are the values of community and teamwork," says Shackelford (BSBA '80), who's been on the faculty since 1990 and was named dean in 2014. "Those are things in which you get drilled into you that it's not about *you*. And that's not the reputation of most business schools. Most business schools have a reputation, and somewhat rightly earned, that this is the place you go to figure out how you can make the most money in the world.

"Kenan-Flagler is a place to which you come and from your first day here, you become part of a team and you learn and your success will be how well your *team* succeeds. If the team wins, then you win."

Dean also recognized the growing power and speed of the internet and wondered how online education might fit into the school's mission and operations. He took the seeds planted in Jones' last days as dean and cultivated them into what would become one of Kenan-Flagler's most important projects, the creation and christening of the MBA@UNC online program in 2011.

One of the last hires Jones made in early 2008 was Susan Cates, a Duke undergrad who earned her MBA from Kenan-Flagler in 1998. She was a partner with Best Associates, a private equity firm with investments primarily in the education sector, based in Dallas, and was on the school's Board of Visitors; in that capacity, she was asked to sit on a search committee for the associate dean for Executive Development. The committee struggled to find the right candidate, and eventually Jones suggested to Cates that she would be ideal for the job.

Better internet speeds, faster laptop computers and innovative production techniques allowed Kenan-Flagler to literally go worldwide with its MBA@UNC program.

"I told Steve that I knew what they were looking for, and I was definitely not it," she says. "Then he said, 'Well, sometimes when you're looking for a point guard, you go find the best point guard you can find, and sometimes you go find a great athlete and you turn them into a point guard.'

"So I said, 'If you think I can be a point guard,' let's talk."

A small group of students at Jones' behest had been brainstorming ideas of experimental ventures the school could undertake to access the growing bandwidth and speed of the internet. (In the mid-1990s a course called "Business Opportunities on the Internet" was held in Carroll Hall at 8 a.m., a period of light usage that allowed the group to connect relatively easily to the internet.)

"One of those ideas was doing an online business certificate for non-business majors," Cates says. "I immediately said, 'That one I want to do.' And so I picked that up and with Executive Development, we launched UNC Business Essentials, which was the first real online initiative that the school took on."

"The internet and technology changed a lot of things about the way education worked," Dean said in 2017. "By '97, email was well-established to the point that it dominated the way everyone communicated."

Dean was approached in 2009 by a start-up company called 2tor that wanted to talk about offering an MBA program online. At first, he was somewhat hesitant.

"I just didn't see how it could work," Dean says. "The MBA Program was all about *interaction* between students."

Dean says his opinion changed when 2tor unveiled a teaching platform dubbed "The Brady Bunch"—a window with small screens for every student and professor in the room, reminiscent of the opening theme to the early 1970s television show.

"The ability to interact with one another was what I feared was going to be missing from the program," he says. "Once I saw we could do that, I was more positive. But still, there were a lot of people who thought it was a really bad idea. They said we were going to ruin the reputation of the school by offering online classes."

Dean promised the skeptics that, as had been the case with the first Executive MBA Program in the 1980s, the quality of the curriculum, the faculty, and the students would not be comprised. Shackelford embraced the idea and took on the role of selling it to his faculty colleagues.

"There literally was nobody else on the faculty that

could have had the same sort of influence as Doug did if he were onboard with it," Cates says. "People knew that he would not back something that wasn't the highest quality, that if he didn't fully believe in it himself."

Kenan-Flagler gave 2tor (which would later change its name to 2U) the thumbs-up and signed a deal in November 2010 for 2tor to provide the technology platform, instructional design, marketing and infrastructure support to deliver the classes online.

"I give the school and Jim and Doug a lot of props for believing. You had to *believe*," says Chip Paucek, co-founder of 2U and later a 2017 MBA@UNC graduate. "There was really no data, no evidence that this was where the world was going. It was not totally obvious. We were able to show what we *thought* we could do, but we had no proof. You kind of had to believe that this was a part of the future of graduate education."

Dean remembers a trip to the University of Southern California to inspect 2tor's operation in a similar venture at USC and asking how Kenan-Flagler should price the online MBA versus the $89,000 cost for the regular program.

"They said to price it the same," Dean says. "If you price it less, people will think of it as being less valuable."

The first classes were held on Independence Day—July 4, 2011.

"We made the decision from the beginning that we were going to be holiday agnostic," Cates says, "that we were going to start classes on the first Monday of every calendar quarter, so January, April, July and October. And the first Monday of July happened to fall on the fourth, and so we said, that's fine. We're going to be a global program, and so we cannot start moving around based on holidays."

The new program had the same admission standards and used the same professors as the full-time program. Ironically, the perceived initial issue of a lack of intimacy wasn't a problem at all. The environment was actually quite the opposite.

"2U's slogan was, 'There's no back row,'" says Cates. "You can't slouch in the back. If you nod off, everyone in the class sees you. The word we got quickly after we started was that the structure felt very intimate."

MBA@UNC has grown considerably over half a dozen years and in 2018 had just under a thousand students enrolled, and other business schools across the country have fallen like dominoes in launching similar programs. Dean was heartened to see that the Tepper School of Business at Carnegie Mellon University, where he had received his PhD, entered the online space soon afterward.

"I was on a review committee there and they were peppering me with questions about the online program," Dean says. "It was a funny kind of conflict of interest, since I am an alum there but was a dean at Kenan-Flagler."

Dean left Kenan-Flagler in July 2013 to move to South Building and become executive vice president and provost under Chancellor Carol Folt (and in 2018 left Chapel Hill to become president of the University of New Hampshire). Susan King, dean of the UNC School of Media and Journalism, led the search committee that landed on a native of North Carolina, UNC undergrad and expert on tax and accounting who had been teaching at Kenan-Flagler for nearly a quarter of a century.

In Doug Shackelford, the committee saw a candidate with an intense love of the institution and a respect for Carolina's public-university mission.

"He loved the opportunity Carolina offered farm boys like him to go to the top of the business world," King remembers. "He talked with passion about growing up on a tobacco farm and his personality and soul was never far from those roots, although he earned a PhD and rubbed shoulders with CEOs and America's world leaders. He wants education and a business degree to take individuals—willing to work hard—to new vistas and to grow a state and a community in the process."

****

MBA@UNC

The New Frontier

Jamie DeMaria once took a class from Kenan-Flagler on a cruise ship in the Caribbean Sea. Kristen Fanarakis was caught in Los Angeles freeway traffic, so she took an exit as class time approached, found a coffee shop and logged on to her operations class. And Allen Baker quietly arose at 2 a.m. at his Navy base in Africa to connect with his professor and classmates on the other side of the globe.

The business of business education changed dramatically in the summer of 2011 when MBA@UNC launched, allowing students to interact with their professors and classmates from anywhere in the world with a laptop computer and good internet connection.

"It was a blessing and a curse," says DeMaria, one of nineteen students in the original MBA@UNC cohort. "It gave you tremendous flexibility to continue your life, but on the flip side, you could never use the excuse, 'I'm on vacation and can't come to class.'"

"The online piece was crucial for me because I didn't want to be married to a city," adds Fanarakis. "It allowed me to do and be wherever I wanted. And I was everywhere. I went to Asia twice. I lived out in San Francisco for a while. I was in Atlanta and D.C. I could accomplish multiple life goals having the flexibility of the online program."

The MBA@UNC program has grown from that original class to nearly a thousand students enrolled per year in 2018. It evolved as turbocharged internet speeds became available and as Kenan-Flagler's production partner, 2U, improved its technical capabilities. And it was also born of necessity in the wake of the 2008-09 recession.

"The state of North Carolina started to decrease its financial commitment to the UNC System during the recession," says Dave Stevens, senior associate dean of business and operations. "So from an entrepreneurial standpoint, we had to start thinking more creatively. You could read where the state was going. So you can either shrink or find alternatives. The online program opportunity came about around that time, and we did take advantage of it."

So did students like DeMaria, Fanarakis and Baker. For each of them, halting their lives and moving to Chapel Hill for the full-time MBA Program was out of the question.

DeMaria was thirty-eight years old and in the pharmaceutical industry. He had a PhD in neuroscience and believed he needed a broader business education.

"I was married with two kids, and the idea of quitting my job and not having an income and going back to school for two years was untenable," he says. "As the program started to evolve, I took a look and said, 'This is just what I'm looking for.' It's a top school and I don't have to quit my job, give up my paycheck and relocate my family."

The commitment means never having an excuse that he was on vacation and couldn't come to class.

"I took class in an airport and at sea," he says. "It was a family vacation that had been planned for some time, my in-laws' anniversary. One class was late at night so I got on the ship's Wi-Fi from the pool deck as we traveled from St. Thomas to Aruba."

When students log on to the 2U platform, they get a screen with their professor's face in the middle and up to fifteen students' heads surrounding it.

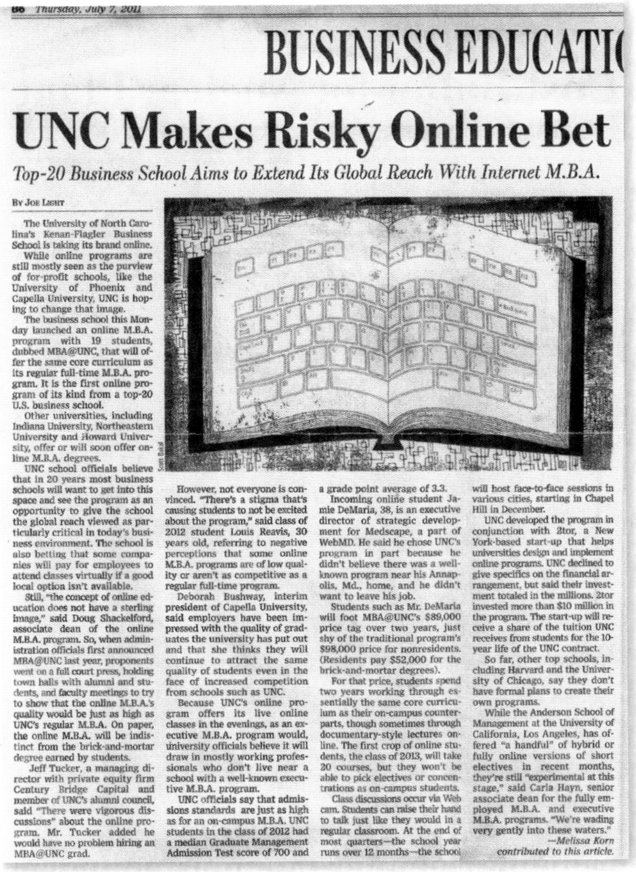

B6 Thursday, July 7, 2011

BUSINESS EDUCATI[O

UNC Makes Risky Online Bet

Top-20 Business School Aims to Extend Its Global Reach With Internet M.B.A.

BY JOE LIGHT

The University of North Carolina's Kenan-Flagler Business School is taking its brand online.

While online programs are still mostly seen as the purview of for-profit schools, like the University of Phoenix and Capella University, UNC is hoping to change that image.

The business school this Monday launched an online M.B.A. program with 19 students, dubbed MBA@UNC, that will offer the same core curriculum as its regular full-time M.B.A. program. It is the first online program of its kind from a top-20 U.S. business school.

Other universities, including Indiana University, Northeastern University and Howard University, offer or will soon offer online M.B.A. degrees.

UNC school officials believe that in 20 years most business schools will want to get into this space and see the program as an opportunity to give the school the global reach viewed as particularly critical in today's business environment. The school is also betting that some companies will pay for employees to attend classes virtually if a good local option isn't available.

Still, "the concept of online education does not have a sterling image," said Doug Shackelford, associate dean of the online M.B.A. program. So, when administration officials first announced MBA@UNC last year, proponents went on a full court press, holding town halls with alumni and students, and faculty meetings to try to show that the online M.B.A.'s quality would be just as high as UNC's regular M.B.A. On paper, the online M.B.A. will be indistinct from the brick-and-mortar degree earned by students.

Jeff Tucker, a managing director with private equity firm Century Bridge Capital and member of UNC's alumni council, said "There were vigorous discussions" about the online program. Mr. Tucker added he would have no problem hiring an MBA@UNC grad.

However, not everyone is convinced. "There's a stigma that's causing students to not be excited about the program," said class of 2012 student Louis Reavis, 30 years old, referring to negative perceptions that some online M.B.A. programs are of low quality or aren't as competitive as a regular full-time program.

Deborah Bushway, interim president of Capella University, said employers have been impressed with the quality of graduates the university has put out and that she thinks they will continue to attract the same quality of students even in the face of increased competition from schools such as UNC.

Because UNC's online program offers its live online classes in the evenings, as an executive M.B.A. program would, university officials believe it will draw in mostly working professionals who don't live near a school with a well-known executive M.B.A. program.

UNC officials say that admissions standards are just as high as for an on-campus M.B.A. UNC students in the class of 2012 had a median Graduate Management Admission Test score of 700 and a grade point average of 3.3.

Incoming online student Jamie DeMaria, 38, is an executive director of strategic development for Medscape, a part of WebMD. He said he chose UNC's program in part because he didn't believe there was a well-known program near his Annapolis, Md., home, and he didn't want to leave his job.

Students such as Mr. DeMaria will foot MBA@UNC's $89,000 price tag over two years, just shy of the traditional program's $98,000 price for nonresidents. (Residents pay $52,000 for the brick-and-mortar degrees).

For that price, students spend two years working through essentially the same core curriculum as their on-campus counterparts, though sometimes through documentary-style lectures online. The first crop of online students, the class of 2013, will take 20 courses, but they won't be able to pick electives or concentrations as on-campus students.

Class discussions occur via Web cam. Students can raise their hand to talk just like they would in a regular classroom. At the end of most quarters—the school year runs over 12 months—the school will host face-to-face sessions in various cities, starting in Chapel Hill in December.

UNC developed the program in conjunction with 2tor, a New York-based start-up that helps universities design and implement online programs. UNC declined to give specifics on the financial arrangement, but said their investment totaled in the millions. 2tor invested more than $10 million in the program. The start-up will receive a share of the tuition UNC receives from students for the 10-year life of the UNC contract.

So far, other top schools, including Harvard and the University of Chicago, say they don't have formal plans to create their own programs.

While the Anderson School of Management at the University of California, Los Angeles, has offered "a handful" of hybrid or fully online versions of short electives in recent months, they're still "experimental at this stage," said Carla Hayn, senior associate dean for the fully employed M.B.A. and executive M.B.A. programs. "We're wading very gently into these waters."

—Melissa Korn contributed to this article.

"The Wall Street Journal" proclaimed it a risky bet when the MBA@UNC program opened in July 2011. Nineteen students in the first cohort have exploded to approximately one thousand eight years later.

"They liked to say, 'There is no back row,' and they were right," DeMaria remembers of his financial accounting class. "The professor would randomly cold-call people. You couldn't be distracted or take your eyes off the screen for two seconds. At any moment he might ask a question. It very intense."

Fanarakis was thirty-six and had worked in finance in Boston and then on Wall Street and was at Morgan Stanley just after the 2008-09 financial crisis. She had tried during free time over the years taking classes toward an MBA but had gained no real momentum, and when her group at Morgan Stanley was let go after the recession, she had the opportunity in 2011 at Kenan-Flagler to pursue that MBA but not be locked into a particular city or campus.

"No one knew what to expect with the format, but it really worked very well," says Fanarakis, founder of an online women's clothing line called Senza Tempo Fashion, now based in Charleston. "I think having the cameras made it feel like you're sitting in a room together. There's just something about seeing everybody's faces, seeing everybody live, it just didn't feel as impersonal as you would think it would."

Baker graduated from the U.S. Naval Academy in 2005 and started the MBA@UNC program while stationed near Seattle. But he was soon deployed as a security officer on a base in Djibouti on the horn of Africa and was living in a containerized living unit (CLU) for eight months while pursuing his MBA.

"I never had good enough Wi-Fi in the CLU, so I had to go to a common area and get on the base Wi-Fi," says Baker, who now lives in Charlotte and is in international sales for Konecranes. "It was usually two or three in the morning, so I'd have to get up quietly and try not to wake up my roommates."

Three days after the first online class was held, *The Wall Street Journal* published a story on the enterprise with the headline, "UNC Makes Risky Online Bet." The story chronicled the evolution of the program, included the requisite yea and nay

Students come from across the nation and the globe four times a year for "immersions" at the mother ship in Chapel Hill, as these MBA@UNC students did in the spring of 2018.

opinions and canvassed several other top business schools for their views on the program.

"We're wading very gently into these waters," the story quoted one associate dean from the West Coast. It added that Harvard didn't have plans at the moment to create its own online program. But in four years, Harvard would launch its Harvard HBX online program.

"It turned out to not be all that risky in hindsight," says Susan Cates, the founding executive director of MBA@UNC and herself a Carolina MBA graduate (1998).

Among the graduates of the program is a man who helped invent the technology that made the program possible in the first place.

Chip Paucek held a bachelor of arts degree from George Washington University and had started three businesses, one of them the company named 2U that provided the online architecture that connected professors and students from every corner of the globe. He coveted a graduate degree in business administration and in 2012 convinced his board and his wife "that I wasn't clinically insane" and received their blessing to enroll in the MBA@UNC program.

Paucek was thick in the weeds of taking 2U public in March 2014, and an investor conference in Vail, Colo., fell smack against a midterm exam.

"I can't remember exactly what class it was, but it was a difficult exam," Paucek says. "I go into the business center at the hotel and turn the camera on, and for three and a half hours, I'm sweating it out. I take the exam and then walk out and meet with twenty-two investors.

"I think one can argue given that I did an IPO during the MBA, that I didn't *need* it, but I really *wanted* it."

Paucek took five years to earn his MBA, but he embraces the memory of attending graduation in the spring of 2017, bringing his wife and two sons to Chapel Hill and having photos taken in cap and gown by the Old Well.

"It was worth it, I would do it again," he says, running down a litany of knowledge in reading balance sheets, negotiating, building a regression and developing company strategy that he gained through the experience. "I didn't just get relationships, I got a lot of knowledge. Now I have a different level of sophistication when I'm talking to my auditors or my chief accounting officer.

"And I love the fact that come basketball season, I've got my Carolina blue on and I've got a rooting interest in the Tar Heels."

Customer Satisfaction

Valarie Zeithaml

As a teenager growing up in Baltimore and then as a college student at the University of Maryland, Valarie Zeithaml was a lifeguard, babysitter, secretary and restaurant worker. She remembers through every job wondering how she was being judged by her bosses and constituencies in the rather subjective world of providing a service.

"Sitting by the pool as a lifeguard, I knew I wasn't supposed to let anybody drown," she says. "But I didn't know what else, what were the criteria? How are the parents and the kids and my bosses judging me? What should I be doing to keep the customers satisfied? It turns out that became my main research topic later on."

From that kernel of an idea has sprouted a career in research and teaching that has had a profound effect on Kenan-Flagler Business School. Today Zeithaml, the David S. Van Pelt Family Distinguished Professor of Marketing, is recognized around the world as a pioneer in both services marketing and service quality.

"People found out that service quality is not as easy to measure and define as product quality," she says of her early days writing and researching. "Over fifteen years and twelve different studies, my colleagues and I worked to quantify what good service meant."

Zeithaml has researched customer expectations in more than fifty industries and consulted with service and product companies that include IBM, Kaiser Permanente, General Electric, John Hancock, Aetna, AT&T, MetLife, Bank of America, Chase, Allstate and Procter & Gamble.

She joined the faculty at Kenan-Flagler in the mid-1990s, and hundreds of Kenan-Flagler students have benefitted from her insights on field trips in her services marketing classes to such businesses as a big-box retailer like Nordstrom to a grocery chain like Trader Joe's to a Chapel Hill restaurant like Kipos Greek Taverna.

Her textbook *Services Marketing* continues to set the standard in that field of study. Now in its seventh edition, it's used in classrooms around the world after being translated into Chinese, Italian, Spanish and other languages. The newest edition includes studies of recent developments in service businesses such as Airbnb, Uber, OpenTable, Mint/Intuit, and others, alongside greater emphasis on technology, digital and social marketing, Big Data, and data analytics as a service.

"Valarie is a really special person—funny, kind, humble, beloved, classy in every way," says Dean Doug Shackelford. "Her work has been cited more than anyone in the school's history. I'm not sure if any current UNC professor has been cited as much as she has."

On the Cusp of a Second Century

Doug Shackelford grew up on a farm outside the town of Hookerton between Greenville and Kinston, and many in his family were N.C. State fans. But he wanted to get off the farm, so his father suggested business or law school in Chapel Hill as the best avenue to accomplish that goal. Shackelford entered Carolina in the fall of 1976 and took a broad range of courses his first two years—from pre-law to political science to business classes such as accounting.

"A lot of people thought accounting was really hard and it seemed to me very easy," he says. "And at some point it struck me—if everybody thinks this is really hard and I think this is really quite easy, maybe there's some opportunity there. That's one of those pieces of advice I pass along to people."

He was still giving some thought to law school when he took a tax class under Dr. David Hoffman.

"I took that course and it was incredible," Shackelford says. "I thought, 'That's what I want to do.' I remember at that time thinking if I could be Dave Hoffman and I could teach as well as he teaches and relate as well as he relates to students, that would be incredible. I didn't at that time think about eventually becoming a professor, but he was just extraordinary and that class stayed with me."

Shackelford received his BSBA in 1980 and went to work for Arthur Andersen, but that "itch" to teach he picked up from Hoffman never went away. He began graduate studies at the University of Michigan in 1986 and earned his PhD in business administration in 1990. He immediately returned to Chapel Hill, where he became assistant professor at Kenan-Flagler under Dean Paul Rizzo. He became a tenured, associate professor in 1996 and a full professor three years later. In 2002, Shackelford was appointed as the Meade H. Willis Distinguished Professor of Taxation, a designation he still holds in addition to the deanship. He was at the right place at the right time to work under the deans Paul Rizzo and Paul Fulton his first decade at Carolina.

"I call them 'the two Pauls,'" Shackelford says. "They just put the school on a rocket shot. Everything changed when they got here. Paul Rizzo was one of the most amazing leaders I've ever been around. I felt like the atmosphere in the room changed when he walked in, even if you had your back to the door and didn't know he had come in.

"I joined and others joined from top-flight universities at the same time, and this was a school that was really going places in the early to mid-nineties. It was exciting to be here."

Shackelford played key administrative roles with Deans Steve Jones and Jim Dean from 2002-2014 and was on the front line of developing what would become the MBA@UNC program—a cutting-edge initiative that would allow a student to take a class from a Navy barracks on the Horn of Africa or while tending a sleeping infant in a Manhattan apartment. At first blush it was controversial: Professors didn't believe they could teach over the internet, and students about to graduate thought their degrees would be cheapened and that an online program couldn't offer the same engagement and community as their on-campus program. Shackelford was charged by Jim Dean to be his liaison with the faculty in devising an online curriculum.

Shackelford thought the concept could be revolutionary. He liked that Carolina was getting out front of its peers in technology. He envisioned something that had never been done before would let schools with outstanding teachers thrive. Shackelford was one of the first professors to go online soon after the program launched in July 2011.

"My approach in leading the faculty with MBA@UNC was, 'Let's design an online program that we would be proud to teach in and that our best faculty in the school want to teach in,'" he says. "This was a great opportunity to lead, instead of catching up.

"When I'm done here and look back, that will probably be one of the things that is most meaningful to me."

In 2018 Shackelford had a number of challenges and initiatives on his plate as Kenan-Flagler dean, among them finding additional space for the school's faculty and students and the never-ending quest of finding new sources of revenue. The school's annual operating budget in 2018 was $160 million and the endowment was $170 million.

"Most of our revenues come from tuition, philanthropy and programs we run that can make money, like Executive Development," Shackelford says.

The school has long outgrown the McColl Building, so plans were in the works and fundraising underway in 2018 to build an adjunct building on land to the northwest of the current facility that services just over 2,700 total students in all programs. It will need the space even more in the next several years as the school got the approval in the spring of 2018 to begin working toward a fifty percent undergraduate enrollment increase over eight years, going from approximately four hundred business majors and minors in the junior and senior classes to six hundred in each class.

Bill Seymour earned his business degree at Carolina in 1964 and went on to a successful career that included a dozen years at IBM, founding a computer software company and later a commercial real estate development firm. He received the 2019 McColl Alumni Legacy Award and has been a supporter of expanding the undergraduate offering at Kenan-Flagler.

"One of the things I learned in business school was the power of leverage," says Seymour, chairman of Primax Properties in Charlotte. "And if you educate someone with the high quality of degree one receives at Kenan-Flagler, you leverage it throughout the state. That individual goes out in the state and plays a key role in economic development, which is good for everyone. But I have heard Doug Shackelford say he could build a *second* top-twenty business school with the students who *cannot* be admitted for space reasons. That's painful—telling an A-student you don't have room for him. That's like turning away a good, clean, high-tech industry at the state border.

"I value the BSBA I received at Carolina and think we should offer more students that opportunity."

Shackelford has also led the school into a major initiative in the $3 trillion American healthcare economy. The Center for the Business of Health is a multidisciplinary effort spanning the Carolina campus and encompassing schools of public health, pharmacy, nursing, dentistry and medicine.

"Healthcare is going to be a huge part of our future," Shackelford says. "We have a major push to build bridges and collaborate in ways I'm not sure any business school has ever done with the healthcare side of the campus. At Carolina, we have the No. 1 pharmacy school in the country, No. 1 public health school, one of top dental schools, one of the best medical schools and an outstanding nursing school. We have been reaching out to all those pockets and saying the Business School wants to be involved in health care. Fifteen percent of our MBAs go into healthcare."

Harnessing technology is a key initiative as well. Virtual and augmented reality and artificial intelligence are new frontiers, and Shackelford brightens telling of how students are transported to a meeting with a town official in the African nation of Cameroon to develop a real sense of how they would respond to questions and circumstances.

"We can create situations where you get sweaty palms and your head's all clouded," he says. "Let's create *real* pressure, so when you get in the real world, it will not be the first time you've ever faced it."

He winces talking about the days of delivering the very same lecture four times in one day. Now many lectures are delivered from state-of-the-art production studios, and class time is used for discussion. In time, Shackelford sees the elimination of "Harvard cases" and instead a student steps

Six deans of Kenan-Flagler Business School gathered in the fall of 2016 for a group photo (L-R): Jack Evans, Steve Jones, Jim Dean, Paul Rizzo, Doug Shackelford and Paul Fulton. Opposite: The new Global Education Initiative is designed to help students learn and master global competencies.

ground as any school in the country, and I think we can do that."

Allen Wilson (BSBA '77), Kenan-Flagler's vice president for strategy and innovation, has known Shackelford for some forty years and agrees.

"I think Doug is the best dean that we've ever had who understands and who can operate both inside the walls and outside the walls," Wilson says. "Normally they're good at one or the other. He can talk to somebody from eastern North Carolina, he can go up to Wall Street and everyone in between, and everybody just sort of warms up to him. They realize what a genuine person he is. There's no ego to him, it's all about what is in the best interest of the school."

Paul Fulton served the school as dean for nearly four years in the mid-1990s and understands the nuances. He likes what he sees in the visionary and pragmatic dean.

"Doug is not like your typical academic who has to ponder things and assemble committees and nothing happens," he says. "He's an action-oriented guy. He's a straight shooter. He gets things done. He's going to take this school to new heights."

Kenan-Flagler has become particularly adept as its centennial arrives practicing what it teaches and preaches. The school is an excellent business enterprise at a time when it's incumbent on it to generate funds to augment its traditional revenue sources. The school's revenue in 2018 was $157 million, with $45 million coming from tuition and fees. Executive Development ($21 million), Executive MBA ($13 million) and online programs ($56 million) counted for more than half that total. Those three lines have doubled over the last five years.

Shackelford often muses on how and why the University leadership decided in the late 1910s to create a School of Commerce.

"For much of our hundred years, we took a lot of people off farms and mill towns in a poor state, and we launched them onto careers and lives that were not conceivable on the farm or the mill town," he says. "So for a hundred years, we've been transforming lives."

To The Head Of The Alphabet

Charlie Loudermilk

Charlie Loudermilk graduated from Carolina in 1950 and went on to success with Aaron Rents, later sharing much of his wealth with UNC and Kenan-Flagler. One of the new buildings comprising the Rizzo Center in the late 1990s is named for Loudermilk.

Countless times over half a century in business, Charlie Loudermilk (BSBA 1950) has been asked, "Who is Aaron?" the name of his Atlanta-based furniture and appliance rental business.

"There never was an Aaron," Loudermilk answers with a smile. "I just wanted to be the first name in the Yellow Pages."

Loudermilk had no idea what he wanted to do after graduating with a business degree in 1950, when he spent much of his time socializing and becoming close friends with some of the football players from the noted Justice-era teams of the post-war forties. He worked briefly as a salesman for Pfizer in Greensboro but decided he wanted to work for himself. He returned to his hometown of Atlanta in 1955 and divined there would always be weddings and always be funerals—ergo the need for folks to temporarily possess tables, chairs, linens, silverware and all the other accoutrements of entertaining.

His first deal was renting out three hundred Army surplus chairs—which he bought with a $500 loan from a bank—for an auction. In the beginning, he kept the business alive by kiting checks, writing them from one account to another and hoping the funds were not deposited by the bearer too soon. But Loudermilk's business grew, and in time he adjusted to focusing on renting office and residential furniture, appliances and electronics.

In the first quarter of 2018, Aaron's Inc. had more than 1,800 company-owned and franchised stores in forty-seven states and Canada with revenue just under $1 billion for the quarter.

"You have to have the basic management skills, the ability to read a balance sheet and know enough about business law to keep you out of trouble," Loudermilk says. "But if I studied the success and failures in the business world, it seems to be without exception, the real success-

es are enjoyed by those who have people skills."

Loudermilk, who stepped down as CEO of Aaron's in 2008 and then as chairman in 2012 at the age of eighty-five, was generous with his alma mater in sharing some of the wealth that Aaron's Inc. generated.

He endorsed the idea in the mid-1990s of his old friend Paul Rizzo being the namesake of a new conference and Executive Development center east of campus and gave money to have one of the buildings named Loudermilk Hall (the other hall was named for trucking and shipping magnate James K. McLean, a 1939 UNC Business School graduate). The Loudermilk Foyer in the McColl Building is also named in his honor.

Another of Loudermilk's gifts a decade later, this one to the Department of Athletics, helped make possible the Loudermilk Center for Excellence at the east end of Kenan Stadium, a multi-purpose building with tutoring, conditioning, entertaining and team headquarters space that serves eight hundred student-athletes a year.

Loudermilk from his early days embodied the business philosophy of doing well by doing good. He put his business at risk in 1965 by renting tents to the Southern Christian Leadership Conference—at half price—for Martin Luther King Jr.'s second march from Selma to Montgomery. People paid in coins and rumpled bills, Charlie wrote in his memoir, ***Charlie, Just Do Better Next Time***.

"They were working out of their back pockets," he wrote. "I knew the feeling."

The experience touched him, deepening his involvement in the civil rights movement. As part of an interracial group of business leaders, he helped establish Atlanta as a role model for integration in the 1960s. He managed Andrew Young's successful campaigns for mayor of Atlanta in 1981 and 1985, which made Charlie unpopular with many of his friends.

"But that was their problem, not mine," he said.

Snapshots | RINGING OF THE BELL

MBA students since 2011 have enjoyed a bell-ringing ceremony to commemorate their landing a summer internship or full-time job. The initiative has expanded to the production of videos with students striking the chimes to the sounds of Anita Bell's "Ring My Bell" song from 1979.

THE UNC
KENAN-FLAGLER
MBA
WILDLIGHTS
Walmart
Save money. Live better.
DO
WHAT
YOU
Deloitte.

Taking The Armed Forces To School

Military Connection

Generals and admirals in the armed forces understand strategy, machinery, ballistics, psychology and leadership. But the business elements of running a branch of the military are a different kettle of fish.

"Most senior military officers have a great deal of technical expertise and are talented leaders, but most have not had much exposure to business principles," says Jim Dean, Kenan-Flagler dean from 2008-14 and a faculty member since 1998.

That realization led the U.S. Army in the early 2000s to begin bringing all of its new one-star generals to the Kenan-Flagler Executive Development program for custom-designed education programs to help soldiers become better businessmen. And it has led to quite an extensive Executive Development relationship with all branches of the military.

"For the most part, one-star generals are basically running a military base or running an installation or a division, which starts to look a whole lot like a business," says Dave Hofmann, a professor of leadership and organizational behavior. "You've got logistics, supply chain, marketing, social media, community relations,

Gen. Mark Milley, chief of staff of the U.S. Army, visited Kenan-Flagler in February 2018 for the Dean's Speaker Series.

and everything else."

When Gen. George Casey Jr. became Army Chief of Staff in April 2007, he took a hard look at the budget and business operation of the Army and realized drastic changes needed to be implemented.

"The Army budget at that time was $254 billion," Casey says. "And I started to realize that there was only one way that was going, and that was down. Yet, we were six or seven years at war and the costs were enormous. I realized that we would have to change the mindset of the officer corps. We had to help our officers learn how to manage and spend our money more effectively. I had all these guys that were spending money who didn't know anything about running a business. And we give them two- and three-billion dollar programs to run and we're surprised when it doesn't work out."

At the time, the Navy was conducting an Executive Business Course at Kenan-Flagler that all new one-star admirals were required to attend. Many new Marine generals attended as well. Casey got an email from a general who attended one of them and immediately said, "This is what I want my officers to learn."

He visited Chapel Hill, met with Kenan-Flagler staff and professors and together they put together a program for the Army's one- and two-star generals. The program started in 2009, and over nearly a decade hundreds of Army officers have attended.

"The course was primarily started for the one- and two-stars, and by the second class they're all telling me, 'You've got to get the three- and four-stars down here,'" Casey says. "They need to see this because they're the ones that need to understand this as well. So we brought them down there for a special session."

"The course has evolved over time," says Gen. Martin Dempsey, who followed Casey in 2011 as Army Chief of Staff. "In the early days, the emphasis was on management of the Army as a business enterprise. More recently, there has been an increased interest in leadership practices."

Today the military is a significant part of UNC Executive Development. Among current programs is a Strategic Thinking Program, where Navy admirals, Marine generals, senior civilians, and admirals/generals from the armed forces of allied countries gather. The school also produces a program for the Marines that helps them manage and operate their retail operations across the nation and the world more effectively.

Kirk Lawrence, program manager for Executive Development, joined the Kenan-Flagler staff in 2011. His background in the military as an Army officer gave him a keen appreciation for the value of the Executive Development program.

"I've got scar tissue from the Army, watching them wrestle with this process," Lawrence says. "I was very impressed with the way the Navy was handling it. The Navy tells us that we've probably saved them and the taxpayer about $1.8 billion dollars over a six-year period because of the work that we've done in educating their workforce."

Gen. Mark Milley, chief of staff

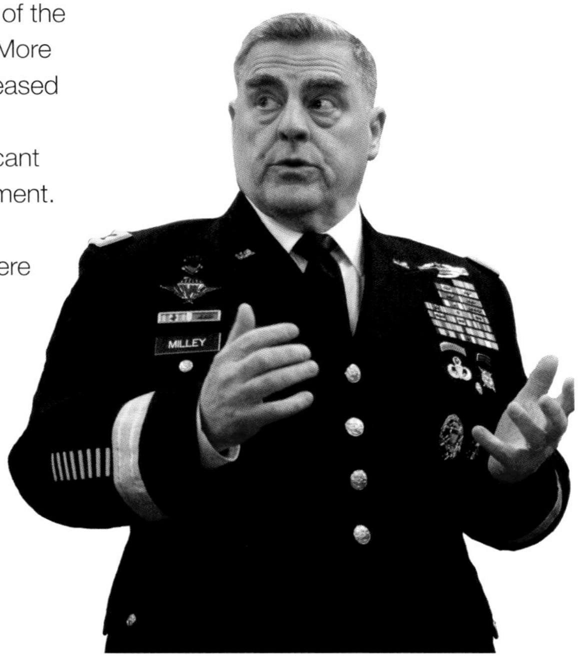

of the U.S. Army, visited Kenan-Flagler in February 2018 for the Dean's Speaker Series and to meet with student entrepreneurs running start-up enterprises in the Launch Chapel Hill incubator. He addressed the corollaries between military operations and business education and spoke of seeking out innovators and visionaries like Tesla founder Elon Musk for ideas that could apply to the armed forces.

"The Army is a big organization—1.2 million soldiers, serving in 140 countries around the world—providing a product called the safety and security of the American people," says Milley, who was appointed by President Donald Trump in December 2018 as chairman of the Joint Chiefs of Staff. "In order to provide that, we have to adapt to the changing operational environment and remain on the cutting edge. You do that by getting exposure to innovators. I seek out areas of innovation around the country, in places like the Triangle, Silicon Valley and Route 128 (in Massachusetts)."

Milley said that Musk's thoughts on emerging technology, artificial intelligence and electric ways of powering vehicles certainly have applications for the military.

"Musk has a brilliant mind and looks at the world differently than I might," he says. "He says that in order to succeed, you have to have a high threshold for pain and failure."

The Kenan-Flagler Veterans Association provides bonding and service opportunities for MBA candidates coming from active military duty. During the 2018-19 academic year, there were thirty veterans pursuing their MBAs at Kenan-Flagler; all were officers and a majority had done at least seven years of active duty.

Allison Hughes (above, MBA '14) flew Black Hawk combat helicopters for the U.S. Army. Michael Burris (opposite, far right, Class of 2019) is a former Naval officer and was president of the Kenan-Flagler Veterans Association for the 2018-19 academic year.

"Just by the nature of our previous employment, we are used to leading people and organizations—from stressful situations like intelligence or combat—and we're used to managing millions of dollars of equipment," says Michael Burris (Class of 2019), president of the association and a former Naval officer. "We try to parlay that into having a noticeable presence at the Business School."

The Veterans Club sponsors weekly social gatherings on Thursdays at the Franklin Street bar He's Not Here, with all students across two classes of MBAs invited. In 2017-18, the group logged seventy hours of community service and raised $10,000 for a charity store.

"Business schools and the military have had a very tight-knit relationship for a very, very long time," Burris says. "The commanding officers that I had when I was in the Navy, every single one of them had an MBA. It's by far the best graduate degree to have to be in a commanding officer role because essentially, you're the CEO. My last tour when I was in special operations with the Navy in San Diego, I led the charge that we design and procure the new naval special warfare 11-meter boat. That involved budgeting, the contracting, the procurement process—that was more business than anything military."

Numerous military personnel have taken advantage of the MBA@

UNC program that gives students the chance to pursue a graduate degree while serving in the armed forces from every corner of the globe. One was Allison Hughes (MBA '14), who received the 2016 Dwight W. Anderson Young Alumni Award for leadership in career accomplishments and exceptional commitment to the school.

Hughes flew Black Hawk combat helicopters in the U.S. Army and later started a new venture named "Heels on the Ground" in the aftermath of her husband Breg being severely wounded by a roadside bomb while deployed as an officer in Afghanistan. The program seeks to enrich and improve the lives of Gold Star spouses and caregivers of severely wounded Green Berets through local support networks, workshops and retreats, and her early organization and fundraising efforts were aided by taking Professor Ted Zoller's New Venture Discovery course.

"It is important for me to work in a role where I can impact change and feel relevant in what I do every day," she says. "Entrepreneurship brings me the intellectual stimulation and idea exchange that I find valuable in a career."

Henry Flagler and his bride Mary Lily Kenan pose with their wedding party following their nuptials at the Kenan family home, Liberty Hall, in Duplin County on Aug. 24, 1901. That's William Rand Kenan Jr. kneeling in front and years later (above) at The Breakers in Palm Beach. Frank Kenan (L) carried the family's legacy into the latter part of the 1900s.

the Namesakes 2

Henry Flagler in later years (above) with wife Mary Lily Kenan and as a young man (opposite) in the early 1850s with first wife Mary (standing) and sister-in-law Isabella Harkness.

The final decade of the 1800s included a market swoon (the Panic of 1893), a new brand of cereal (Shredded Wheat), life-changing technological innovations (tractors and radios) and the first eighteen-hole golf course in America (St. Andrews Golf Club in Yonkers, New York). Americans continued to refine and drive the "horseless carriage" from the previous decade and develop more and more uses for the thick black liquid being drilled in Pennsylvania and Appalachia. Grover Cleveland became the first and only President to serve two non-consecutive terms, winning in 1892 over an incumbent, Benjamin Harrison, who refused to campaign because his wife was dying of tuberculosis.

The names Kenan and Flagler were fused during this decade as well, first on a purely social level and a second time along business dimensions. Henry Flagler and Mary Lily Kenan were first acquaintances, then friends, later husband and wife. Flagler and William R. Kenan Jr., Mary's younger brother, had an immediate connection as businessmen, builders, scientists and entrepreneurs.

Life at the University of North Carolina, across the state and down the East Coast of Florida and beyond has never been the same since.

Mary Lily grew up in Wilmington, North Carolina, and was in her early twenties in 1890 when she, her sister Jessie and Sadie Jones played the piano and sang for the entertainment of guests at the Wilmington estate of Sadie and her husband, Pembroke. Among those present were Henry Flagler and his wife, Alice. The Joneses entertained the upper crust of Eastern society at their Airlie Gardens estate with guests coming for leisurely visits. Flagler, one of America's richest men by virtue of his being a founding partner in the Standard Oil Company in 1870, ran in the same circles as the Joneses.

"Mary Lily and Mrs. Jones had both majored in music [Mary Lily attending Peace Institute in Raleigh] and used to sing at the parties the Joneses had at their home," says Tom Kenan, a 1959 UNC graduate in economics and a relative of William Kenan (his grandfather was a cousin of William's) and his sister. "Mr. Flagler's wife took a liking to Mary Lily and asked her to travel with them to Florida and to their mansion in Newport."

Prominent biographers for Flagler and Kenan both write that Will, as he was known among friends and family, and Henry met in 1899, with Walter Campbell, author of the Kenan story with his book *Across Fortune's Tracks*, specifying the date as July and the occasional house party Flagler hosted at his Lawn Beach mansion on Long Island Sound. By that time, Ida Alice Flagler had been institutionalized and Flagler had taken a shine to the vivacious young Mary Lily. "I am living in hopes each day to hear that the ladies of your family are coming to Mamaroneck at a very early day," Flagler wrote to Mary and Will's uncle, Colonel Thomas Kenan. Will joined the group by traveling from Niagara Falls, where he worked for the fledgling Union Carbide Company. Will, twenty-seven, and Flagler, sixty-nine, discussed a subject that would define much of their relationship to come: Technology, specifically, the incandescent gas light burners Flagler had ordered for his house. That common ground prompted Kenan to call on Flagler and propose selling chemically treated railroad crossties to Flagler's Florida East Coast Railway.

A Long List Of Corporate Icons

Kenan-Flagler Guests

The "Oracle of Omaha," the founders of the Wendy's hamburger chain and of FedEx overnight delivery service, and the top two bankers in Charlotte in the late 1990s are just a few of the noted business leaders who have visited Chapel Hill and Kenan-Flagler for various speaking events over the years.

Legendary investor Warren Buffett visited in 1996 and spoke to some 250 Kenan-Flagler students, faculty and invited guests at the George Watts Hill Alumni Center. Buffett's appearance, headlined "Warren Buffett Talks Business," was taped by the UNC Center for Public Television, and the format was essentially an informal Q&A. Buffett opened the session by telling the students of a seminal hiring event in the early 1990s and how what he looked for in naming a CEO for a Wall Street firm applied to each of the young students and their impending business careers.

Buffett had taken a major stake in the venerable Wall Street firm of Salomon Brothers in 1987, and in August 1991 the firm was under siege from the Federal Reserve of New York for bond trading improprieties. Buffett was roused from bed at 6:45 a.m. on August 14 in his Omaha home and told by regulators the company was leveraged by a 30:1 margin and top management was out. Buffett jumped on the first plane to New York, and one of his challenges was to pick someone to run a far-flung business with eight thousand employees.

"I met twelve people, roughly, and I knew four or five by sight," Buffett told the group. "I did not ask their grades in business school. I didn't even ask if they'd even *been* to business school. I never looked at their résumés. I knew all twelve had the I.Q. to handle the job. It was more about hearing and seeing how their machinery worked.

"You can tell the people who are very full of themselves. You can detect those who perhaps didn't have the courage for what was to come. You looked for the qualities that Ben Franklin wrote about two hundred years ago—who is willing to give others credit? Who will not cut corners? Who will deliver their promise and a little extra?

"I picked a guy named Deryck Maughan. I tapped him on the shoulder and said, 'You're it, pal,' and he immediately walked down to a press conference with a room full of people with zero preparation. He worked eighteen-hour days for months and months and never asked what his salary was, if he got more stock options. But he showed uncanny judgment and helped us through a very difficult period.

"I tell you this story because all of you are at the age when you can develop the habits that a man like Deryck Maughan exemplified. It wasn't about running the hundred in 9.6 or high-jumping seven feet. It wasn't about being the smartest

Kenan-Flagler Professor Dave Hartzell (L) welcomed Warren Buffett (C) to Chapel Hill in 1996; they visited with Frank Kenan before Buffett's address at the George Watts Hill Alumni Center.

guy or the best looking. Every quality that goes into the issue of 'character' is obtainable. It's simply a matter of deciding at a young age to be that person or not. You have time to form the right habits."

The nineties were the heyday of aggressive bank expansion across interstate lines, and perhaps the most active city in the nation was two and a half hours southwest of Chapel Hill in Charlotte, where rivals NationsBank and First Union competed to build the biggest towers in uptown Charlotte and expand their brands across the Southeast and beyond. Hugh McColl (BSBA '57) of NationsBank and Ed Crutchfield of First Union appeared at Kenan-Flagler in October 1999 as the part of the Dean's Speaker Series. Bill Friday, the former president of the UNC System, moderated the discussion.

"That event was so popular that they had several overflow classrooms," remembers Professor David Ravenscraft. "It was the first time they had ever met to discuss banking. The press showed up unannounced and filmed their introduction and then we made them turn off the cameras."

Professor Dave Hofmann remembers Fred Smith, the founder and CEO of FedEx, visiting Chapel Hill and telling students about how in the 1970s he formed the idea to create an overnight delivery service that was originally named Federal Express (and shortened to FedEx in 2000). Smith had a particular interest in Carolina during the early 2000s because his son Arthur was an offensive lineman on the Tar Heel football team.

"He gave a great talk," Hofmann says. "What struck me is how rare it is to see the same person form the idea, start the company and still be the CEO and president some thirty years later of a multibillion-dollar company. I was reflecting during the talk how much he must have grown and learned continuously to keep up with the changing nature of his company and the industry."

Over the years Jack Welch of General Electric, Ken Langone of Home Depot, Ross Perot of Electronic Data Systems and Hilton Head Island developer Charles Fraser have appeared before Kenan-Flagler audiences. Federal Reserve Chairman Alan Greenspan spoke at

the opening of the McColl Building in 1997. Carolina grads and Wall Street titans Julian Robertson, Dick Jenrette and Sallie Krawcheck have delivered speeches, as has David Gardner, a Morehead Scholar and English major who was a co-founder of The Motley Fool, one of the early online stock and investing advisory services. Phil Knight, the co-founder and chairman of Nike, spoke on the company's labor management practices to the class taught by Professor Nick Didow and two colleagues. Former U.S. Senator Olympia Snowe delivered the 2016 Weatherspoon Lecture.

Peter T. Grauer, chairman of Bloomberg L.P. and a 1968 Carolina graduate, had just finished speaking to a group in the Koury Auditorium one Friday in 2012 when he noticed some students working on Bloomberg terminals in the Capital Markets Lab. The students were completing a self-directed certification program as directed by Professor Chip Snively, and Grauer struck up a conversation with them and told them he'd offer summer internships to the first two of them to send him an email.

Michele Buck (MBA '87), president and CEO of The Hershey Corp., told a Chapel Hill audience the story of starting working at age ten, first delivering papers, then babysitting. She's been a waitress, sold Avon products door-to-door and worked in a bank—all of that before ascending to the top of Hershey management in early 2017.

"I wasn't always aspiring to be a CEO," she told MBA students. "When

I came out of undergrad, I never thought I'd get a master's. After my MBA, I just wanted to be a brand manager. I had to see myself accomplish one thing to know I could do another."

Buck realized early on that her strength was her ability to inspire others with creativity and passion. "I don't want to be sitting in the office sending memos all day when my strength is inspiring others in person," she said.

Senator Lowell Weicker of Connecticut spoke on Nov. 11, 1977, on the silver anniversary of the Executive Education Program and congratulated the school for having graduated more than a thousand business executives in their continuing education.

The Archie Davis Lecture Series started in 1983 to honor the former chairman of the board of Wachovia Bank and Trust Co. The first speaker was Alfred Kahn, a professor of economics at Cornell and a former Carter Administration official. Former President Gerald Ford spoke in 1987 to an audience of thousands in Carmichael Auditorium as part of the series.

Michael Bloomberg visited Chapel Hill in 1999 and told Kenan-Flagler students about having evolved from the investment banking arena at Salomon Brothers to creating Bloomberg LP and entering the financial news and data dissemination business. Bloomberg launched his business in 1981, and eighteen years later had 110,000 Bloomberg terminals in banks, trading houses and media outlets.

The Q&A touched on the current state of the stock market, which was nearing dizzying highs in 1999. Asked if he worried about the rapid rise of internet stocks like Yahoo and Amazon, Bloomberg said, "I wouldn't own them in a million years." And he cautioned against day-trading: "It's like going to a gambling casino."

Guest speakers over the years (beginning opposite, L-R): Wendy's founder Dave Thomas; Home Depot founder Ken Langone; Wall Street tycoons Julian Robertson and Dick Jenrette; and General Electric CEO Jack Welch.

ENTRANCE TO WHITEHALL, HOME OF H. M. FLAGLER, PALM BEACH, FLA.

Copyrighted 1912 by Harris.
Mr. H. M. Flagler's arrival with First Train to enter Key West, Fla. Jan. 22nd, 1912.

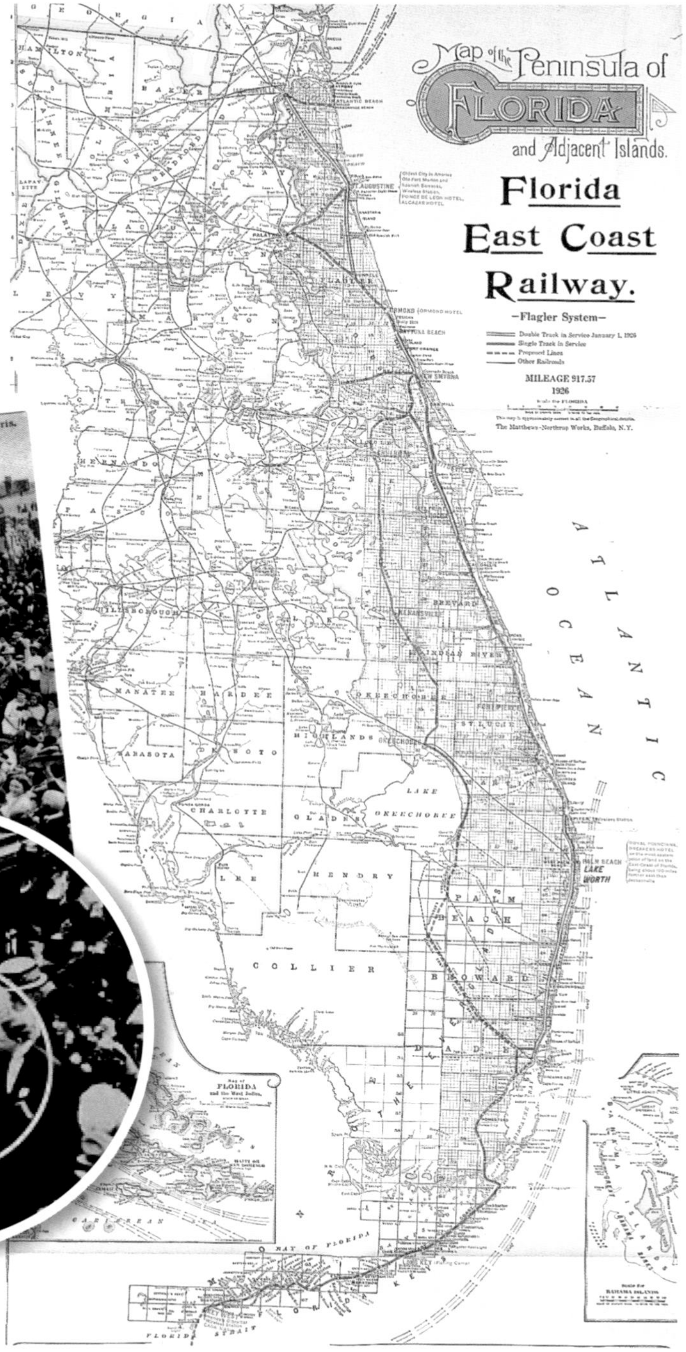

Henry Flagler built the Florida East Coast Railway and along the way positioned the Whitehall Mansion as a wedding gift for his wife in Palm Beach. His dream of a Jacksonville-to-Key West rail was realized when his tracks reached Key West in January 1912. The photo opposite shows Flager (L) and Will Kenan (R) on the rear of a train car used to traverse the Florida coast along with an associate named Jack Metts.

Flagler soon retained Kenan, an 1894 UNC graduate with a bachelor of science degree who'd spent his early working years traveling the world for Union Carbide, as a consulting engineer to travel to Palm Beach and oversee the installation of electric and heating systems for Flagler's new Breakers Hotel, one of a half dozen opulent properties Flagler owned and operated from St. Augustine south to Palm Beach (and later to Miami). Kenan handled the job with dispatch and economy, as Flagler noted in 1901 when he directed the supervisor of another hotel construction project, The Continental Hotel in Ormond Beach, to cede to Kenan's opinion on the installation of that facility's infrastructure.

"I want it to be vised by Mr. Kenan, and if there are any differences of opinion, I want Mr. Kenan's views adopted," Flagler wrote to J.A. McGuire. "There are very few men of his age who have had as much experience and who are as competent as he is. The successful work of The Breakers plant proves this. We have got a plant in there with a greater measure of efficiency, and at least half the cost of other plants of equal size."

Another Flagler biographer, Sidney Walter Martin, concurred in his 1949 book, *Flagler's Florida*, writing that after the Breakers project, "The elderly capitalist depended strongly on the opinion and judgment of his younger associate."

Author Thomas Graham, in his book *Mr. Flagler's St. Augustine*, noted the relationship had been cemented by the time Flagler traveled to Nassau in early 1901 to inspect construction on his grand new hotel there, The Colonial.

"On his voyage to the Bahamas, Flagler was accompanied by several of his lieutenants and by a newcomer, William R. Kenan Jr., the younger brother of Mary Lily," Graham wrote. "Flagler had become intrigued with the abilities of Mary Lily's brother and wanted to show him around the East Coast system. Perhaps he saw young Kenan as the possible heir to his empire, and that would be how things eventually turned out, at least in part."

And so evolved a relationship between the two that could be defined by various boundaries—friends, business partners, boss-and-subordinate and mentor-and-mentee. They were also brothers-in-law; after several years of low-profile courting and Flagler eventually obtaining a divorce from his wife, the seventy-one-year-old married the thirty-four-year-old Mary Lily in 1901.

It's clear studying the correspondence as early as the spring of 1900 that Henry and Will had a friendly and cordial relationship: "Can't you run down to see us while we are marooning, so to speak, on the beach this summer?" Kenan wrote to Flagler in May 1900 on personal letterhead that listed Wilmington as a return address. "We would be delighted to have you."

Later in September, Kenan wrote: "By the way, I congratulate you on your victory before the Supreme Court of Nebraska. Will that end the persecution? For it is nothing more."

All In The Family

The Breakers Hotel

"You think corporate politics are tough? Go work for your Mom and Dad."

Entrepreneur Gary Vaynerchuk strikes a chord addressing how family businesses have a set of dynamics unlike any other enterprise. Kenan-Flagler Business School recognized years ago that parents, siblings, cousins and second-aunts once removed can make for strange bedfellows running a widget factory or pouring over spreadsheets. Thus it has evolved from offering one course on family business in 2006 to operating the Family Enterprise Center in 2019.

Cooper Biersach and Steve Miller co-founded the Family Enterprise Center. Biersach (BA 1991, MBA/JD '96) came to Kenan-Flagler from a career in human resources and Miller (BA '77) from a long tenure in Asheville at The Biltmore Company working for the Cecil family, the heirs to the 250-room chateau and grounds built in the late 1800s by George Vanderbilt.

Miller began teaching a class at Kenan-Flagler in 2006 as an adjunct professor and since 2011 has been teaching two classes, one an introduction to family business and a second dealing with governance and wealth management.

"There are essentially three systems going on in a family business," says Miller. "One is the business system, which is just like any business—the marketing and operations and finance and that kind of stuff. Then there are the family dynamics, which play a role. And then there's the ownership and governance. All three of these provide a different set of challenges to running a family business."

Frank Kenan's widow Betty is pictured front-right of this gathering of the Kenan family in 2017. The generation in charge of furthering the family's legacy with The Breakers calls itself "The Cousins."

There happens to be an interesting petri dish of family business right under the nose of Kenan-Flagler Business School.

The Breakers in Palm Beach was originally built in 1896 by Henry Flagler, twice rebuilt after fires by protégé and brother-in-law William R. Kenan Jr. and today is owned by two trusts controlled by the Kenan family. The Breakers is listed on the National Register of Historic Places, and its

"The Breakers represents something very special to our family, both as a valuable long-term asset and as a business that has a positive and meaningful impact on its employees, community and environment."

Frank Kenan II (MBA '11)

owners re-invest a minimum of $30 million a year in capital expenditures. The AAA Five Diamond property has earned numerous accolades for its commitment to the quality of life of its more than 2,000 employees, the environment and community service.

"The Breakers is kind of like Biltmore—there is only one," Miller says. "There just aren't really any properties like that left any more that are still under family control. The family through the generations has been excellent owners and good stewards of the property. They are very committed to providing a world-class hospitality experience at The Breakers. They are very committed to the preservation of that wonderful national historic landmark property."

Top management of The Breakers in recent years has included James Graham Kenan III (UNC 1968) of Lexington, Ky., as chairman of the board and his cousin Tom Kenan (BA 1959) of Chapel Hill as vice chair. The next generation is in position to assume the leadership mantle, including Frank Kenan II of Charleston, S.C., a Kenan-Flagler graduate (MBA 2011) and one of the family members three generations down from siblings and UNC benefactors William and Mary Lily Kenan. This generation calls itself "The Cousins" and since 2004 has conducted biennial gatherings to learn about strategy and operations of the business as well the unique culture created by the senior generation.

"The Breakers represents something very special to our family, both as a valuable long-term asset and as a business that has a positive and meaningful impact on its employees, community and environment," Frank says. "As such, the ongoing integrity and success of The Breakers are extremely important to me and to the entire next generation. Our generation is grateful for the extraordinary leadership provided by the senior generation of the family, the board of directors, and The Breakers' management team, and we are determined to work hard to protect and grow this special legacy.

"The next generation is proud that The Breakers' history dates back more than a century, and we are also well aware that excellence can be fleeting and that most family businesses fail to transition successfully from one generation to the next. As such, our generation has taken several steps to prepare for the generational transition and continued responsible family ownership."

Management pays attention to its history. In 2017, it opened an ice cream and candy shop called "Mary Lily's" on the anniversary of the death of Mary Lily Kenan Flagler. ❖

Henry Flagler was one of three partners instrumental in the evolution of Standard Oil, the others being John Rockefeller and Samuel Andrews. This stock certificate from Standard Oil hangs in the lobby of the McColl Building in Chapel Hill.

And later in the same missive: "Our Spirittine business is gradually and securely growing and when we get a customer he always sticks. I write about thirty letters daily to every corner of the country. So you see it is no small job to look after the correspondence." ("Spirittine" was apparently some sort of pitch pine product, judging by references in other correspondence.)

Flagler sent one urgent message to Kenan in August 1903 to Kenan's Lockport, New York, residence, asking for help getting telephones installed in The Breakers: "Mr. Parrott telegraphs as follows: 'Don't you think we had best put telephones in rooms at Breakers as fast as possible?' Will you please hurry the necessary material forward as fast as possible?"

For four years, Kenan gave part-time commitment to Flagler. Then in 1904, he went to work for Flagler Systems full-time. Kenan was a brilliant scientist and engineer and chafed at times that he was seen mostly as "Mr. Flagler's brother-in-law" by other company workers, but nonetheless he poured every ounce of brains and energy he had into Flagler's enterprises. His father, Buck Kenan, once sounded a bell of caution, according to Campbell's book: "I dislike to hear that you're working eighteen hours of the twenty-four and, unless you quit very soon, you will surely break down, for no one can abuse nature in that way without paying very dearly for it."

Kenan was a consulting engineer but also an officer, serving directly under Flagler. He was made a director of all of Flagler's corporations and could sign papers or checks at any time. Over the first fifteen years of the 20th century, Kenan helped Flagler in his mission to turn the state of Florida from a dense, swamp-infested outland to one of America's hottest growth areas. When Flagler died in 1913, his last accomplishment in business secure with the opening

Entrepreneurial Spirit

Frank Kenan died one year before the McColl Building opened in 1997, but he was around to salute Hugh McColl two years earlier in a ceremony to recognize McColl for having the new Kenan-Flagler Business School head quarters named for him. Kenan waxed about the entrepreneurial spirit and what it meant to business and the nation.

"I can remember sixty-five years ago, while I was serving in the Navy, North Carolina decided they would try regulating interstate trucking," Kenan said. "I called back to Durham and asked the manager of my small oil company to buy an older water truck and a second-hand Ford and start hauling gasoline from Wilmington to Durham. The total investment was about $1,000. That investment grew into the Kenan Transport Company, with terminals from Washington to Miami. It's the largest bulk hauler in the region. The stock is worth $20 a share now, my cost is nine cents. That just shows you what happens when an entrepreneur creates wealth."

one year earlier the Over-Sea Railroad to Key West, Kenan became his designee to run a far-flung business empire that included hotels, railroads, steamships, terminals, bridges and newspapers.

Kenan died in 1965 at the age of ninety-three, and his branch of the Kenan family tree that included Mary Lily and sisters Sarah and Jessie Kenan had only one child among them. So Frank H. Kenan, whose father was a cousin of William Kenan, was left to take the reins on the family's far-flung financial and philanthropic endeavors.

"Father went to the aid of the older Kenans who desperately needed him, his counsel and his ability," Tom Kenan said in 1991. "From that moment on, our lives changed. Father, as the conservator of his family fortune; Father, as the trustee of charitable foundations; Father, as a builder of new enterprises."

Each step that Frank Kenan would take would forever be governed by appreciation for what he and his ancestors and his immediate family had engendered during their years in Chapel Hill.

"I learned just about all that was necessary for me to cope during the Depression in the relatively highly competitive field, oil marketing," Kenan said.

So just who were the Kenans?

And who was Henry Flagler?

And why does the Business School in Chapel Hill bear their names?

***

In Chapel Hill there are the bricks and mortar of Kenan Stadium, Kenan Residence Hall, Kenan Music Building, the Frank Hawkins Kenan Institute for Private Enterprise, Kenan Laboratories, the Kenan Science Library, and, of course, Kenan-Flagler Business School. Kenan Street runs one block and connects Franklin Street and Cameron Avenue. And there are the entities—the William R. Kenan Jr. Trust, the William R. Kenan Jr. Fund and the Kenan Distinguished Professorships, created and funded in 1917 upon the death of Mary Lily Kenan. Many are the children and dogs who have been named "Kenan" because their parents and masters thought the name was quintessentially Chapel Hill and UNC. And that's not even traveling to the town of Kenansville in Duplin County or to the Kenan Chapel in Wilmington or Kenan Library at N.C. State University.

It's difficult to measure and fathom the impact one family has had on one institution like the Kenans and the University of North Carolina. The family through the mid-20th century had provided six successive generations of trustees, students and benefactors, and five Kenans had served as trustees.

"The Kenan Professorships have made the name of the University known to the whole civilized world, they have advanced the front of human knowledge in the humanities, the arts and the sciences, both natural and social," A.C. Howell wrote in his 1956 book, *The Kenan Professorships*. "Their works are read and studied by thousands of scholars and students. From their inspiring classrooms and laboratories have gone leaders in many fields."

"The thing about Kenan giving is this: It reflects an extraordinarily sophisticated understanding of higher education, from the aspect of students, teaching and budgets," said Holden Thorp '86, a former Kenan Professor of Chemistry and chancellor of the University. "For one public university to have such a benefactor at this level is unusual. If someone asked what makes UNC stand out, especially among Southern universities, this kind of philanthropy is it."

Meanwhile in Florida, the name of Henry Morrison Flagler lives on in avenues, drives or streets in most every city along the East Coast. Flagler made his fortune in the oil business—a 1901 calculation put him as the sixth-wealthiest man in America—and then spent much of it developing the East Coast for nearly three decades from the mid-

Frank Kenan (at left opposite) shakes hands with a new Tops Petroleum distributor in Wilson in the mid-1900s; his portrait hangs today in the Kenan Center in Chapel Hill.

1880s. Flagler spent approximately $50 million developing Florida, but at his death he was still able to leave an estate valued at nearly $100 million. There is Flagler University and Flagler Hospital in St. Augustine, Flagler Museum and Flagler Steakhouse in Palm Beach, Flagler Beach just north of Daytona, Flagler Park in Stuart, Flagler Hall at the University of Central Florida. The Flagler Memorial where he is interred sits in St. Augustine. How does the sound of the Flaglerville Dolphins or the Flaglerville Heat strike you? It could have happened. The city of Miami was originally to be named Flaglerville upon its founding in 1896, but Henry suggested instead that the burgeoning south Florida town be christened for the Mayaimi tribe that once populated the land around Lake Okeechobee. Early maps also identify the river running through the area as the "Miama" River, which why is some old Miamians still say "Miama" rather than "Miami."

"Much of what he did in Florida was a personal adventure," Thomas Graham wrote. "It seems that the challenge of creating something new outweighed the desire to make money. One might hazard the speculation that he saw continuing innovative activity, ever moving on to the next endeavor, as a way of maintaining his vitality. When he finally reached Key West, he died."

A business school in the 21st century can learn much from the legacies of a group of four individuals collectively bearing the Kenan and Flagler names—Henry Flagler, a founder along with John D. Rockefeller of Standard Oil; Mary Lily Kenan Flagler, who inherited Henry's fortune and passed much of it along to the University; Will Kenan, a scientist who played a part in the discovery of acetylene gas, helped Flagler build Florida and continued his sister's legacy of giving; and Frank Kenan, who created his own wildly successful business empire and in the mid-1900s stepped in to manage the extended family's business and philanthropic endeavors.

There are the lessons of overcoming defeat and horrible misfortune. Flagler and Frank Kenan both went bust early in their careers, Flagler in the salt business just after the Civil War and Kenan in fuel distribution out of college in the 1930s. Both Flagler and Will Kenan were devastated that fire on two occasions took down their opulent hotels on the Palm Beach coast, but Will persevered in 1925 and, in a mind-boggling case study in logistics and operations, rebuilt The Breakers in just over one year, installing dormitories, a commissary and hospital so that 1,200 workers could live on-site and work around the clock and open in December 1926 the grand hotel with the twin-towered facade inspired by the famed Villa Medici in Rome.

Kenan-Flagler Business School pays homage to its namesakes with a bust of Henry Flagler in the lobby of the McColl Building.

As a young man growing up in Ohio, Flagler started out in the wholesale grain and liquor business but was quick as the Civil War began to note that the army's need for salt to preserve food sparked a steep rise in the price of the commodity. He and his brother-in-law each invested $50,000 in a salt mine in Saginaw, Michigan, and made good money while the war was on. But when it ended, the price of salt collapsed and the business went bust, with Flagler owing a $50,000 debt that he covered by borrowing from his father-in-law and then clawing it back in a business he knew and understood—the grain industry.

"He said what he learned from the salt business is you'd really better understand a business before you go into it," says John Blades, the former executive director of the Flagler Museum in Palm Beach. "His debt after the war in today's money was about $2.5 million. Imagine trying to bounce back from that. But he did. He paid off the debt."

Frank Kenan learned the motivational power of failure as a teen. He went to Woodberry Forest from his home in

Atlanta at age fourteen, and one of his early low grades was posted on the wall for all to see.

"It made me furious," he said. "It took five years, but I graduated right up close to the top of the class."

After graduating from the University of North Carolina in 1935, Kenan wanted to follow his grandfather into the banking business. But Frank Hawkins instead gave him $3,000 to buy a Pure Oil gas distributorship in Durham. Kenan lost his money in two months, closed the business and started over.

"It was a good lesson," Kenan said. "I advise young people don't be afraid of going broke, but go broke *early*. Adversity is the greatest teacher in the world."

An eight-year-old Frank also learned the importance of sizing up your potential market and the risk of going into debt. He was at summer camp near Asheville, and the campers were given a dime to buy candy at a country store before starting up Mt. Pisgah. Most of the campers scarfed down junk food before the journey, but Kenan bought a box of Uneeda Biscuits and thought he could sell them on the hike back down the mountain to his hungry friends on credit for a nickel. He made a nice profit on paper—but then had trouble collecting.

"Don't sell to people who can't pay," he later said with wry understatement.

The Kenans were big on the concept of a healthy mind and healthy body. Will Kenan played baseball at Chapel Hill and his senior year joined the football team. In later times he remembered that his body during his college years had been as "hard as nails," and he didn't think he could have withstood the pressures of his working career and incessant travel by train and automobile over rugged roads "were it not for the resistance built up by my years of athletics."

Frank Kenan was a tenacious and competitive athlete from boyhood—in gymnastics, football, golf, any number of pursuits. Archie Davis, later the chairman of Wachovia Bank, was a fifteen-year-old at Woodberry Forest in 1926 when he first met Frank, a year his junior. "As I walked into the gym that night I saw this young fellow on the parallel bars," Davis said. "He was swinging up into a handstand position and vaulting to the floor with apparently little effort."

Tom Kenan marveled at his father's lifelong attention to physical fitness. During Tom's boyhood years in Charleston—Frank was stationed there in the Navy during World War II—Tom remembers waiting for his school bus and looking back at his house. "Father would be chinning himself on a broom placed between two French doors, in plain view," Tom says.

Frank loved football but said as his professional career evolved, "Business is the greatest game in the world. Business has replaced football long, long ago."

Kenan was quite adept at sizing up people and proposals. Allen Wilson, a 1977 business graduate from Carolina who worked nearly forty years in accounting before joining Kenan-Flagler in 2016 as vice president of strategy and innovation, remembers early in his career when one of his tax clients, a venture capital firm, asked if he'd set up a meeting with Kenan, who Wilson knew through his firm's relationship with Kenan Transport. Wilson told them, "Mr. Kenan doesn't suffer fools lightly" and they'd best get their twenty-five page pitch book down to ninety seconds if they stood a chance to pique Kenan's interest in a deal.

"I'll give these guys credit, they whittled their pitch down, were quick and to the point," Wilson says. "Mr. Kenan listened a few minutes, flipped through their book and all of a sudden he closed the book. He said, 'Boys, at my age, I don't invest in green bananas.' That was that. He quickly sized them up and made a decision. That was Frank Kenan."

UNC Athletic Director John Swofford went to see Frank in the mid-1980s to talk about expanding the football stadium that bore the family name. Specifically,

Tiger of Wall Street

Julian Robertson

Julian Robertson Jr. is giving a visitor a tour of Tiger Management's forty-first floor offices in midtown Manhattan in June 2017 when he comes to a modest workout facility complete with treadmills, stair-steppers, free weights and assorted other fitness accouterments. At eighty-five years of age, Robertson hits the workout "pretty hard" every other day.

"I tell young people, the business world is not a one-way street," Robertson says. "There are detours. It's a helluva lot easier to make it through the rough spots with a wonderful wife and family and a treadmill. I almost feel like putting the treadmill right there with the wife and family."

He smiles and nods toward the exercise room.

"That's why we have this room. Everyone is welcome to use it and they have a great time."

Robertson is one of many Kenan-Flagler graduates (BSBA 1955) who went on to notable success in business—in Robertson's case on Wall Street via his talents in stock-picking. Robertson evolved from an admitted "under-achiever" in college to turning $8 million in 1980 to $7.2 billion in 1996 via the Tiger Fund he created and managed.

"I learned to pick stocks from my father and told him that's what I wanted to do," Robertson says of growing up in Salisbury, N.C., the son of Julian Robertson Sr. "He said New York was where I could learn the business best. Then when I learned the business, it would be all right for me to come back to North Carolina."

He smiles.

"But I never really learned the business, so I stayed here. I'm still trying to learn it."

Robertson spent two years in the Navy after Chapel Hill and then moved to New York. He was a stockbroker for Kidder Peabody & Co., where he began cultivating his skills to spots trends and undervalued businesses.

"Early on I tried to get to know management," he says. "I visited companies. I remember the first company I visited was Frito Lay. Here were these filthy potatoes going in one end of the machine and coming out as packaged potato chips at the other. I just figured that was kind of the next best thing to making gold I could find. Those were fun times. But there was a lot of legwork involved."

Robertson started the Tiger Fund in 1980 and was, according to *Businessweek*, "ahead of the curve on every major trend in investing from the surge of Europe after the fall of Berlin Wall." Said one Tiger executive of the era, "When he's convinced he's right, he bets the farm."

The success of his fund spawned many from his staff of talented traders and stock-pickers to take off on their own, forming the group of "Tiger Cubs" to make their marks on Wall Street as well. Two of the most notable are Lee Ainslie (MBA '90), the founder of Maverick Capital, and Dwight Anderson (MBA '94), who worked for Robertson for five years before launching Ospraie Management, a commodities hedge fund. Anderson serves on the Kenan-Flagler Board of Advisors, funds three MBA fellowships and in 2000 and 2007 won the Outstanding Young Alumni Award. That honor in

Robertson addresses a group of Kenan-Flagler administrators, graduates and friends during a 2017 reception at his Central Park apartment; among those present was Paul Parker (BA 1985), Co-Chairman, Global Mergers & Acquisitions at Goldman Sachs.

2016 was renamed the Dwight W. Anderson Young Alumni Award.

Robertson is perhaps most visible around Chapel Hill today by virtue of the Robertson Scholars, a program he conceived that has students taking classes at both Carolina and Duke. The idea was spawned when one son, Alex, matriculated at Chapel Hill (BA 2001) and another, Spencer, graduated from Duke in 1998.

"It occurred to me they both had interesting groups of friends, but they never met each other's friends," Robertson says. "I looked back on my time, and I never knew anyone from Duke. I thought it would be a good idea. I think it's worked out well. Several have changed schools. A lot of people feel Carolina is less formal and more inclusive. It's been a good experience and I've enjoyed doing it."

Also noticeable in Robertson's Park Avenue suite are dramatic photographs of his Cape Kidnappers Golf Club in New Zealand, which he built in 2001 on land that served for centuries as sheep and cattle farms. The Robertson family has long had a love affair with New Zealand, ever since Robertson moved his family—wife Josie and two sons at the time—there in the late 1970s so he could write a novel.

"I never published it, I'm glad I didn't publish it," he says. "It was a complete exercise in narcissism. My kids put it together for my eightieth birthday. I was the hero of the book, I was also the villain. I wanted to write about a Southern boy on Wall Street."

Swofford needed to install permanent lights in the stadium to accommodate the coming wave of televised games. The long-held story went that Will Kenan donated the stadium that opened in 1927 with the stipulation that no part of the structure ever rise above the trees and clutter the venue's natural beauty. But Swofford found no opposition from Kenan when he went to talk about expanding the structure.

"Frank was a very competitive man by nature," says Swofford, who left Carolina in 1997 to become commissioner of the Atlantic Coast Conference. "He understood change and the need to have some vision in terms of the future and things you needed to do to stay competitive. He said, 'John, you have a program to run, it needs to be successful, we all want it to be successful. If you need to put lights in that go above the pine trees and put in a new press box, you need to do that. I'll be one hundred percent supportive.' He did say this pine tree thing was a myth. That's the exact word he used. It was probably good mythology, though, but not the truth."

Successful businessmen are generally adept at watching from twenty thousand feet as well as zooming in with a microscope. Will Kenan would later say that Flagler had the "most remarkable memory of any person I have ever met. He read everything, talked to everybody on any subject, and always recalled what he read or heard. Should you discuss some subject, be it engineering or scientific, with him, and a year or more later you related the same thing, be sure to have the exact wording, because he would surely say: 'Now let me see, on such and such occasion you told me so and so and this is different. Now which is correct?'"

The original members of the Rockefeller, Andrews and Flagler partnership that began refining and selling oil in Cleveland in the late 1860s offer a textbook example of the importance of marrying skills at the top of a business's hierarchy. Rockefeller was the operations expert with a keen eye for waste and inefficiency. Samuel Andrews was the chemist dubbed a "mechanical genius" by a journalist of the time and the man who developed the process of separating crude oil into its components. And Flagler was the big-picture impresario who, despite not being a lawyer, convinced Rockefeller to incorporate and set up the complicated structure of corporations operating in multiple states. In later years, a reporter asked Rockefeller whose idea it had been to transform the partnership into the corporation called Standard Oil. "I wish I'd had the brains to think of it," Rockefeller replied. "It was Henry Flagler."

"If Flagler never came to Florida, he should still be in the business hall of fame because he basically established the first multi-state corporation," John Blades says. "He figured out how to do business across state lines. We talk about 'multinational' today, and you can create that by going online. In Flagler's day, you had to go to each state to get a corporate charter limited to that state. He figured out how to work around that in order to essentially create a multi-state or national corporation."

Blades spent more than two decades running the Flagler Museum, housed in the Whitehall Mansion in Palm Beach that Flagler built for Mary Lily in 1902, and in the process became the *de facto* Flagler family historian.

"We were changing from an agrarian society to a corporate society, and there were no handbooks on capitalism," he says of the post-Civil War times. "There were no other countries one could look to as examples of how capitalism should work. There were no business schools. They had to make it up. America had created this legal entity, this corporation, you can invest your money in without risking your house or other businesses. That idea of creating a corporate entity was huge and powerful. Flagler and his contemporaries realized that and off they went."

Flagler and the Kenans had immense wealth but all were vigilant for opportunities to help their fellow man.

Will Kenan purchased Randleigh Farm in Lockport, New York, in 1921 with the goal of producing safe milk from the highest quality Jersey cattle. The farm was a leader in dairy research, and Kenan collaborated with veterinarians and scientists on breeding, feeding, milking, milk production leading to "a cleaner and better milk supply for mankind," he said. Direct descendants of Kenan's cows from his New York estate graze today on a farm at N.C. State University.

Frank Kenan's legacy of charitable endeavors stretched far and wide. Some were big and visible—from hospitals to schools to churches to museums. Others came quietly in the middle of the night—late one Christmas Eve, he got dressed and drove a Kenan Oil truck downtown to the *Durham Morning Herald* office and filled the newspaper's empty tank so the Christmas paper could be delivered. He gave money to Chapel Hill in large amounts—$10 million in the early 1990s to help fund the new South Campus Business School facility; and in smaller sums—$30,000 from the Kenan Family Foundation in June 1993 to Interim Dean Carl Zeithaml to assist in "updating the school's promotional materials."

Flagler believed that creating a viable and productive business climate and economy was the biggest contribution he could make to mankind and his fellow Americans, but he nonetheless was generous with his wealth. A document in the Flagler Museum Library lists hundreds of beneficiaries that are known to have received his largesse in the state of Florida alone. He donated land—in 1904 he bought a parcel and donated it to West Palm Beach to use as a cemetery. He looked out for his employees—spending $50,000 on a YMCA building for use by Florida East Coast Railway workers. He built parks—he purchased land in West Palm Beach in 1899 and transferred it to the city; that land stands today as Flagler Park. And he took care of little things as well—in 1902 he paid for Thanksgiving dinner for Cuban children under the care of the Sisters of St. Joseph School in St. Augustine.

"He was a great, enigmatic man who kept his distance from most people and attempted to conceal his private life from the world," Graham wrote. "In Florida, he spent money in prodigious amounts on ventures that benefited the state and its people but not necessarily Flagler himself."

And at their cores, they wanted to be *in the game*.

"What's important to remember about Flagler is this: He wanted to be productive and contribute to make a difference," Blades says. "Whether it was Standard Oil, where he happened to make a ton of money, or Florida, where he spent that money, that's what he wanted to do. What brought meaning to his life was to be productive."

Blades talks of a group of railroad barons that met every year and in 1891 drew up a plan for a centralized railroad system out of Milwaukee that would cover the United States and have a double-track line over the North Atlantic to Europe. He equates it to modern times and getting Steve Jobs of Apple, Jeff Bezos of Amazon and Elon Musk of Tesla together for a brainstorming session.

"That's how big they thought," Blades says. "They thought technology was going to free us to be the best version of ourselves and finally realize what western culture was always meant to be. Free society, meritocracy, technology are going to free us from the daily drudgery of just surviving, do it in a new world and get it right. Destiny has chosen us. We're already a nation of risk takers anyway, populated by people who took risks to get here. Everything came together in the late 1800s. They believed America had a real destiny and they were lucky enough to be part of how we fulfilled that destiny.

"Henry Flagler was in the center of that."

So was Will Kenan—on his own at times and at the right hand of Flagler for more than a dozen years.

Kenan knew from boyhood he wanted to be a scientist. The family was visiting its estate in Duplin County, Liberty Hall, one time when young Will wanted to understand how the meat grinder worked. He inserted his finger in the wrong place at the wrong time and the tip of his finger was lopped off and had to be sewn back on.

Wall Street To UNC

Capital Markets Lab

One of the earliest initiatives to give Kenan-Flagler students hands-on experience in the investing world came in 1952 when Charles Babcock of the Reynolds and Co. investment firm of Winston-Salem gave $10,000 to the school to be invested by students in an investment class. It was known as the "Babcock Fund" and had risen as high as $17,000 toward the end of 1958—and that included making annual donations to the Chapel Hill Community Chest. Avery Cohan, a lecturer in the school, taught the class, but all investment decisions were made by students.

Babcock, who was married to Mary Reynolds, daughter to tobacco magnate R.J. Reynolds, wanted students to learn with real money how to analyze stocks, sectors, bonds and other financial instruments.

That ten grand had risen to $473,000 by the middle of 2018 and today is managed by the Applied Investment Management (AIM) class that is taught in the Capital Markets Lab, which was built in 2008 at a cost of $1.2 million. The room has fifteen Bloomberg terminals and was reconfigured in 2017 to allow the trading monitors to be visible for the

The Capital Markets Lab provides a hands-on, real-time environment for students to learn skills in investing, trading and risk management.

AIM class but recede into the desks for a standard class.

Dr. Mustafa Gültekin teaches the class that manages the Reynolds Fund; the class might range from fifteen to forty students in any given year. Students are assigned specific roles and responsibilities and collaborate on decisions regarding investments in the fund. There is a portfolio manager, strategists for domestic and global portfolios, risk/compliance manager, securities trader, sector analyst and coordinator of investor relations—just as there is on Wall Street.

Will Kenan (UNC 1894, right) on campus years later with two of his contemporaries: George Stephens (1896, left) and Jesse Oldham (1894, center), who was the Tar Heels' baseball coach for one year in 1895.

At Carolina, Will was involved in a number of extracurricular activities—Glee Club, Germans, Sigma Alpha Epsilon fraternity and a society known then as the Gim Ghouls (later changed to the Order of the Gimghoul) among them. He played football as a senior, but baseball was more his passion. He was an infielder but also ran the team as the student manager with responsibilities for scheduling, purchasing equipment and conducting practices. He showed an early business acumen by insisting that the existing athletic field be enclosed by a fence, an idea that met strong resistance because it would detract from the aesthetics of the campus. But Kenan was resolute—a fence was the only way to control spectators and thus charge admission.

Kenan had a front-row seat and a hand in the discovery of chemical technology that would change the world. John Motley Morehead III earned a B.S. degree in 1891 and returned to Chapel Hill for graduate work in chemistry under Francis Venable, UNC's chemistry department chair and professor. Morehead and a Canadian inventor and business associate of his family, Thomas Willson, were looking for a way to manufacture aluminum and in the process created a dark, glassy rock that upon submersion in water, released a gas they thought was hydrogen. The rock, it turned out, was calcium carbide. They brought their process to Venable, who discovered in experiments conducted with Kenan at his side that the gas was acetylene and their method of producing it was cheap and as yet unknown. The dominoes started falling—from calcium carbide came the ability to frame skyscrapers and from the clear gas evolved new methods of welding.

"The story goes that there was an explosion in the old chemistry building, the pre-Venable Hall building, that resulted in the formula used in the development of acetylene gas," says Tom Kenan. "Before then, buildings could only go up five or six stories because they didn't have the structure supports. Acetylene gas allowed you to weld the steel frames together, and then the skyscraper era started."

Will graduated in 1894 and within two years had moved to Niagara Falls to work at the Carbide Manufacturing Company (the precursor to Union Carbide). His "offer letter" from Carbide to manage one shift in its plant specified he would be expected to work "ten hours a day, seven days a week." Soon Will was promoted and sent around the world to help establish plants key to the fledgling industry, two of his outposts being in Australia and Germany, and he left the company in 1900 when he didn't want to move to Austria for a year. But for someone as smart and energetic as Kenan, there would always be another opportunity. And it came fast when he met Flagler in 1899.

"There is nothing I can say in his behalf that he does not deserve," Flagler said of Kenan in an introductory letter to a business associate. "During his college course, he was first in everything—studies and games."

When Flagler died in 1913, Kenan became the trustee of his estate and at one point ran Flagler's interests in railroads, steamships, hotels, power, electricity and water. He designed the central heating system for Whitehall, the 1902 Palm Beach mansion Flagler built for Mary Lily as a wedding present. By the 1920s, Kenan was in middle age and had ascended to dizzying heights in business. He spent much of his time pursuing passions of gardening, the cultivation of dairy cows and also rebuilding the Flagler hotel system with modern structures to replace the unwieldy firetraps built in the late 1800s.

Kenan in 1926 received a prospectus from University administrators outlining plans for a new football stadium to replace Emerson Field, which with a seating capacity of 2,400 was overrun for big games of the day, particularly against arch-rival Virginia. He was inclined to contribute an amount to match the ballpark of dollars given by other alumni and donors, but the idea also occurred to him that the stadium might be a fitting memorial he'd been thinking of creating for his mother, Mary Hargrave Kenan, and his father, William R. Kenan Sr. Kenan visited with University officials and was shown the site for the proposed stadium, a ravine in a forest south of campus, and decided to underwrite the entire venture—just over $300,000 that included a field house at the east end of the playing field. Kenan Stadium opened in November 1927.

Kenan's prudent management of the estates left in his hands—including retention of substantial holdings of shares in Standard Oil Company, now Exxon Mobile Corporation—grew enough that upon his death his estate was worth more than $100 million. He left $95 million to become the corpus of the William R. Kenan Jr. Charitable Trust and wrote in his will: "I have always believed firmly that a good education is the most cherished gift an individual can receive, and it is my sincere hope that the provisions of this Article will result in a substantial benefit to mankind." Over half a century, the Trust had distributed more than eight hundred grants worth nearly $500 million; the Trust's market value in 2018 was in excess of $650 million.

"Even if he had not met Henry Flagler, William Rand Kenan Jr. would almost certainly have made a noteworthy journey on his own," posited Walter Campbell.

Meanwhile, after Frank Kenan's early hiccup in the gas business, he founded Kenan Oil and soon started a transportation concern to move gas between Durham and Wilmington. Kenan Transport would grow into a $60 million annual business. Kenan was at the vanguard of the self-service gas station business after World War II when his friend Watts Hill had a lot at the corner of Duke and Chapel Hill Streets in Durham that he couldn't build on because of post-war construction restrictions.

"Watts called me and said, 'Do you have any idea what we could do with that corner lot?'" Kenan said. "We had an old concrete block building and took twelve old pumps and put them up there and sold more gasoline at cut prices than anybody. Agents came from all over to see how we did it."

That concept would lead some years later to Tops Petroleum, with the company's distinctive look of buildings made of glass fronts and red roofs appearing across the Southeast. Kenan also ran the Westfield Company (a developer of shopping centers) and had other interests in commercial real estate, including the University Square retail and office project on Franklin Street in Chapel Hill. In a world-class example of "coming full circle," Kenan in the late 1980s became a major investor in the Landfall golf and residential community between downtown Wilmington and Wrightsville Beach—the very land where his ancestors had hobnobbed on the Pembroke Jones estate.

"I like to build things. I like to see success," Frank said.

Indeed he did. That building process to Kenan was the very essence of capitalism. Jack Kasarda replaced Rollie Tillman as head of the Kenan Institute of Private Enterprise in 1990 and remembers a quote that hung near Kenan's portrait on the third floor of the Kenan Center as the bedrock to the Institute's very existence: "Free enterprise is the backbone of a prosperous society. If you lose that, you lose all that is good in society."

"Frank Kenan really believed that," Kasarda says. "He also believed in setting up the Kenan Institute, and I think he was probably on target, that there was a strong drift to the left of the academy, and business was viewed as not positive but negative. He very much wanted to utilize the Institute to get the word out that business was good for society and that people prospered and that the best social program was a permanent job, a permanent *meaningful* job."

Longtime family friend Mary Semans paid tribute to Kenan when he was given the 1991 North Caroliniana Society Award. "In his quiet, cheerful manner, he has served the state and its people in countless ways—many times few are aware of," she said. "He works on so many projects behind the scenes, never seeking recognition. The variety of Frank's interests is staggering. Philanthropy and

Kenan-Flagler administrators have used the Flagler Museum in Palm Beach for special events over the years. The atrium that houses Henry Flagler's railroad car is a perfect spot for an evening meal function.

service are his watchwords."

Mack Brown, the Carolina football coach from 1988-97 who returned as head coach in 2018, was impressed in his dealings with Kenan in the early 1990s that Kenan "was eighty years old and was talking deals twenty years down the road. And he had no intention of not being around for them. He was tough and smart." Lee Shaffer, a former Carolina basketball player and the long-time president of Kenan Transport Co., termed Kenan "a once-in-a-lifetime man" and one "who had no patience for failure."

Kenan died in June 1996—just months before the opening of the opulent new football center at the west end of Kenan Stadium bearing his name and a year shy of the opening of Kenan-Flagler's new campus on the hill above the Dean E. Smith Center.

"He was a person of the great Southern tradition of grace and sense of duty," UNC President William C. Friday said. "The remarkable quality about the man was that his mind was always looking for ways to use the funds he controls to ensure they're maximized."

"He's been everything to the business school—visionary, motivator, philanthropist," said Paul Fulton, an alum and, at the time, Kenan-Flagler dean. "Where this school is today is as much the work of Frank Kenan as anyone."

His widow Betty Kenan has remained engaged and supportive of the school since Frank's passing. One of her gifts helped convert the fifth floor of the McColl Building for use by the PhD program, and she has contributed to

Mary Lily Kenan Flagler was described in various journals as a "talented young woman of grace and charm." She loved music and was an accomplished singer and pianist.

retrofitting DuBose Home bedrooms. She often joins stepson Tom Kenan in sponsoring events such as the Leaders Weekend at The Breakers in Palm Beach.

Kenan valued and cherished his days at Woodberry Forest and was generous and active the rest of his life in giving back financial support and pearls of wisdom. He addressed the graduating class in 1989 and told the boys: "Don't be afraid to be the best. Don't be afraid to be a leader. Be compassionate but have strong convictions and go for the top in whatever you do. Too many people had rather blend in—had rather be average, be comfortable. The greatest thrill is succeeding in a difficult task. Set impossible goals."

Often Kenan cited the "Sermon on the Mount," Matthew 7, Verse 7, as providing inspiration and a framework to his life:

"Ask, and it will be given you; seek and you will find; knock, and it will be opened to you. For every one who asks receives, and he who seeks finds, and to him who knocks it will be opened."

***

James Kenan was a member of the University of North Carolina's first Board of Trustees and contributed fifty dollars in 1790 to the construction of Old East, the first state university building in the nation. From there, a long line of Kenans would serve as students, trustees and benefactors, creating what UNC Chancellor James Moeser (2000-08) once characterized as "one of the oldest philanthropic partnerships in American higher education."

Four generations and a century later, Mary Lily Kenan in the late 1880s was perhaps too early for the idea of women succeeding in business. The "cult of domesticity" as historians have pegged the 19th century held that women could best serve the political and social needs of a growing America by focusing on the creation and nurturing of the household, providing a haven for husbands and sons from the rough-and-tumble world of the streets, the fields and the factories. Given the times, she was the ideal partner to a busy and successful businessman like Henry Flagler.

Mary Lily was described in various journals as a "talented young woman of grace and charm, she was always the center of a gay group, and it was said of her that her greatest desire was to make others happy." She loved music and enjoyed singing and playing the piano as she traveled the social circuit of Newport to St. Augustine and later Palm Beach. The *Times-Union* of Jacksonville once described her as "a sweet, pretty young lass, a typical flower of North Carolina."

"Her pretty clothes, her attractive manners and her many accomplishments representing the flower of Southern womanhood attracted her to the best society of the resorts she frequented with her friends," wrote A.C. Howell.

She and Flagler were married at Liberty Hall, the Kenan ancestral home in Duplin County, on August 24, 1901, with Will Kenan in attendance and had a happy twelve-year marriage.

Sidney Walter Martin in *Florida's Flagle*r wrote that Mary Lily was "cultured, well-trained and had an excellent background. She was Flagler's equal socially and intellectually. She was a good wife to him and during most of their married years, his interests came first with her. She was socially included and loved excitement and a good time."

When Henry died in 1913 after complications from a fall down a staircase at their Whitehall home in Palm Beach, Mary Lily inherited much of his vast fortune—estimated by various reports as being worth from $90 to $100 million. Over the next few years she would give considerable thought to what to do with her vast millions. Though Mary Lily didn't attend Chapel Hill, she held the University in high regard for what it had meant to her family, particularly her father and brothers. She heard bits of news of how the University was faring and had every intention of remembering the institution in her own will.

Real Estate Sets Template For Excellence

Wood Center for Real Estate

Dean Doug Shackelford says one of his goals for Kenan-Flagler Business School as it enters its second century is to "play to our strengths." To double-down, if you will, on programs and initiatives in which the school is holding a full house.

"Our real estate program is second to none in this country," Shackelford says. "Our goal is to be number one in everything we do. This program sets the standard."

The real estate curriculum was launched in 1976 and run throughout the 1980s by professor Mike Miles, who left in 1991 to enter private business and would later become managing principal and portfolio manager for Guggenheim Real Estate Partners.

Succeeding him was Dave Hartzell, a graduate of the PhD program who started as a professor of finance in 1988 and remains so today while adding the title in 2007 of Steven D. Bell and Leonard W. Wood Distinguished Professor in Real Estate. Hartzell says his father was "kind of a George Bailey in *It's a Wonderful Life* kind of banker" back in Wilmington, Delaware, in the 1960s and '70s. "I always wanted to be like him," says Hartzell, explaining his early interest in banking and real estate.

So when Miles left, Hartzell was the next man up.

"Mike was a legendary professor, he was on the level of Dick Levin and Jack Behrman and those guys," Hartzell says. "When he left, there was a huge hole in the MBA Program. I was kind of the only man standing, so I took the real estate program over. I hired a guy to come in the next year and we hovered between one and two faculty members for many years."

An important cog in the evolution of the real estate program was Steve Cumbie (BA '70, MBA '73), a highly successful CEO and principal of NV Commercial Inc., NV Retail and Metro Realty Group—companies in the D.C. Metro area with projects exceeding $1 billion. Cumbie served as an adjunct professor and executive director of the Wood Center from 2008-10, spending two days a week in Chapel Hill for three years while managing his commercial businesses back in D.C. He was honored in 2017 with the Kenan-Flagler Business School Leadership Award.

"Steve brought real-world stories and examples to our students as an adjunct professor and provided numerous networking opportunities for our graduates," Hartzell says.

The program made a quantum leap in 2013 when the real estate center was renamed the Leonard W. Wood Center for Real Estate Studies. Wood is a 1972 Kenan-Flagler graduate who cut his teeth on residential and commercial projects working for Charles Fraser at Hilton Head Island and later for the

Trammell Crow Company. In 1998, he founded Wood Partners LLC of Atlanta; the company's focus was the development of apartment and condominium homes, and at the time of Wood's retirement in 2007, the company had started over 38,000 multi-family units representing an investment of more than $5.3 billion.

The Wood Center was also facilitated with the largesse and vision of another successful Kenan-Flagler grad, Tom Harvey (MBA '72), who was the former Pulte Homes area president for Florida. Harvey was the first executive director of the Center for Real Estate Development at Kenan-Flagler.

"Both these guys are incredible idea and deal guys," Hartzell says. "Leonard had the original vision for a center to formalize a lot of what we do now."

Hartzell was able to add classes and professors—it now has four full-time professors—and expand the work of the Kenan-Flagler Real Estate Funds, which was launched in 2007 and furthers the school's emphasis on experiential learning. Through the spring of 2018, three separate real estate investment funds operated by students had invested $8.1 million in over thirty-four deals. The program's tagline is "real-world real estate."

Real estate students explore construction site at Hudson Yards in New York in 2015.

The students have full responsibility for the management of the funds, subject to oversight by a faculty advisor and an investment committee. They cold-call investors to raise capital for a new fund and are then responsible for sourcing deals, doing due diligence and financial underwriting. Students present a pitch to the investment committee, work with the sponsor on legal documents and create quarterly and annual reports to investors, who often call to address inconsistencies and ask questions.

"You can simulate decision making with cases, but this is real-world experience," says Hartzell. "They sit in the seat of an investor and make actual investment decisions for the benefit of real investors with real capital at risk. I don't think any other schools have had the confidence in their students or faculty to allow them to do something like this."

One example of the kind of project the students take on was a mixed-use project in 2017 with East-West Partners in Chapel Hill that included a new fire station, parking garage and 48,000 square feet of office space over four floors on a site just east of the UNC campus.

"We had a financing gap to fill, this was a project they liked and it was right in their backyard," says

Ben Perry of East-West Partners. "We dealt only with the students managing the fund. They asked pointed but fair questions, got to the heart of the issue and weighed the risks with the potential rewards. They did so very knowledgeably, not unlike many of the other larger investors we work with."

"We've done deals from Albuquerque to Milwaukee to Florida to Austin," Hartzell says. "Literally everything from a small rehab of fourteen apartments into twenty-one apartments a mile from campus at UT-Austin to being a small part of a big industrial portfolio in Dallas.

"The students get an unparalleled experience, and they really feel ownership of it."

One of the Wood Center signature events is an annual real estate conference that in April 2018 drew nearly a thousand attendees to the Dean E. Smith Center for a variety of programs and speakers, the keynote being delivered by real estate mogul Sam Zell.

And all MBA students benefit immensely from the Global Immersion Electives, where students and faculty travel to get inside looks at international business. Four trips are made per year, and one is generally real estate focused. Hartzell estimates he's taken sixteen or seventeen GIE trips over the years and in the spring of 2018 escorted a group of some two dozen MBA students to Israel and Dubai.

"That was a remarkable trip in many ways, but one thing that stuck out to me was the strength of the Carolina network or, what many refer to as the 'Carolina family,'" says MBA student John McColl Jr. (2019). "Each stop on the trip was set up by Kenan-Flagler alumni and their associates, and we were able to meet with the top real estate firms and companies in both Tel Aviv and Dubai, companies that we would normally not have access to. It is a testament to the program that Dave Hartzell has created and the relationships that he continues to keep with former students. That is something that is especially unique that I think every Carolina graduate experiences everywhere they go. The GIE trip reinforced the strength of that network for me." ❖

Washington was the destination in 2016 for this class of real estate students to tour construction sites and meet industry executives.

Howell's juggernaut of a book about the evolution of the Kenan Professorships includes profiles of the original fifty-five faculty honorees and is shelved in various libraries around campus. One chapter tells the backstory of the bequest and includes intricate detail of how it came to pass, including letters from Colonel Robert Bingham (UNC 1857), the father of Robert Worth Bingham (UNC 1891), who was an old beau of Mary Lily's and the man who in 1916 would become her second husband. Col. Bingham in the early 1900s was headmaster at the Bingham School in Asheville and used Mary Lily's visits to the Grove Park Inn with her invalid mother to soft sell her on the many financial needs of the University, at the time having a thousand students, thirty-six full professors and a total teaching staff of sixty-six.

"She got as many as fifty letters, begging letters, in a single day sometimes and she got very sore about it and seemed to turn her against anybody who asks her for money," Bingham wrote in an October 1915 missive to University President Edward Graham. "But she listened to me right through.

"I said the University could not house more than half its pupils and that the other five hundred must live in the village in unsanitary quarters, and that the professors were constantly being offered larger salaries elsewhere."

Separately more than a year later, Josephus Daniels, the publisher of *The News & Observer* in Raleigh and also Secretary of the Navy, wrote Graham to say, "I am hoping she is going to do something handsome for the University. My wife had a long talk with her Friday night .... I am going to urge her to give the money to build a Kenan Building to be the Law Building of the University and also to erect a dormitory."

Graham responded in early 1917 that a Law Building and a dormitory would be wonderful, but he had his sights set higher. Graham was going to suggest she underwrite a Student Union—"a student club house building, large enough to center and contain all religious, social and general student activities for the whole college .... I understand she has in mind giving an important memorial of some sort to her father and uncles together .... A really splendid gift."

While University officials and friends were planting seeds in Mary's head over how her resources could benefit education in Chapel Hill, she was moving on in her personal life. Newspaper reports said it had been twenty-two years since she and Robert Bingham had courted when they reconnected in Asheville in 1915. Bingham was born in Mebane and attended law school at Carolina and Virginia and later earned his law degree from the University of Louisville. He was married and had three children as he began his law career in Louisville, but his wife died in a car crash in 1913. Judge Bingham, as he was universally known after having served a temporary appointment to a local bench, and Mary were married in November 1916 at the New York home of Pembroke and Sadie Jones, but it would be a very short union.

Some in Mary's circle suspected Bingham of being a fortune hunter as the relationship evolved, so he had to forswear any share of her vast riches. But months after the wedding, Mary added a codicil to her will, leaving her husband $5 million—which he would use in 1918, one year after her death, to purchase the *Louisville Courier-Journal* and *Louisville Times.*

The newlyweds went on a honeymoon on their private rail car and then settled in Louisville, a town where Mary Lily had no history and no close friends. Their marriage was heralded by a series of well-publicized dinners, socials and afternoon teas given in their honor, and in late November, writes William Campbell, she sent a telegram to family members saying she was "the happiest woman in the world." Sadly that would not last long as Mary Lily's health started deteriorating that spring. In June she fell ill and went into a tailspin from which she never recovered. She died on July 27, 1917, after suffering what was reported to be the

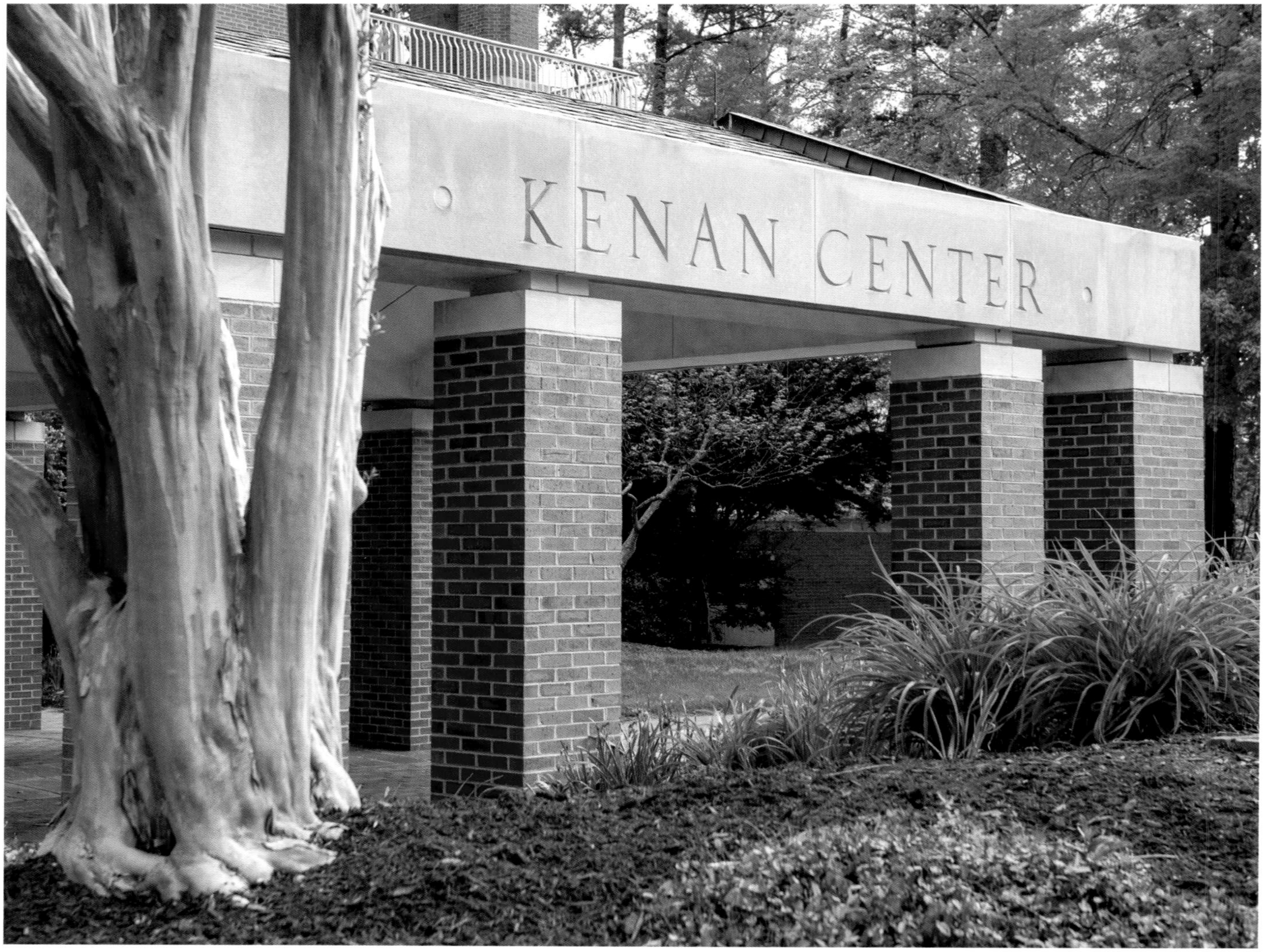

The buildings are multiple on the UNC campus that have benefitted from the largesse of the Kenan Family.

third heart attack in three weeks. She was buried a few days later in Wilmington at Oakdale Cemetery.

Her bequest to the University of $2.3 million to establish the Mary Lily Kenan Professorships at Chapel Hill was misinterpreted by most newspapers statewide, the news hitting that she had left a *principal* amount of $75,000 to be used for paying salaries of professors. Only *The Asheville Times* correctly understood it to be an amount that would generate $75,000 in *interest* on an annual basis in perpetuity, an editorial saying she had "bequeathed to humanity a gift which will benefit thousands yet unborn and forever render blessed the memories of her great generosity." Many saw the first reports that the donation was $75,000 and were disappointed. "When it was announced she had given only $75,000, I was downhearted, because when I had my talk with her she intimated she intended on doing something handsome," Josephus Daniels wrote to President Graham. "But she has done better than even I expected, and I will rejoice with you and all other friends of the University."

The bequest "insures the strengthening of many of the present schools and departments," noted the *Carolina Alumni Review* in October 1917. "It makes possible the establishment of others long needed but not provided on account of lack of funds; and it vitalizes the entire life at the University at the very moment when North Carolina supremely needs the full service of every one of her educational institutions."

Five professorships were appointed in 1918, one of them to Francis Venable, who had been a great friend and mentor to Will Kenan a quarter of a century earlier. By 1920 the professorships paid $5,000, basically doubling the standard salary of a professor just three years earlier, and the story of William Branson, a Kenan Professor of Rural-Social Economics, was emblematic of the good works being generated by Mary Lily's generosity.

Branson was a pioneer in the organization and development of rural social economics and came to Chapel Hill from Georgia Normal College in Athens in 1914. The theme of his courses, according to Howell's book, was "the need to reawaken rural North Carolina" and the goals of his department were the "gathering, disseminating and interpretation of facts and the study of problems" of rural life in North Carolina.

He led men out of "mourning for the lost cabins in the cotton, the plantations and the mansions of a romantic antebellum civilization; he led them onto the high-road to the New South of good roads and schools, of erosion control and reforestation, of well-kept farms and prosperous communities."

The University of Virginia in 1920 tried to pirate him away to start a similar program in Charlottesville. But Carolina had the resources to make a counter-offer through the Kenan Professorships and enticed him to stay in Chapel Hill.

"It may well be that Mrs. Bingham's far-sighted investment in the alma mater of her fathers was the spark which touched off the almost explosive growth and expansion which took place in the next twenty years," Howell wrote.

President Graham did not get those buildings he had hoped from the Kenan estate. Instead, Mary Lily's will stated she was interested in "the instruction of the youth of North Carolina," that she wanted to build lives and the way to do that was to invest in the procurement and retention of talented teachers. A portrait of her was commissioned by the University and hung on commencement weekend in May 1958 in the library of Kenan Hall, the women's dormitory named for her that opened in 1939 in a three-building court on the northeast corner of campus.

A.C. Howell presided over the ceremony and addressed a group that included twenty of the current Kenan Professors. He noted that Mary Lily grew up in a time when women were not admitted in Chapel Hill.

"She would, I am sure, be pleased to know that now they are admitted and that this hall, bearing the honored name of Kenan, houses the women graduate students who have come from near and far to complete their education," he said.

The University has long been considered one of the nation's top public institutions. When *U.S. News & World Report* first launched its rankings of colleges and universities across America in 1983, Carolina was listed ninth. In the most recent rankings of 2018, the University was listed fifth among public institutions, behind the University of California, UCLA, Virginia and Michigan. And in September 2018, it was named the best public university for financial value by *The Wall Street Journal* and Times Higher Education; the University ranked second overall among the

Dr. Jim Johnson (R) poses with Kenan-Flagler graduate Brittany Curry (C) and students enrolled at the Global Scholars Academy in Durham.

Making A Difference

Dr. Jim Johnson

Dr. Jim Johnson Jr. joined the Kenan-Flagler faculty in 1992 as professor of strategy and entrepreneurship and brought with him a deep reservoir of experience in geography, urban studies, poverty and social justice. He made the acquaintance of Frank Kenan, who had built the Kenan Center on UNC's South Campus and had just pledged $10 million toward the Business School's eventual new home next door.

"One of the first times we met, he talked about how kids from the inner city needed something other than drug dealing and basketball," Johnson remembers.

Johnson had spent years researching, writing and lecturing on inequality and on demographics and sensed that Kenan might be an ally in attacking the problem. Johnson proposed the Durham Scholars program, an after-school, weekend and summer initiative to provide mentorship and wholesome activities to disadvantaged youngsters. Kenan, through the William R. Kenan Jr. Charitable Trust, contributed $3.6 million to fund the program and it launched in 1995. One tenet of the program has been to establish ways to apply business tools and principles to social problems, and students at Kenan-Flagler have been volunteers for more than two decades.

"There are pressing social problems we should be addressing, and I had to do something," says Johnson, today a Kenan Distinguished Professor. "I've always believed I was put on this earth to make a difference."

The program was successful, but Johnson and Durham Scholars administrators soon discovered it wasn't enough.

"We decided we needed our own school to ensure kids get a consistent message for as long during the day as possible," Johnson says.

The Durham Scholars evolved into the Global Scholars Academy, which used a $10 million commitment from Union Baptist Church to build a 49,000 square-foot facility in downtown Durham, just across Dowd Street from the church. GSA opened in 2009 as a K-8 laboratory charter school.

"We start at 7:30 in the morning, we go to 6 p.m. daily, and we're a year-round school," Johnson says. "It's a culture that you have to create and a set of expectations."

GSA enjoys a state-of-the-art early learning center, thirteen classrooms equipped with the latest education technology, a media center, a gymnasium with a circular walking/jogging track, a fitness

"We decided we needed our own school to ensure kids get a consistent message for as long during the days as possible."

Dr. Jim Johnson

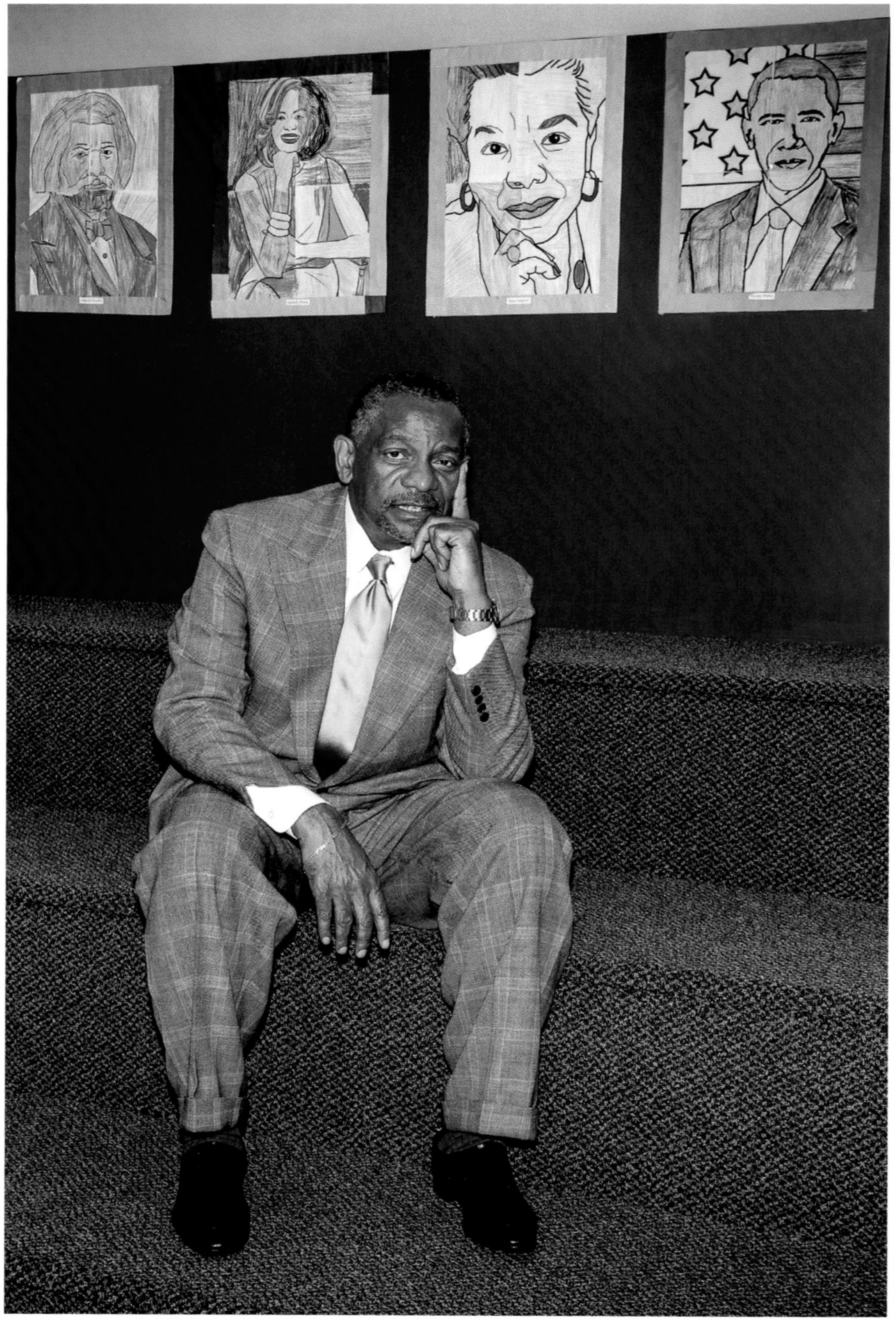

center, a health and wellness center, an industrial sized kitchen and dining area, a dance studio, an animation studio/photojournalism lab, and secure outdoor recreation areas with age appropriate equipment. It has a capacity for 225 students.

One volunteer from the 2010-12 era was Brittany Curry, who was pursuing her MBA at Kenan-Flagler (which she completed in 2012). She developed a connection with Johnson, the school and the children and helped recruit fellow MBA students to tutor and mentor the children.

"At the end of my second year, I just felt like I had really done something that I really, really had cared about for the past two years. It was a great feeling," she says.

After a five-year stint in global marketing and brand management with Johnson & Johnson, she moved to Durham in April 2017 to become managing director of the school. Her domain at GSA is everything non-academic—marketing, finance, accounting, grant-writing and fundraising.

"This school is about changing the narrative of their lives," Curry says. "We have a rigorous academic program and our goal is to make sure that the kids are able to compete in a global economy once they leave here, that they are set up in a really big way for success." ❖

"These professors are what set Carolina apart from our peer universities and give us an opportunity to be a standout university."

Dr. Ronald Strauss

top 250 institutions in that listing.

"Dr. Frank Graham told me the University would not have existed except for the help given by Mary Lily Kenan," Frank Kenan, the family's mid to late-20th-century patriarch, said of the University president from 1930-49. "She established the Kenan Professors, the original ones. I don't know whether that's true or not, but it was very helpful, I'm sure."

"Over the years I have heard people say that those first Kenan professorships, taken together, were like the keystone in an arch, holding the university's faculty together through the Depression," adds Jack Evans, a Kenan-Flagler faculty member since 1970 and dean from 1978-87.

Tom Lambeth is a 1957 Carolina graduate who worked in philanthropy much of his life, serving for nearly twenty-five years as executive director the Z. Smith Reynolds Foundation in Winston-Salem. He cites a letter written by Nancy Reynolds, daughter of R.J. Reynolds, where she said, "The best kind of giving is that which encourages others."

"I think the Kenans have every right to claim that the example they set leveraged a lot of other money—from faculty strength to buildings and much more," Lambeth says. "The original Kenan gift was really, really important in that moment in the University's history. We had the great tragedy for the flu epidemic robbing us of one president and then his successor. We had the University effectively taken over by the military during World War I. It was a difficult period and that was a considerable sum of money."

Stroll around the town and campus today and you'll pass many entities and buildings named for esteemed faculty members who held these early Kenan professorships—Francis Venable in chemistry, William Coker in botany, Edwin Greenlaw in English, Robert Connor in history, Horace Williams in philosophy, William Dey in literature, Joseph Hamilton in history and Maurice Van Hecke in law among them.

And within some of those buildings and many more you'll find the twenty-eight faculty members appointed to Kenan Distinguished Professorships one century later doing the work they were ordained to do. There is Jodi Magness in religious studies, Bland Simpson in English and creative writing, Arturo Escobar in anthropology, Barbara Fredrickson in psychology, Jacqueline Hagan in sociology and Fabian Monrose in computer science among them.

"These professors are what set Carolina apart from our peer universities and give us an opportunity to be a standout university," says Dr. Ronald Strauss, executive vice provost and chief international officer. "They would be assets to any major university in the world. If they were not on our faculty, this would be a much diminished place."

President Edward Kidder Graham in his 1916 *Annual Report* wrote of the demand on the University to recruit and maintain quality faculty. Good professors produced "work of distinctive quality," he said, and he wanted to create an environment that would "keep the best men at their best."

Little did he know at the time of the rich font of resources that soon would begin flowing from the Kenan and Flagler names—and would continue for a century, with no end in sight.

3 the Culture

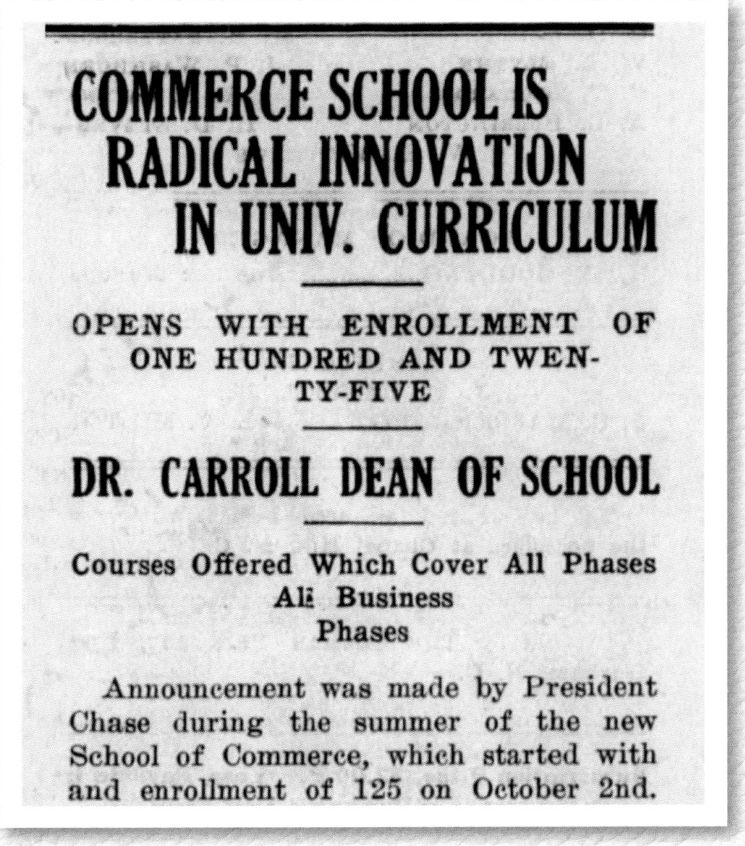

COMMERCE SCHOOL IS RADICAL INNOVATION IN UNIV. CURRICULUM

OPENS WITH ENROLLMENT OF ONE HUNDRED AND TWENTY-FIVE

DR. CARROLL DEAN OF SCHOOL

Courses Offered Which Cover All Phases Ali Business Phases

Announcement was made by President Chase during the summer of the new School of Commerce, which started with and enrollment of 125 on October 2nd.

The School of Commerce opened its doors in 1919 because of the need to develop business leaders within North Carolina and beyond, and a century later the school's reach was literally worldwide, as this group of undergraduates demonstrated in their 2018 trip to Cape Town, South Africa, as part of Kenan-Flagler's global programs.

John Townsend III arrived at 140 Broadway in the financial district of Lower Manhattan in July 1982 and took his spot in the Donaldson Lufkin & Jenrette MBA recruiting class along with seven other bright and shiny investment bankers. As he remembers it, two were from Harvard, two from Wharton, two from Stanford and one from Columbia.

"I put the over-under on me at about six months," Townsend says. "*Maybe* I'd make it six months. I was so intimidated."

This, after all, was the financial big leagues, where the old and established firms of Salomon Brothers, Merrill Lynch, Goldman Sachs, Morgan Stanley, Lehman Brothers, Bear Stearns and First Boston bought, sold, traded, invested, merged and acquired the assets of America and beyond. Then you had smaller firms like DLJ and Drexel Burnham nipping at the big dogs' heels.

"I had a handful of offers," Townsend says, "but ultimately I went with DLJ because I thought it was a place I might differentiate myself a little sooner than at other firms."

Townsend earned a degree in English with a minor in American history from Chapel Hill in 1977 and moved with his bride Marree to Lumberton, where John grew up and where a tidy career awaited him in the family business—growing tobacco, corn and soybeans, operating a tobacco warehouse and raising some hogs just to diversify. Three years in, he hit the brakes.

"I could have stayed in that, done very well and been in the family business for a long, long time," he says. "By small-town standards, it was pretty successful. But I just had a feeling I might wake up one day when I was sixty years old and realize I never really tried to see what I could have accomplished on my own, and I might regret that."

So Townsend applied to what was then known as the UNC School of Business Administration to pursue an MBA. The Townsends sold their house, moved back to Chapel Hill and rented an apartment. Marree went to work at the State Employees Credit Union and John dove headfirst into the wilderness of business school.

"I made a very conscious decision that if I did this for two years with the opportunity cost and moving expenses and everything, I would really commit myself to it," he says. "And I did. I was pretty disciplined. I was really committed to making the most of the experience."

Townsend thought he was relatively good at math—certainly for an English major—but when he got into financial accounting in August 1980 under Professor Harold Langenderfer, "It was like a foreign language, and I didn't understand a word.

"But Professor Langenderfer, while very demanding, was a likeable guy and he made you believe that anyone could learn accounting," Townsend remembers. "Not that it would be easy. It was challenging. It was hard. But then one day, the lightbulb pops on and you say, 'Oh, I've got it.' You understand what double-entry means, income and balance sheets, debit and credit, all that stuff. It becomes very intuitive and logical."

Townsend was similarly tested by Professor Dick Levin's integrated management class. Students read one case study each week about issues and problems facing companies across a broad spectrum; their analysis covered the disciplines of accounting, finance, operations, management, marketing, statistics and more. The core of the class was distilling the case into a one-page paper.

"You had to identify the problem, develop the narrative, then make a recommendation," Townsend says. "You learned to grasp the core issue and then write with economy. Dick graded the papers on the business elements and had someone else grade the writing part of it. It was all very beneficial. It was something I thrived in. Dick was quite demanding. But we became good friends. He was just one of an all-star cast of faculty stars at the time."

When it came time to look for a job, Townsend consid-

Five years in, Goldman Sachs offered Townsend a position "with my name written all over it—to run the firm's business across the entire southern part of the country." He accepted it and began work at Goldman in May 1987 and "crammed forty years of work into the next sixteen." When Goldman went public in 1999, Townsend became profoundly wealthy. He retired from Goldman in 2003, then spent several years helping fellow Kenan-Flagler alumnus Julian Robertson (1955) run Tiger Management. Today Townsend devotes his time and energy to philanthropy, board service and outdoors interests from skiing to golf.

He's proud that his career was bookended with Tar Heels—Jenrette at the front end and Robertson at the rear.

"In-state tuition in the early 1980s was about $250 per semester," he says. "That's amazing. It's crazy. What I received versus what I paid is far out of balance. I have a long way to go to make it up. In the big picture, what we offer students even today and the price they pay is really extraordinary."

Stories like Townsend's are legion among graduates of UNC Kenan-Flagler Business School—students from multiple backgrounds converging on Bingham Hall in the forties or Carroll Hall in the seventies or the McColl Building today and immersing themselves in two years or more of classes. At the end they emerge with a sheepskin, a set of technical skills, a loyal network of classmates and colleagues and a battery of essential values standing them in good stead for a long and productive life.

"Our graduates' job is to go back and make their families, companies, communities and countries better," says Doug Shackelford, Kenan-Flagler dean since 2014. "If that is what we're achieving, then we are providing a great social good."

"A typical student at UNC wants to have a successful career, but they want to have a *meaningful* career," adds David A. Hofmann, a faculty member since 2001 and today the Hugh L. McColl Jr. Distinguished Professor of Leadership and Organizational Behavior and Senior Associate Dean for Academic Affairs. "And I define 'meaningful' as making a positive impact on society. That's partly the type of students that UNC gets, but I'd like to think that we as a business school help reinforce that and grow that notion while they are here."

Bill Moore received his Carolina MBA in 1967 and was working for Legg Mason in Washington in 1970 alongside others with experience on Wall Street and from top business schools like Harvard.

"I realized I knew as much and I was at least as well trained as they were," says Moore, now retired from a successful investment banking career and since 1999 a professor of finance at Kenan-Flagler. "In fact, I thought I was *better* trained. And I had several guys from Harvard who I worked very closely with, and I just realized this school is as good as any of them. I just knew Carolina was hands down the best business school in the Southeast."

Lewis Burton was the first African-American to graduate from Kenan-Flagler, earning his degree in 1965 and going on to a half-century career in accounting with Arthur Andersen in Chicago. He cites as an invaluable resource the guidance and mentorship from Accounting Professor Isaac Reynolds, who was also his academic advisor.

"He was a very direct and firm individual," says Burton, who retired in 2015. "He took an interest in me. I followed his instructions. I figured out as time went on that the more I followed his advice, the more advice he gave me. He would suggest courses to take and the sequence to take them. He also told me to take a speed-reading course, which I did and which proved very valuable."

Early in 1965, Langenderfer told Burton to come by his office after class, and he asked if Burton had any plans after graduation.

"That was a great question to hear, because it meant he knew I was on track to graduate," Burton says with a smile. "But no, I was clueless. I had no plans."

Langenderfer handed him a package and told him, "Read what's in here, and follow the instructions."

It was an employment package from Arthur Andersen. Burton filled out the paperwork, sent it in and soon got a letter inviting him to Chicago for a formal interview. He made that trip in March and soon afterward got a letter offering him a job. He started on July 5, 1965, and before he left, had one more meeting with Reynolds.

"He told me what I had to do in terms of being successful, which was really make sure you do not go to the big city and party too much," Burton says. "In the big city, there was tremendous exposure to a lot of things. On many occasions I would be in situations, and in the back of my mind came a voice. It was Ike Reynolds."

Richard "Stick" Williams graduated in 1975 and went to work for Arthur Andersen for three years and then to Duke Power (later to become Duke Energy), where he worked in corporate finance his entire career.

"I didn't realize how prepared I was leaving Chapel Hill," he says. "Three years in public accounting and then moving to Duke in corporate finance, I was just astounded at how well prepared I was. I thought of myself as a struggling college student. When I got out and started practicing public accounting and then corporate finance, I *knew* that stuff."

Jeff Tucker got his undergraduate degree at Southern Methodist University in Dallas and his MBA at Kenan-Flagler in 2000. The SMU experience, he says, provided a solid education that allowed him to check the box that he had earned an undergraduate business degree.

"UNC, however, *changed my life*," says Tucker, managing director and COO of Century Bridge Capital, a private equity investment firm focused on China. "The quality of the faculty, students and the program were first rate. Moreover, the culture of the entire school was one of support, shared success and teamwork. That fit so well with my personality and aspirations, both in my career and my life. So I came to UNC for a business education but received so much more."

Frank Kenan (BSBA '35) and Julian Robertson ('55) both credit a rigorous accounting class with helping their business careers.

"It was a vicious thing, the accounting exam," Kenan said in a mid-1980s interview. "It's all day long. You went in with a set of books and ran a company for a month, made all the entries, closed the books, and got out the trailing balance. That usually came at four o'clock in the afternoon. Strong men cried when the damn thing wouldn't balance. That was the best lesson I ever had in that business school. I can read a balance sheet so quick now, and it came from then. Success in business comes to a fellow who can read figures and read a balance sheet in the proper way. That's the biggest lesson I learned in Chapel Hill."

Robertson left Chapel Hill for a stint in the U.S. Navy, then moved to Wall Street to become a stockbroker with Kidder, Peabody & Co. In 1980 he founded Tiger Management, the name a suggestion from one of his sons who noted that his dad called everyone "Tiger" if he couldn't remember their name. The Tiger Fund was fabulously successful and was one of the early true "hedge" funds that shorted individual stocks as well as owning them based on a bullish hypothesis.

"That accounting course was tough, but it was great and exactly what I needed," Robertson, chairman and general partner of Tiger Management LLC, said in June 2017. "I realized later that I had such an advantage over everybody else because I had taken it. It was Accounting 101 or something like that. I can't remember my grades but I do know I did well later on because of it. I wasn't a great student. I've always been very appreciative of the business school at Carolina."

Charles "Eddie" Sams Jr. is a 1971 graduate who went on to a career in accounting in High Point, helping build the Dixon Hughes Goodman firm into a regional giant that today has some 1,700 employees in eleven states. He warmly remembers professors like Reynolds, Langenderfer, Levin and Junius Terrell, pegging Langenderfer as "probably the smartest man I've ever known" and Reynolds with giving him the key contact that got him his first job.

"They were fabulous," says Sams, who's retired today. "They were our role models. They were the last group that got a shot at us before we went out into the world of business."

Sams says the trigger in building a successful firm was getting good people—and a significant boost to that came from annual recruiting at the Business School.

"And when you came back, it was *Ike*, it was *Harold*, it was *Junius*. They were now your friends. It was just a great time," he says.

John Ellison Jr. received an offer on Wall Street when he earned his MBA in 1972, but his father had recently suffered a heart attack and asked him to come home to Greensboro to run the family business. Over more than half a century, the Ellison Company grew into a multi-faceted holding company with interests in textiles, international manufacturing and real estate, and Ellison's children Lucien and Gray went to work for the company.

Ellison was impressed enough by Professor Gerald Bell and the leadership tenets he learned in a business psychology class that years later he hired Bell on a regular basis to consult with him, his children and the business's top executives. Bell had evolved into an expert in leadership and in 2004 co-authored with Coach Dean Smith his book, *The Carolina Way*. Today Bell remains an adjunct professor of organizational behavior but his focus is running a consulting firm, the Bell Leadership Institute.

"Jerry ran these very interactive sessions with us," Ellison says. "He addressed questions like, 'How do you handle success? How would my children handle the business if I died?' He gave them homework to do before the sessions and asked them to answer questions like, 'What were your

Julian Robertson (L) opened his home to Kenan-Flagler staff and alumni during a reception in the fall of 2017, among them Dwight Anderson (MBA '94), one of the so-called "Tiger Cubs" who got his start in the hedge fund arena by working for Robertson.

three biggest successes last year? Your biggest failures or embarrassments? What were your dad's biggest achievements last year? Your dad's three biggest screw-ups?' So he really improved personal interaction in the family. And if you ask my children today, they would say those sessions were huge."

The first two-year MBA Program class graduated in 1968, and this group formed a tight bond, playing intramurals in flag football and basketball, living together in some instances and getting help from spouses in typing papers into the night. Smedes York played basketball for Coach Everett Case at N.C. State and graduated in 1963. After two years of military service, he entered Carolina to get an MBA. All along he planned to go to work for his father in

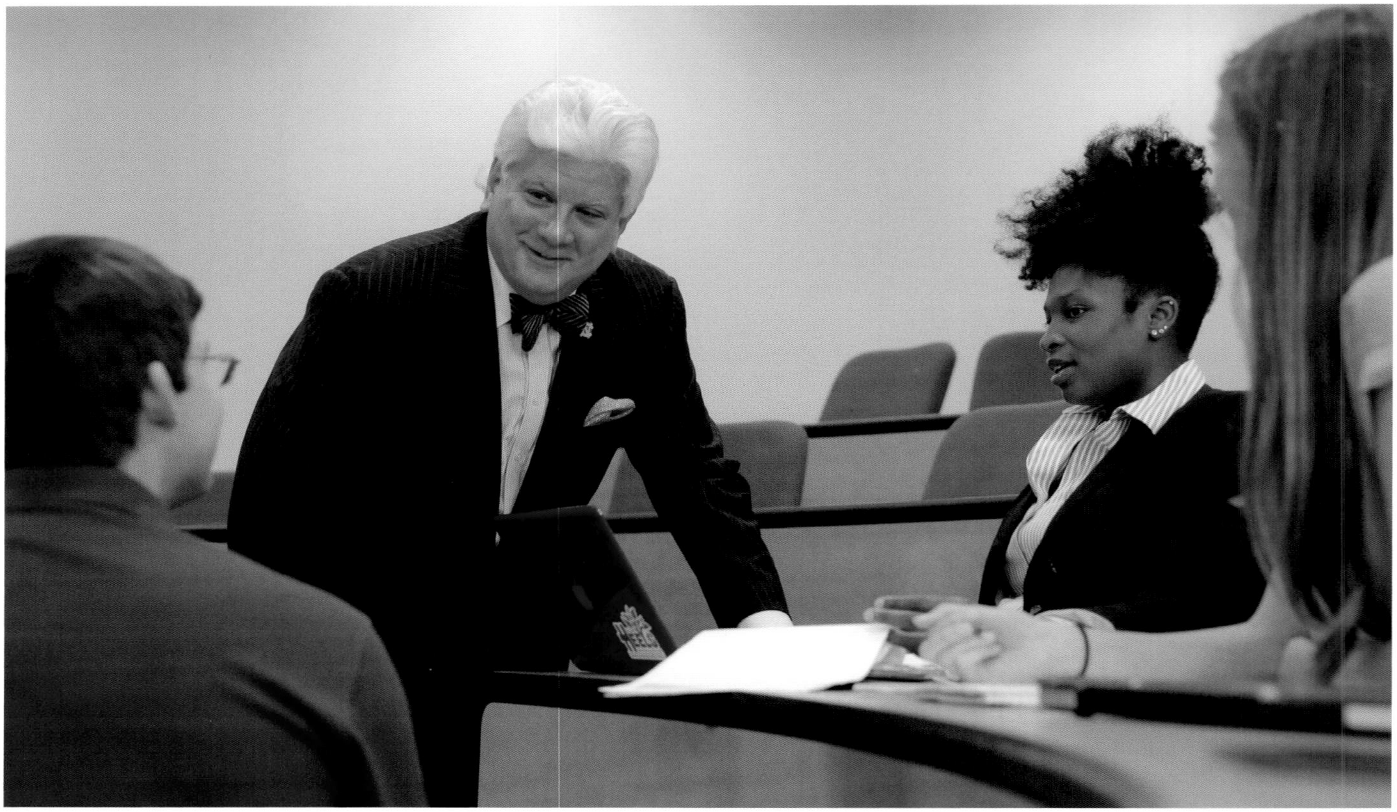

C.J. Skender has been a full-time professor of accounting at Kenan-Flagler since 1997 and reflects the culture of the school as well as anyone. He holds eleven accounting industry designations and more than two dozen teaching excellence awards and is known for his colorful assortment of bowties, matching socks and suspenders. One of his teaching tenets has been to "imagine each student is your own child"—and that comes naturally since he has taught all three of his children in various accounting classes. "C.J.'s love of teaching and devotion to students is unmatched," says Dean Doug Shackelford. "None of his students ever forget him, and although he has taught about one-quarter of all UNC undergraduates over the last twenty years, he remembers details about many of them. He is truly a Carolina precious gem."

the family business, York Construction Co., in Raleigh.

"But I wanted an MBA because I didn't want everything I knew about business to come from my father," York says. "As smart as he was, I wanted to know a full range of issues. My son George came back to the Executive Development program in 2006. I told him he would learn a lot, but mostly what he would get would be confidence. You won't go into a meeting with someone and not know what they're talking about. That part never changed. It was a great experience."

York, Bill Simpson and Ben Rudisill sat side by side in the same seats for two years. York remembers once staying up all night working on a marketing case for Gaines-Burgers, at the time a popular dog food made to resemble hamburgers. Simpson and Rudisill were Duke undergrads and all three had some background in engineering and math. DeWitt "Bulldog" Dearborn was a finance professor who tried his best to flog the devout technical leaning out of these scientists. Simpson remembers whipping one financial document to a pulp and Dearborn having fun with him in class.

"When you finished those numbers, Mister Simpson, did you put them under your pillow and *sleep* on them?" Dearborn asked. "Did you *caress* them? Did you get up this morning and look at them again?"

Simpson smiles fifty years later.

"He never told us *not* to do the numbers, but the point he taught us was don't try to get to .01 percent accuracy," says Simpson, one of a dozen class members to return for a reunion in 2018. "In business, nothing is *that* accurate. Make judgments about the numbers and put them in their proper place. They are part of the total picture, they are not the *whole* story. I needed that. With four years of engineering and a master's in engineering, I firmly believed you could solve the world with algorithms and fancy mathematics. Professor Dearborn taught us otherwise."

Several members of that 1968 class met for a dinner in 2014 honoring Rollie Tillman, a 1955 Business School graduate and long-time professor, administrator and fundraiser. They began reminiscing about their professors, among them Tillman and Bell. York suggested they use those two as benchmark examples and create a Faculty Excellence Fund that would assist the dean in retaining and recruiting faculty who would provide experiences similar to the ones they enjoyed. Through the spring of 2018, the fund had generated $65,000 with a goal of hitting $100,000.

"The only computers at the time were huge mainframe units that operated on perforated tape," York says. "There were no cell phones, no laptops. The upside was you had to communicate face to face, you had to write things down. When you talked to someone, they weren't looking down at their phone. You were able to develop a relationship with your professors. I remember some great ones. We got to know a couple of them pretty well playing golf."

Mary Shelton Rose thrived through the personal relationships she made with her professors in her Master of Accounting program in the mid-1980s.

Adds Rudisill: "I made an eagle at Hillandale once with Professor Langenderfer as my partner. We made a little money that day. We worked very hard and studied hard, but it was nice getting to know some professors outside of class."

Mary Shelton Rose learned the value of investing in relationships and nurturing them over many years from her experience at Kenan-Flagler in the 1980s and her classes under the late Professor David Hoffman, who counseled the 1987 BSBA major that she would benefit from the Master of Accounting program, so she added that degree in 1988.

"I was struck by the personal interest he took in me and all of his students," says Rose, now a senior partner with PwC headquartered in New York City. "He demanded excellence as a professor but was always there if you were challenged by something and needed some help. He was a mentor. He enjoyed having his teaching assistants to his house for cookouts.

"I learned how the relationships you develop along the way make your career and your life more interesting and more fulfilling. And they make you better at what you do because you invest in people."

That's the kind of culture Shackelford has hoped to

Snapshots | ALUMNI REUNION WEEKEND

The 1968 MBA class (opposite) reflected the times of the overall University of North Carolina with its preponderance of Caucasian males. Among the members who returned in the spring of 2018 for a reunion were (L-R) Tom Ogburn, Ben Rudisill, Smedes York, Shade Mecum, Henry Blair, Rusty Edminster, Ed Tennent and Ed Robbins.

CLASS OF '07
State Farm
ELITE
BACK AGAIN

Snapshots | ALUMNI REUNION WEEKEND

These images from Alumni Weekend in 2017 and '18 illustrate that Kenan-Flagler spans all genders, races and nationalities. A Saturday night dinner at the Dean E. Smith Center is a highlight each year.

build on during his tenure as dean. He and other faculty members take pride in the feedback they get from recruiters.

"My first year as dean I talked with a recruiter and asked him why he recruited here," Shackelford says. "He said because Kenan-Flagler students can tackle any job working with any group anywhere and be highly successful. But then he paused and said '*without drama.*' I really think that captures a lot of who we are and who we want to be. We are a 'without drama' place."

"Recruiters say our students are great team players and they do the work, they get it done," adds Hofmann. "There's not a lot of commotion in the process."

Moore once asked a recruiter the same question Shackelford did.

"I've been to a lot of good schools, and at every school the faculty talk their career," the man told Moore. "This is the first school where the faculty talk about the *students*."

Tucker York is director of global wealth management at Goldman Sachs and is a 1982 Kenan-Flagler graduate. He keeps a close eye on the talent pool at his alma mater, and Goldman has Kenan-Flagler grads in cities all over the country—San Francisco, Dallas, Miami, Houston, Atlanta, Philadelphia and New York among them.

"I am a buyer of the product that comes out of here," York says. "They get a great education and they are terrific people."

York visited Chapel Hill in April 2018 and spoke of his affection for his experience nearly four decades ago.

"There is a big difference between elite and elitist," York says. "This is an *elite* place. The caliber of people who come through is remarkable. The educational process works. And yet the spirit of the place is not elitism. A public school vibe has kind of seeped into the atmosphere here. 'We're in this together' is the feeling you get. It's much more a 'we thing.' It's a very convivial place. It's a great environment."

That spirit is captured in the five "core values" that were formally articulated under Jim Dean's tenure as associate dean of the MBA Program in the late 1990s—Excellence, Leadership, Integrity, Teamwork, and Community. Each year students sign a Core Values Pledge, and the document is framed and hangs in the McColl Building second-floor hallway.

"The core values capture something of the spirit of this place," Shackelford says. "They were based on what we have been for many years and what we are committed to being forevermore. The world changes, and we might teach a class on Mars one day. But we'll still have these values.

"Each of them is equally important. I tell our students, 'Integrity, please don't be good in the other four and be bad in that one.'"

Catie Venable was convinced she made the right decision to leave the workforce and pursue an MBA at a Kenan-Flagler Fellows Weekend in February 2015.

"It struck me in conversations with students that they considered giving back to their community a defining part of UNC Kenan-Flagler experience and identity," says Venable, who earned her MBA in 2018 and was a Teamwork Core Value Award winner in the process. "As I saw how much the student culture centered around servant leadership, I knew this was an environment I wanted to be part of."

Pearce Godwin, a 2018 Weekend Executive MBA graduate, found support from his kindred spirits at Kenan-Flagler in developing an initiative he calls the "Listen First Project." Godwin spent five years from 2008-13 in Washington as a political consultant and realized what a stark contrast that posed with the next six months in a fellowship in rural Uganda with Samaritan's Purse, a Christian international relief and development organization. He came to the conclusion that what America needed most was less noise and more listening, and he harkens to one of his favorite quotes, Sir Richard Branson saying: "If you want to stand out as a leader, a good place to begin is by listening."

"Community" is a core value at Kenan-Flagler, and faculty, staff and students toward that end created Business Cares in 2014 to provide philanthropic support for local non-profit organizations. One of its annual efforts is to stuff charity bags that go to Ronald McDonald House, UNC Children's Hospital Pediatric Cancer Unit and the Souper Cooper Little Red Wagon Foundation.

Mixing Business And Politics

The Hodges Family

Luther H. Hodges arrived in Chapel Hill in September 1915 from a farm in Leaksville in Rockingham County, N.C., with two and a half years of high school experience and $62.50 in his pockets. He worked his way through Carolina waiting tables and washing dishes in Swain Hall, repairing shoes, working as a mill hand and a traveling book salesman. He earned his degree in economics in 1919 and was voted "best all-around man."

Hodges left Carolina and went to work for Thread Mills in Eden (later to become Fieldcrest Mills) for $1,000 a year. He worked his way up, was given charge of one mill, then several mills and, in time, was general manager for the entire textile operation and supervised four thousand employees. Among the employees were members of his immediate family who lived nearby—including seven siblings. Being a "mill town," Fieldcrest was about the only place in the area for the family to get work.

"Over more than thirty years, I made it a point never to have a single member of my family into my office to discuss a job and never to intercede for any of them," Hodges said. "I never placed one on the payroll nor did I interfere when one was hired, fired, transferred or refused employment by the personnel office."

Hodges' strict code of ethics stood him well over a noteworthy career in business and politics. He retired from Fieldcrest in 1952 to run for lieutenant governor. He was elected and ascended to the governor's chair two years later upon the death of William B. Umstead. Hodges was elected on his own in 1956 and served one term through 1960, and was a moving force in the establishment of the Research Triangle Park. He was then appointed by President John F. Kennedy as U.S. Secretary of Commerce from 1961-65. Hodges returned to North Carolina and finished his career working as chairman of RTP.

Meanwhile, son Luther Hodges Jr. attended Carolina, graduated from the UNC School of Business Administration in 1957 and then earned his MBA at Harvard. He taught at the school for one year out of Harvard, went on to a long banking career with NCNB (later to become NationsBank) and returned to Kenan-Flagler in 2006 to become an adjunct professor.

Hodges Sr. once summed up his philosophy of public service as follows: "Businessmen ought to come into government because of their experience in business—government, after all, is big business. I feel that many of them, instead of sitting on the sidelines, sniping and quarreling about what the government is doing, should come in and help. That's what I did at the age of fifty-two. It's a bit frustrating at times, but I've never regretted it."

Luther Hodges Jr. (BSBA '57) addresses a Kenan-Flagler event at the unveiling of a plaque honoring his father, also a UNC graduate (1919). The elder Hodges studied economics before there was a formal business school and later was Governor of North Carolina.

Hodges died in 1974 and friend Hugh Morton led a campaign to raise $500,000 and establish the Luther H. Hodges Distinguished Professorship of Ethics at Kenan-Flagler. The professorship was funded in 1977, and its first recipient was Jack Behrman. The Luther H. Hodges Leadership Center was established in 2005 with the mission of developing MBA students as exceptional leaders who positively impact the organizations they lead and the communities they serve.

In addition to teaching at Kenan-Flagler, Luther Jr. has served on the Board of Advisors.

"My father was an economics major before they had the Business School," Hodges Jr. says. "Our family has long had a close relationship with the Business School. I think leadership and ethics go together. Neither one is easily taught. It's hard to learn from a textbook. They were important to my father, and these programs we've had at Kenan-Flagler have been a fitting memorial to him."

A Good Knight At UNC

Nick Didow Jr.

Dr. Nick Didow Jr. is a 1970 BSBA graduate from Carolina and 1973 MBA who earned his PhD at Northwestern in 1980 and has been a professor of marketing at Kenan-Flagler for nearly four decades, collecting the Weatherspoon Award for Excellence in Undergraduate Teaching in the process. One of his guiding principles has been a 1998 quote from long-time UNC System President Bill Friday:

"Every morning a million North Carolinians get up and go to work for wages which leave them below the poverty line so they can pay taxes that finance the education you receive at Carolina. Your job is to figure out how you're going to pay them back."

Against that backdrop, Didow joined with Jim Peacock of the Department of Anthropology and Pete Andrews of the Department of Public Policy in 1998 at the request of Chancellor Michael Hooker to research outsourcing and labor practices in the wake of Nike partnering with the UNC Department of Athletics to provide millions of dollars in shoes, uniforms and clothing for Tar Heel athletic teams.

The workshop was titled "Economics, Ethics, and Impacts of the Global Economy: The Nike Example."

On the last day of class, student teams presented their recommendations on "What changes would you make if you were in charge of Nike?"

Nike founder and CEO Phil Knight appeared in class unexpectedly that day.

"Two weeks later, I took some of the students up to D.C. at Phil's invitation as he spoke at the National Press Club about Nike assuming global leadership in manufacturing practices and outsourcing policies," Didow says. "Six major policy changes were exactly what he had heard recommended by the students two weeks earlier in Chapel Hill."

The Rev. Dr. Craig Kocher (BA '98) was one of the students in that class and today, as chaplain at the University of Richmond, reflects warmly on the experiences from Knight, Didow and his teaching colleagues.

"Many of the students in the class had a less than favorable opinion of Nike and thought of Phil Knight as a shadowy power-broker behind the curtains, pulling all the strings on what felt at times like a zillion-dollar empire of cheap labor exploitation," Kocher says. "To have him show up in class was an extraordinary moment. He was engaging, funny, articulate, and answered our questions with depth and substance. He took us seriously as students. He wasn't defensive, was eager to share and listened carefully to our concerns and feedback. I was impressed then, and in retrospect, even more impressed now that a leader of his stature would engage a group of students the way he did. It was a wonderful example of engaged leadership by a corporate titan who could have easily avoided the setting.

"Reflecting on all this makes me all the more grateful for my time at UNC and the phenomenal education I received from professors like Dr. Didow and others."

Godwin launched the "Listen First Project," which he explains as a "movement to mend the frayed fabric of America and bridging divides one conversation at a time." He drew on his Kenan-Flagler classmates for his leadership team in what has become an initiative covered close to home by *The Daily Tar Heel* and from afar by *The New York Times*.

"Teamwork creates a culture of collaboration, mutual support and genuine interest in each other's success," Godwin says. "That value extends beyond the classroom when students team up with classmates to start new ventures."

Ravi Maniar (MBA 2016) was Kenan-Flagler's first international student elected as leader of the MBA Student Association. He chose to come to Chapel Hill from his homeland of India because of its culture.

"When I first visited UNC Kenan-Flagler, the extremely helpful and tight-knit community of students, professors and staff left a strong impression," he says. "After two more visits, I knew this was the environment I would thrive in. The students I met were willing to go out of their way to help another student, even a prospective student. The professors I met were very approachable and genuinely loved working with students."

India native Ravi Maniar was Kenan-Flagler's first international student elected as leader of the MBA Student Association. The school's culture helped attract him to Chapel Hill; he earned his MBA in 2016.

Jennifer Conrad joined the faculty in 1985, served as senior associate dean under both Jim Dean and Doug Shackelford and today is the Dalton McMichael Distinguished Professor of Finance. She says that Kenan-Flagler was "all about teamwork before teamwork was cool. Teamwork was an important concept here long before the *Businessweek* rankings were born. We had a very strong commitment to our MBA students having the ability to work in teams. We were definitely a leader in that area. Certainly some business schools foster a more competitive atmosphere among their students. I think most top business schools now do have an emphasis on teams."

Stevie McNeal and Charlotte Farmer came to Chapel Hill to pursue graduate degrees in business, and each had a challenge to overcome—McNeal had a liberal arts degree and Farmer a family that included three children. Both found an inclusive and helpful culture that taught the kind of values important to them.

McNeal entered Kenan-Flagler in 1985 with a degree from Texas Christian University and admits that some of the concepts of her initial micro-economics class "might as well have been Swahili." She was surprised to see her classmates help her rather than leave her in the dust and took a lasting impression from their joy when she was named winner in 1987 of the Norman Block Award, which has been given since 1981 to the graduating MBA student with the highest academic record.

"The spirit of camaraderie and collaboration was remarkable," says McNeal, today an adjunct professor at Kenan-Flagler. "There was no sense of competition among your classmates. There was never a sense of it being a zero-sum game, and I think that's key and one of the lessons I've applied in leadership. If you view the world or you view

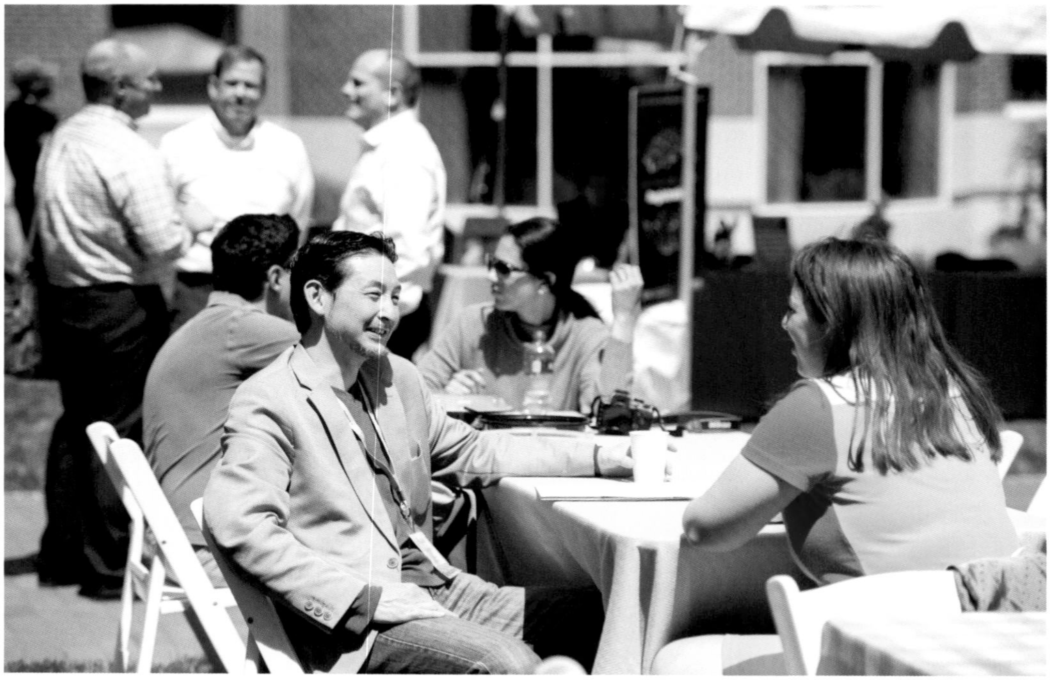

Koichiro "Kane" Nakamura (MBA '08) socializes at the 2018 Kenan-Flagler Alumni Weekend.

your career as a zero-sum game, it brings out very aberrant leadership behaviors and behavioral dimensions. I left Kenan-Flagler with the idea that it's not about dog-eat-dog and stepping on another person."

When Dr. Charlotte Mitcham Farmer entered Kenan-Flagler in the late 1990s, she had a husband and three children aged four to seventeen living in Kingsport, Tenn. She moved into student housing, and her husband Derek and kids drove six hours each way to visit on weekends.

"I was at a point in my career that I needed to pivot to something else because I was not living up to my full potential," says Farmer, today managing director operations for The MITRE Corporation, a technology think tank in Washington, D.C. "My husband is the hero of this story. He worked full time and took care of the kids for two years. But it was worth it. I went from being a very technical, operations-focused individual to a strategic businesswoman."

On one of his first days in the full-time MBA program, Koichiro "Kane" Nakamura (MBA '08) recalls Dean Steve Jones asking all 285 members of the Class of 2008 one question: How can you make a mark at UNC during the next two years and after?

"That message was very striking because I had been only thinking about what to *gain* from business school," says Nakamura, a director with SoftBank U.S. in Palo Alto, Calif. "Since that moment, I shifted my mind 180 degrees and tried to take action based on what I could do to make my study group members, classmates and community happy and successful."

Jamie DeMaria was thirty-eight years old with a PhD in neurosciences and was working in the pharmaceutical industry in 2011 when he decided he needed a broader business education. He earned his MBA online from Kenan-Flagler in 2013 and four years later was working as a group vice president at WebMD in New York when he made what he considered to be a common sense decision around his division's Fourth of July holiday.

"At Carolina, it was always about, 'Treat people with respect,'" he says. "In managerial accounting, where you learn about base compensation, it would come back to the theme of trying to be respectful of people. Kenan-Flagler really taught you there are numbers you have to crunch and understand, but there is a human element. I lead an organization of over two hundred people. This year the Fourth of July was on a Tuesday. The company planned to close early on the third. I said, 'This is crazy, what's half a day?' We shut down my division for a day. That gave everyone a four-day holiday. The response was, 'Wow, that's awesome.'"

George Felix (MBA '09) discovered his passion for marketing at Kenan-Flagler and took very little time leading two successful, high-profile campaigns to revitalize aging, iconic brands at Old Spice and KFC. The campaigns to "Smell Like a Man, Man" at Old Spice and to engineer a makeover of the iconic Colonel Sanders to appeal to a younger audience at KFC led to several Cannes Lions, Effie awards and an Emmy. He was noted by *Ad Age* magazine in 2016 as being "one of the bright young minds who are reinventing and reshaping the future of marketing."

"The school's emphasis on leadership and collaboration

Many are the stories of women who've juggled family life and business education, including 2019 MBA graduates Angela Gurtsishvili (L) and Mariana Thomas.

To The Next Level

Michele Buck

Michele Buck (MBA '87) was one of thirty-two members of an elite club at the beginning of 2018—a woman CEO of a Fortune 500 company. When she was named CEO of The Hershey Company in March 2017, she became the company's first female chief executive and made Fortune Magazine's 2017 list of the 50 Most Powerful Women in Business.

So how did she get from a career that began at age ten delivering papers and babysitting and later included being a waitress and selling Avon products door-to-door?

"Hard work," she told Fortune.

"I grew up in a very humble family. My mother lived on a farm with no indoor plumbing. My father was the first in his family to graduate from high school. I learned very early the values and virtues of hard work. I think there is no substitute for hard work."

Buck has been at Hershey for a dozen years and seventeen before that at Kraft, and over three decades was always eager to accept tough assignments—whether she felt ready for them or not.

"The times I learned the most and developed the most are when I took those opportunities that were outside my wheelhouse," she says. "I grew so much as an individual and learned that I had something in me that I didn't realize before."

Now two years into her post atop Hershey, Buck talks about energy and trusting her gut and says she was intrigued by an article that referenced the corporate CEO as being the "chief energy officer."

"That rang so true for me," she says. "I think during this time of accelerated change in the marketplace, the importance of powerful leadership and the importance of energizing an organization are even greater. I need an organization that has more than just technical competence but leaders who create energy and will support and encourage our people to take bold action to move with speed."

Buck has spoken to Kenan-Flagler students on multiple occasions, including at the 2014 Carolina Women in Business Conference. Among the snippets of advice she gave to attendees was to "make an impact in every single assignment that you are given.

"Look at it as how can I take this to the next level?" she says. "And be confident in yourself. I think women just don't have as much inherent confidence in themselves. They tend to be harsher critics of themselves than they need to be. So go for it."

is crucial to succeeding in the real world," Felix says. "Textbooks and lectures can only take you so far. Kenan-Flagler puts you in situations where you have to learn how to work with people from diverse backgrounds and find a way to lead those people to achieve a common goal."

That's why the school is so nimble at the intersection of art and science and was an important appeal for a move to Kenan-Flagler for Dr. Sridhar Balasubramanian, known around campus as "Dr. B," when he came to Chapel Hill in 2001 from the University of Texas as a marketing professor.

"Kenan-Flagler really resides at the intersection between the science and the heart of business," he says. "There are a fair number of schools that are very good at the *science* of business. There are fewer schools that are good at the *heart* of business. There are very few schools that do as well as we do thriving at the intersection between the science and the heart of business. And that comes through in the way we live our daily lives."

Farmer likes "trust" as a word identifying a Kenan-Flagler grad and says it is instilled in the value of teamwork.

"If somebody comes to me as a leader right now and says ***I*** did it, I don't talk to them," she says. "Because in this life today, how can you create something on your own? It just baffles my mind."

In other words, Gordon Gekko need not apply.

"You can do well by doing good," she says. "Make no mistake, you can do *very* well. Crowdsourcing is teamwork at its best, and it is *the* platform in this age of our economy. You've got Lyft and Uber and Blue Apron and all of these thinned-layered organizations who are making money by putting a small fee on the work of others. Crowdsourcing—that's teamwork at its best."

Jack Evans was on the faculty since 1970 for nearly half a century—serving nine years as dean in the late 1970s and into the 1980s—and remembers when the school quit producing class ranks in the 1970s.

"We did not want students to feel that if they succeed, someone else had to fail," Evans says. "We did not want a zero-sum mentality. It was part of this notion of building a culture of people getting along with each other and not seeing fellow students as competitors but as colleagues."

Adds Bill Moore, "There's just an atmosphere here that is competitive, and they have very high standards, but it's not cutthroat. It's people helping each other."

Evans remembers the idea for eliminating class ranks came from a group of professors that included Jack Behrman, Dick Levin, Rollie Tillman, John Pringle and DeWitt Dearborn, who wanted to tweak the MBA program to distinguish it over other universities. Their concept was to make the program to be more than just the accumulation of sixty credit hours over two years.

"They envisioned an 'integrated professional learning experience,'" says Evans. "I was on the periphery, but those guys were the core leaders. We wanted the learning experience to be cumulative, advanced blocks being built on top of basic blocks. Much of this was accomplished through what was initially called the Core Course Coordinating Committee. For this to work, it required getting the faculty to give up a bit of autonomy in individual course sections in support of the goal of each student getting the same foundation."

Dave Hartzell remembers the collegial spirit among the faculty when he came to work at Kenan-Flagler in the 1980s. There was a lounge on the second floor of Carroll Hall where faculty members gathered to talk shop and dissect the stat sheet from the latest Tar Heel basketball game. Being square in the middle of campus gave the faculty easy access to many town-and-campus gathering spots.

"We'd all walk over to the Daily Grind for coffee and meet with faculty from all over the place," Hartzell says of the long-time coffee shop in the Daniels Student Union. "The old cafeteria at The Carolina Inn, that was a place where Dick Levin used to take me all the time and we'd go

"The school is this beacon for North Carolina that connects across the world. Kenan-Flagler truly is a global institution, and it's delivering great young people into the world, people who are making a difference."

Segun Olagunju (BSBA '04)

in and there'd be faculty from everywhere in there, and of course he knew everybody and would introduce me. Everybody was all part of the team and sort of moving the ball forward and trying to do what was best.

"And we still have that. The idea that I try to instill in our students is that, you've gotten into a great business school, and your affiliation is from the day you agree to come here until the day you die. And I think what that inspires is just a really, really loyal alumni base which supports us in all ways."

"We have a very warm and supportive culture, but at the same time it challenges you," says Dr. B. "Our students are known for working—our recruiters will often tell us that our students are the kinds of people that they want to have next door to them as colleagues. They don't have a chip on their shoulder. That they work excellently in teams. That they are capable from leading not just from the front but also from the middle and from behind if they need to. And ultimately they don't hesitate to get the team together, dirty their hands and get the job done."

Dr. B talks of his outlook each week during the school year as Sunday afternoon rolls into evening. "I miss my colleagues, I miss the students, I miss the institution and I can't wait to get back and meet my colleagues and really get rolling all over again."

The special memories he has of late night study sessions with students in his MBA marketing classes capture the fiber of the Kenan-Flagler experience. As many as two dozen students would routinely gather in his office suite, find spots on the floor to sit and pore over their notes and ask questions.

"Those used to be magical moments, truly magical moments," he says. "It's a special relationship you forge with the students in taking questions and answering them, having other students listen in and probe with other questions at 10:30 or 11:00 in the night—the students never forget that and I never forget that," he says.

As Kenan-Flagler hits its century mark, its graduates are scattered around the globe.

"The school is this beacon for North Carolina that connects across the world," says Segun Olagunju (BSBA '04), an entrepreneurship and leadership consultant with Global Leadership Advisors, LLC. "Kenan-Flagler truly is a global institution, and it's delivering great young people into the world, people who are making a difference."

Tucker York in the spring of 2018 considered his undergraduate and graduate degrees and his place of work—Carolina, chartered 1789; Harvard, launched 1639; and Goldman Sachs, founded 1869.

"I didn't pick it this way, but I'm proud I've gone to the

oldest public school in this country and the oldest private school," he says. "Over time those things have mattered more to me. It's not like I said I was going to work at Goldman because they started in 1869, I didn't know it at the time. But for something to have been around a hundred years or more is profound. These great institutions that endure, it wasn't because no one was doing anything, and it isn't because everything was fine the entire time. Adversity is going to come, you just don't know when or why. The key thing is, 'What happens next?' That's when you build resiliency."

York pauses. Outside the Koury Auditorium where he is about to speak in a "fireside chat" format as part of Kenan-Flagler Alumni Weekend, several hundred returning graduates are enjoying breakfast on Latané Plaza. Among them are members of the 1968 MBA class when the school was all male and lily-white interspersed with graduates from every corner of the globe bearing a battery of names that have originated from India to Korea to Latin America. Flapping in the breeze are the dozens of flags hanging from the McColl Building portico representing home countries of Kenan-Flagler students.

"A hundred years," York says. "That's impressive."

Several weeks later, Hartzell is having coffee and ruminating on his three-decades-plus life at Kenan-Flagler, first as a PhD candidate and later as a professor of real estate and finance.

"I always tell people that I'm an academic and I'm a state employee, so I'm a salary man, if you will," Hartzell says. "I'm not a real estate guy who gets equity or options or restricted shares. So for me and hopefully everybody in the program, our equity is in the people, the people that come through and the alumni.

"We're not rich. But we certainly are rich in so many other ways."

The international element of Kenan-Flagler is represented by the array of flags representing the native countries of its students that hang from the portico running the front length of McColl Building.

Entrepreneurs Chase Dreams

Ideas Into Reality

From selling burgers and pizza to hungry dorm rats at 1 a.m. …. to establishing a come-to-you car wash …. to creating an app to allow folks to tune-out from their phones and the web and social media—entrepreneurs in and around Kenan-Flagler Business School are thriving in generating ideas and opportunities and learning the tricks of execution and adjusting on the fly.

"It's the entrepreneurial generation," says Ted Zoller, T.W. Lewis Clinical Professor of Strategy and Entrepreneurship. "The rise of entrepreneurship has been a staggering result of the development of the web, the proliferation of information and insight and of the American value of independence. People are giving themselves permission to go out and do things. I see new ventures started virtually every day all around me. It's extraordinary."

A generation or two ago, the template was to find a good job, have a nice career and retire with a comfy pension. Not any longer.

"Chasing your dream is not a crazy idea anymore," says Amy Linnane, program director of Launch Chapel Hill startup accelerator of which Kenan-Flagler is a founding partner. "You've got to take care of yourself. You can have your autonomy, you can chase your own dreams, be responsible for your own success and failure. Entrepreneurship can be a scary way to do it, but it can be a really exciting way, too. I read a quote recently where an entrepreneur said, 'I work a hundred hours a week for myself so that I won't have to work forty hours a week for someone else.'"

The entrepreneurship program at Carolina is well-regarded—*U.S. News & World Report* in 2018 listed it in the top four nationally—and is fulfilling the vision of Frank H. Kenan, one of the school's benefactors and the founder of the Kenan Institute of Private Enterprise.

"Mr. Kenan believed the school should always have a countervailing orientation toward entrepreneurship, not just the corporate form," says Zoller, who joined the faculty in 1998. "He would always support the people building those companies. He felt like prosperity and economic opportunity were the great equalizers in society. The Kenan Institute of Private Enterprise and then the

The winners of Professor Jim Kitchen's "Ready-Fire-Aim" competition in October 2018 were (L-R) Alexa Pibl, Mary Laci Motley and Emily Jerman with "Late Night Bites."

Entrepreneurship Center which he established were to create an orientation toward entrepreneurs which, I believe, has made us *the* entrepreneur business school."

Approximately sixteen full-time professors combined with nearly a dozen adjunct faculty and entrepreneurs-in-residence lead Undergraduate Business and MBA students through a variety of classes and programs—from the basics of learning the tools and skills necessary to conceive, plan, execute and grow a successful new venture to more complex issues such as private equity capitalization strategies.

In keeping with Kenan-Flagler's "hands-on" and "learn by doing" touchstones, the opportunities abound in and around the school for students to conceive and launch their own businesses.

Since starting in 2005, the Carolina Challenge awards up to $50,000 in total prize money to promising ventures, and participants have the opportunity to be mentored by experienced entrepreneurs and network with business experts. The "Pitch Party" held in early November in the Blue Zone in Kenan Stadium has become the premier entrepreneurship event each fall as dozens of teams pitch their ideas to over 150 judges in hopes of winning prize money to fund their ventures.

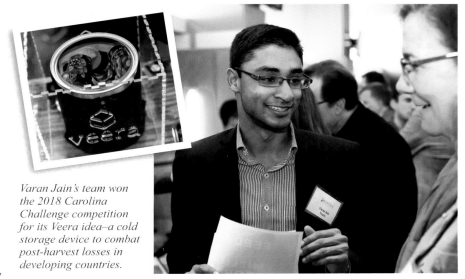

Varan Jain's team won the 2018 Carolina Challenge competition for its Veera idea–a cold storage device to combat post-harvest losses in developing countries.

One of the winners in 2017 happened to be a young man who plied his athletic trade on that very field in Kenan Stadium. William Sweet is a 2018 graduate and a starting offensive tackle for the football team who injured his knee in September 2017 and missed the rest of the season. Sweet's team focused on a technology concept called cold-compression therapy, which combines ice and pressure into a full-length leg sleeve. The team believed such a device could help patients with leg injuries like ACL tears mend from surgery more quickly at home.

"I recently recovered from an ACL surgery, and we want to implement a device for people like me," said Sweet, who talked about the long recovery process such injuries entail. "This is a huge problem with people being out of work, and we want to get them back to the workplace faster. We want to implement recovery at home: be with your family, be with your kids and recover while doing so."

Ideas floated at the event in 2018 included the concept of using the blockchain to make safe and secure payment for internet services available in third-world countries like Colombia; an automated letter-writing service that allows politicians, fund-raisers and business and college athletics recruiters to send ghost-written letters in their handwriting to constituencies; and an online venture that seeks to be the "Amazon of weddings" by integrating purveyors of wedding services at a fraction of the market norms.

"I had never considered being an entrepreneur, but my classes have opened my eyes," says Alex Graves, class of 2019 and one of the partners in the EasyWrite concept. "I've seen how rewarding it can be to actually own your own business, where everything's on you to succeed or fail."

Jim Kitchen is a 1987 Carolina grad in political science who started a travel company during his senior year at Carolina; the company grew into one of the largest student tour companies in North America, and he sold the business in 2005. Kitchen joined the Kenan-Flagler faculty as an adjunct professor in 2010 and teaches the entrepreneurial tenets learned in his business career in his Entrepreneurship and Business Planning class.

Each semester he leads students through a "Ready-Fire-Aim" exercise in which they conceive, plan and execute a business, with the proceeds going to local charities. The seemingly out-of-order steps of firing before aiming are a key part of Kitchen's philosophy.

"The point is to emphasize doing by learning versus over-planning," he says. "Most people never get around to 'doing' because life gets in the way. Being able to learn while executing and adjusting is an invaluable experience that stays with these students their entire lives."

The winning team in October 2018 was comprised of Mary Laci Motley, Alexa Pibl and Emily Jerman and their business Late Night Bites. They solicited food from Franklin Street restaurants and fast-food eateries and sold $8,500 worth of burgers, pizza, chicken wings and sub sandwiches between midnight and 3 a.m. on three separate nights to students at Granville Towers and other dorms and fraternities and sororities. That total was the best-ever in Kitchen's class and eclipsed the previous high of $7,500 set in 2014 by Casey Harris, who sold glow-sticks to students and fans at a night football game.

Aspiring entrepreneurs (L-R) Vivian Zhou, Anisha Datta and Raven Selden use the setting of the Old Well on a football Saturday to ply their venture; the headquarters of Launch Chapel Hill (opposite) provide office space and mentoring for promising businesses emanating from Kenan-Flagler students.

Motley, a sophomore from Asheville in the class of 2021, hatched the idea the previous year after having to wait forty-five minutes for pizza delivery to her dorm. Required class reading material includes the books *Lean Startup* and *Zero to One*.

"Both books emphasize having the ability to pivot," she says. "We had to change locations to find better foot traffic. We had to start a delivery system and take orders directly to a party where we knew there would be hungry customers. Adapting to the market and circumstances is crucial."

It's that execution that leaders at Launch Chapel Hill stress to those with fledgling businesses.

"We go by the idea that lots of people have great ideas, and you think your idea is the best one," says Linnane. "But the idea is really not what's important. That's not what will make you successful. Chances are, someone already thought of it. It's the *execution*. That's the important thing."

Through 2017, Launch had served seventy-five companies, with sixty percent still in business. Thirty-one of the companies were founded primarily by a student. Launch has an office facility in downtown Chapel Hill with seven thousand square feet of space that startups can use for their headquarters.

Among the enterprises that have come through Launch have been Get Spiffy (now known as Spiffy) a mobile car-wash service that goes to parking garages near office complexes and sets appointments; Freedom, a productivity computer application started by UNC professor Fred Stutzman that locks you away from the internet and social media for up to eight hours at a time; and Amirabilia, a digital learning platform created by Lucia Binotti, a professor of Spanish at UNC, that can take you, for example, on a virtual tour of a European city like Rome or Paris.

Another important component of Kenan-Flagler's entrepreneurial program is the Adams Apprenticeship, which brings together mentors who can share their experiences and wisdom with the next generation of entrepreneurs.

"You could think of it like a Phi Beta Kappa of entrepreneurship that strategically connects our more serial entrepreneurial alumni with our most entrepreneurial students to advance their careers," says Zoller. "We begin with talented students. We end with high-performance entrepreneurs."

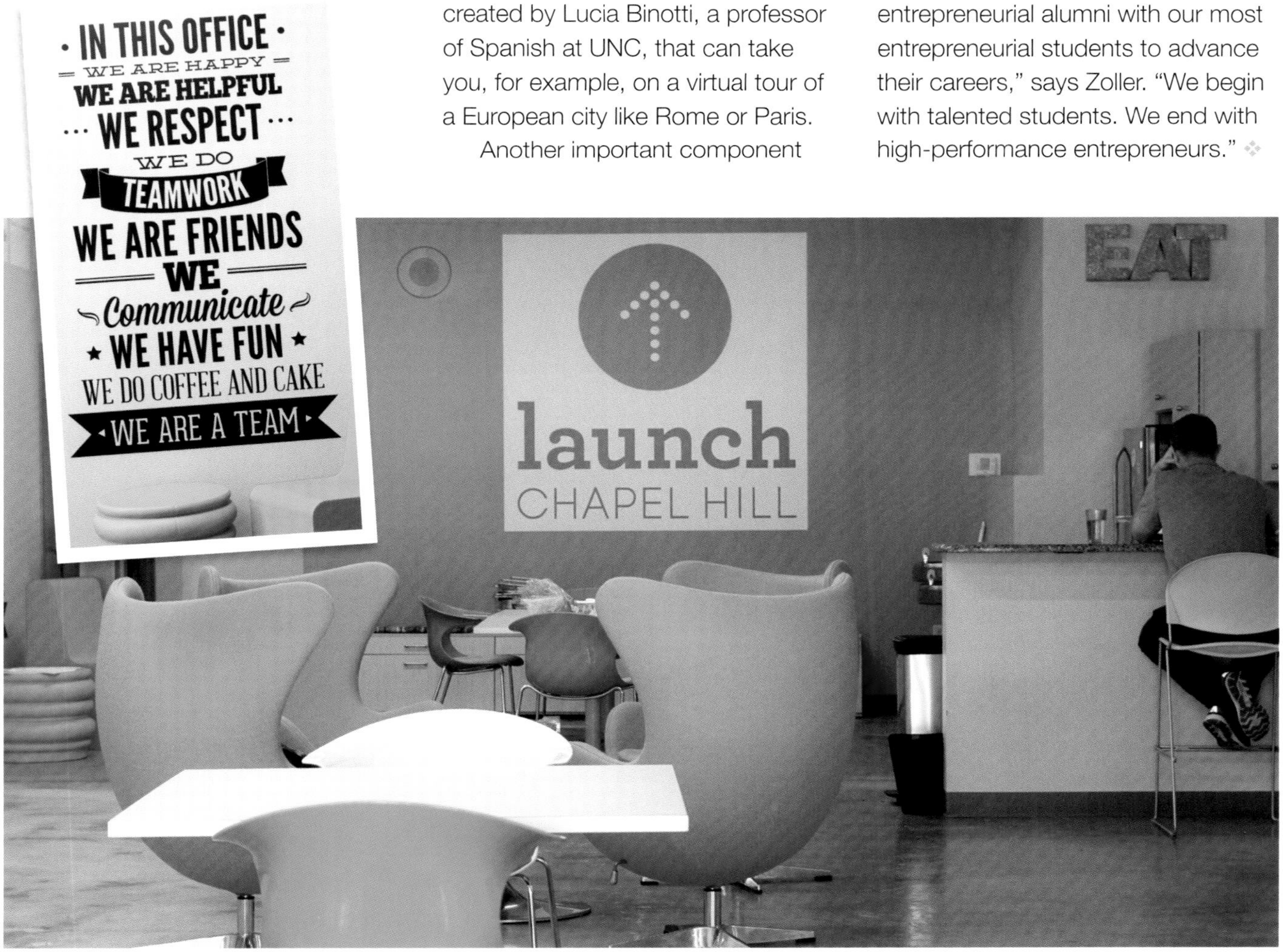

Tar Heel Hoops Is All Business

Sports and Academia

Tar Heel basketball player Luke Maye made national headlines and became a highlight reel icon in March 2017 when he hit a twenty-foot jump shot at the buzzer to lift Carolina over the University of Kentucky and land a berth in the NCAA Final Four.

His legend took another step the next day when a video clip went viral on social media showing Maye getting a standing ovation at his 8 a.m. Kenan-Flagler accounting class.

"The life of Luke Maye," wrote classmate Jack Sewell in a tweet that launched the story. "7 pm: hits game winning shot against Kentucky to send UNC to final four. 8am next day: Busi 101 class standing O."

Tar Heel forward Luke Maye (BSBA '19, fourth from left) was hailed on social media for attending his Kenan-Flagler class at Monday 8 a.m. in March 2017 just hours after a game-winning shot in the NCAA Elite Eight.

The class was conducted by Professor C.J. Skender, who opened class by showing a gas receipt totaling $32. He had filled his car at a gas station the Thursday before the Tar Heels' South Regional appearance, and when the machine clicked to a stop at an even $32—Maye's jersey number—Skender thought it a good luck omen. He asked Maye to sign his receipt and the class went on as normal.

Given that the Tar Heels' home of the Dean Smith Center is next door to the Kenan Center and McColl Building, it's appropriate that Carolina hoops and Kenan-Flagler have had a close relationship. Tom Kenan remembers his father Frank, who conceived and built the Kenan Center in the mid-1980s, asking two workmen on the Kenan Center job if they would build cement steps from the Kenan Center down to the Smith Center in time for the basketball arena's opening in January 1986.

"Father told them if they'd finish by the opening game, he'd get them tickets to the game," Tom says. "They worked day and night and finished on time."

Kenan-Flagler Professor Dr. Gerald Bell in 1990 invited Dean Smith to speak to a group of international business executives in St. Moritz, Switzerland. The group was the Young Presidents' Organization and was comprised of executives under forty who had risen to the top of their business or corporation. Bell, a professor of management and organizational behavior at Kenan-Flagler, suggested Smith speak on "Coaching is Management," and Smith agreed but switched the title to "Coaching is Management?" with the question mark.

Smith at the outset wasn't sure the connection was relevant. But after hitting the highlights of his coaching philosophy that would eventually lead to 879 wins and two national titles and how they might apply to leading a business, Smith was peppered with questions about managing personalities, dealing with selfish individuals and the art of putting team before self.

"There I was in this business environment talking to these dynamic young leaders about motivation, teamwork, and how to get people to work hard for team goals, and it suddenly seemed abundantly clear that coaching a college basketball team and managing a business do have some common issues," Smith said.

Just over a decade later, Smith and Bell co-authored a book titled

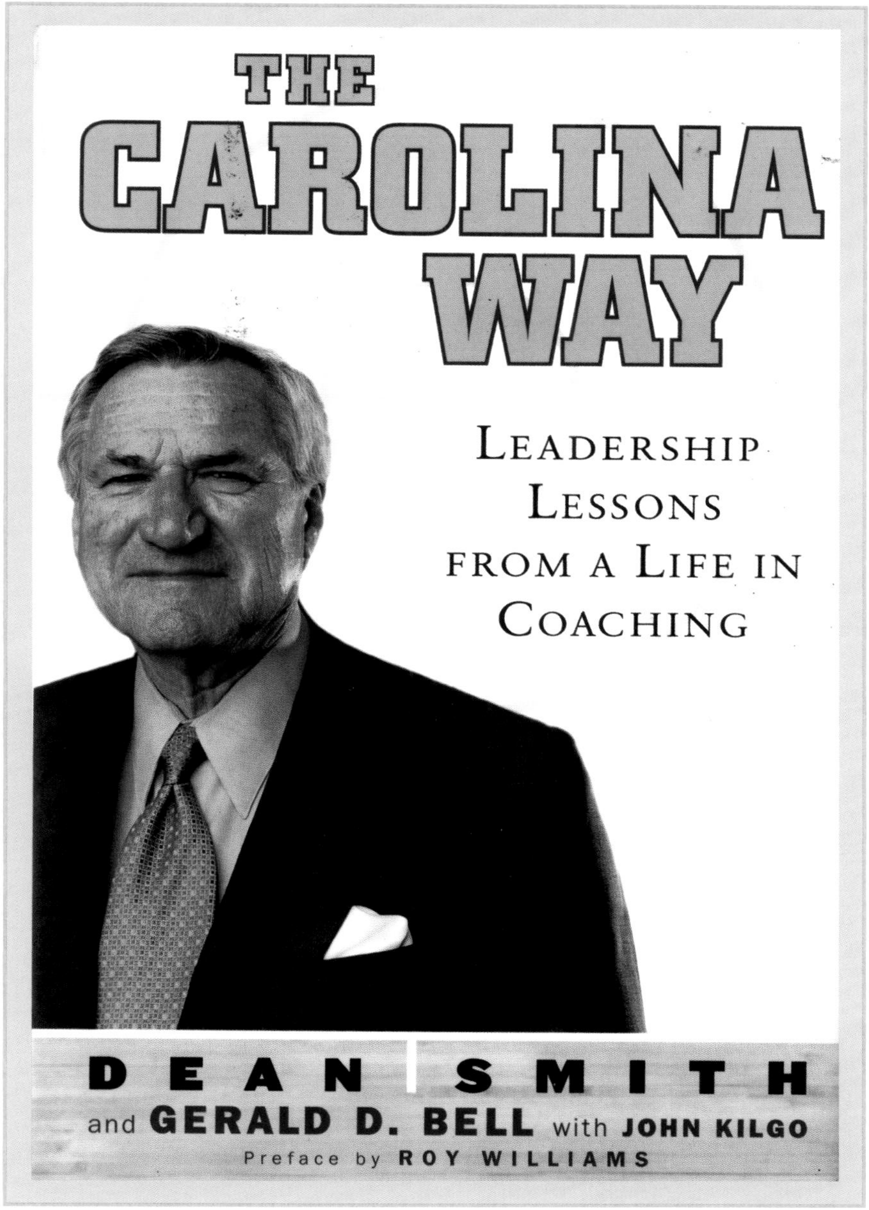
THE CAROLINA WAY
LEADERSHIP LESSONS FROM A LIFE IN COACHING
DEAN SMITH
and GERALD D. BELL with JOHN KILGO
Preface by ROY WILLIAMS

Kenan-Flagler Professor Gerald Bell collaborated with coach Dean Smith on a book that threaded coaching and business together.

"Coach Smith developed three keys for coaching. He focused on getting his players to play hard, play smart and play together."

Dr. Gerald Bell

The Carolina Way, in which Smith espouses his coaching and teaching philosophy in twenty-six chapters and Bell follows with a subchapter on how Smith's message can be applied to business.

Smith devoted one chapter, for example, to his Tar Heel teams' pride in "taking care of the little things" that helped produce a mindset that allowed them to conquer the big things. Bell followed with examples of the varying skills CEOs have with the "little things"—that attention to detail in customer service parlays into increased profits while obsessing over the color of paper clips leads to office dysfunction.

Smith wrote about meting out discipline, building confidence and why unselfishness works, among other subjects.

"Coach Smith developed three

Former Tar Heel All-America point guard Phil Ford (opposite) is a 1978 Kenan-Flagler grad and frequent participant in the Alumni Weekend festivities in the museum and on the playing floor of the Dean E. Smith Center.

keys for coaching," says Bell. "He focused on getting his players to play hard, play smart and play together. What business is all about is getting people to do things effectively and in orchestration with each other."

Matt Doherty (BSBA '84), the Tar Heel head coach from 2000-03, wondered years later how much better his tenure might have been had he had more formal leadership training like that offered by Bell. Doherty was dismissed after his third year and in 2018 was associate commissioner for the Atlantic 10 Conference; he also offered speaking and consulting services to coaches on leadership development.

"Leadership is a learned behavior, and that's become my mission in teaching leadership," Doherty says. "I feel we need to coach coaches. They are running programs worth millions of dollars and have never been trained in leadership. To have them in these positions and never have been trained in leadership is asinine."

Socialshots

unckenanflagler • Following

unckenanflagler #tbt to last Spring when Kenan-Flagler students Zander, Brenna, Zeke, Liz, Justin, and Pete watched @unc_basketball beat Duke while studying abroad in Hong Kong! We can't wait to see where our #studyabroad Kenan-Flagler students cheer on the Heels tonight!

.

.

.

Tag @unckenanflagler in your pictures where you watch the big game tonight!
Photo: @acmagee
#BeatDuke #BlueVBlue #BusiAbroad
#KenanFlagler #GoGlobal

ellieejay 😂😂 where is this taken?!

148 likes

FEBRUARY 8

Add a comment...

unckenanflagler • Following

unckenanflagler Rameses is back on the road visiting alumni in D.C.! Join us on Facebook and Instagram Live on May 18th at 8:30 AM EST at the UNC Kenan-Flagler Alumni Breakfast in D.C. Dean Doug Shackelford is looking forward to seeing our alumni. Want to join the conversation? Use #UNCForAll to interact with us! #minirameses

alliealphagam I love following mini Rameses!

unckenanflagler @alliealphagam he loves following his #unckfalumni! 🖤

picklesandjenny Poor Ramses looks like he needs a raincoat!

unckenanflagler @picklesandjenny Thankfully, it stopped raining enough for #minirameses to stop and enjoy the view 😊. #goheels!

169 likes

MAY 17

Add a comment...

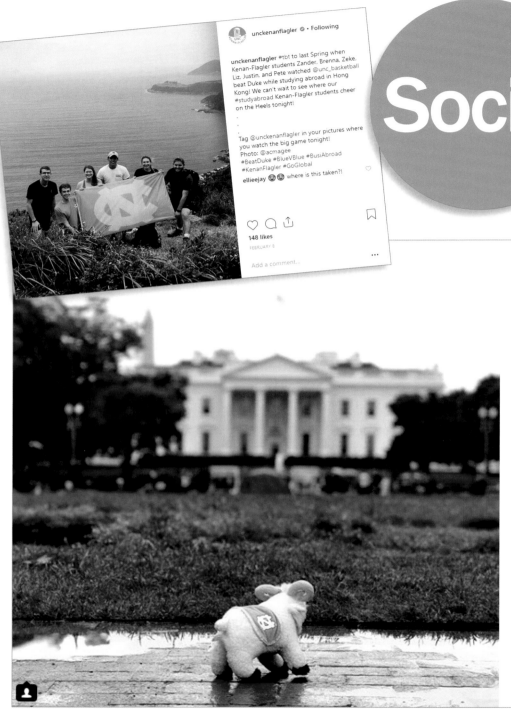

unckenanflagler • Following
unckenanflagler Carolina blue sky/water tower on a beautiful spring day @uncchapelhill @unckenanflagler
putitonmytabb @wardeaux3
168 likes
APRIL 2
Add a comment...

unckenanflagler • Following
unckenanflagler "Getting accepted into the #UNCKenanFlagler Business School restored an academic confidence in me that I would not have been able to restore any other way," said Kenny Selmon BSBA '18. "I'm able to carry myself within my sport as a businessman instead of just an athlete. And that type of confidence allows me to understand that there's more to life than just athletics."
139 likes
JUNE 15
Add a comment...

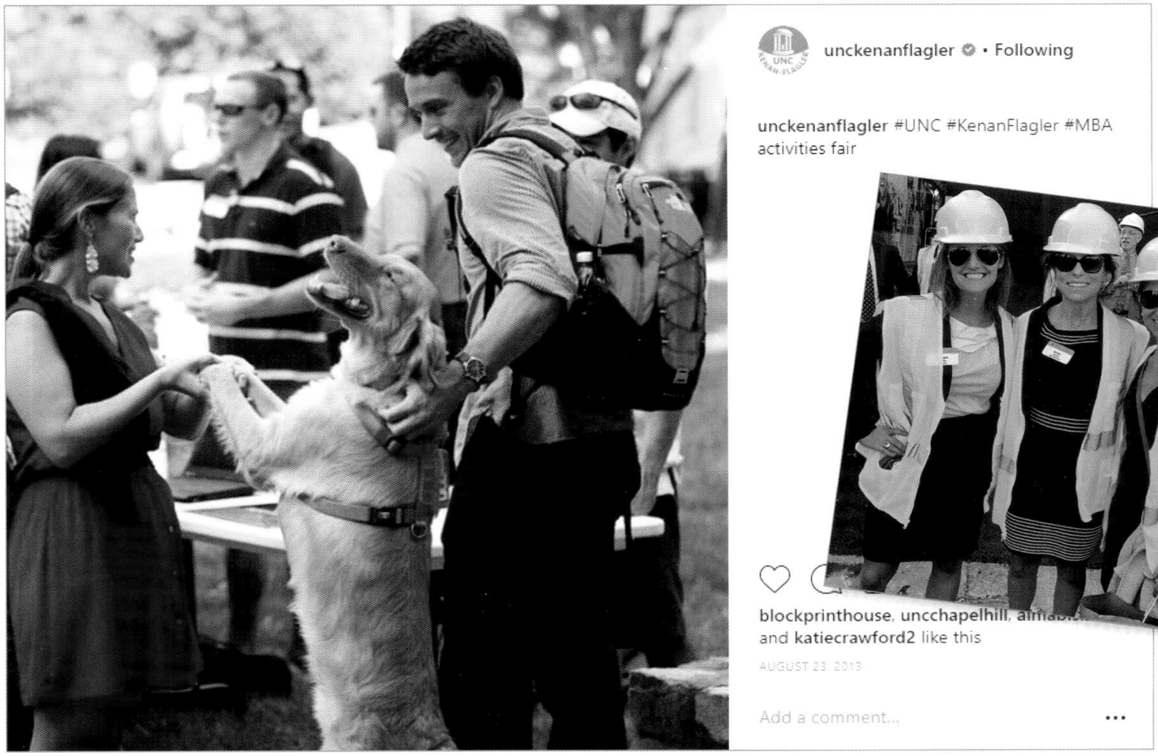
unckenanflagler • Following
unckenanflagler #UNC #KenanFlagler #MBA activities fair
blockprinthouse, uncchapelhill,
and katiecrawford2 like this
AUGUST 23, 2013
Add a comment...

unckenanflagler • Following
unckenanflagler Tar Heels take DC! Our #MBA Real Estate Club is spending fall break career trekking their way through the DMV. (: @ayishaswann)
#RealWorldRealEstate #UNCMBA #BSchool #career #networking #TARgram
unc_real_estate This is actually in DC. ATL last week and NYC next!
62 likes
Add a comment...

The Green Lights

Sustainability

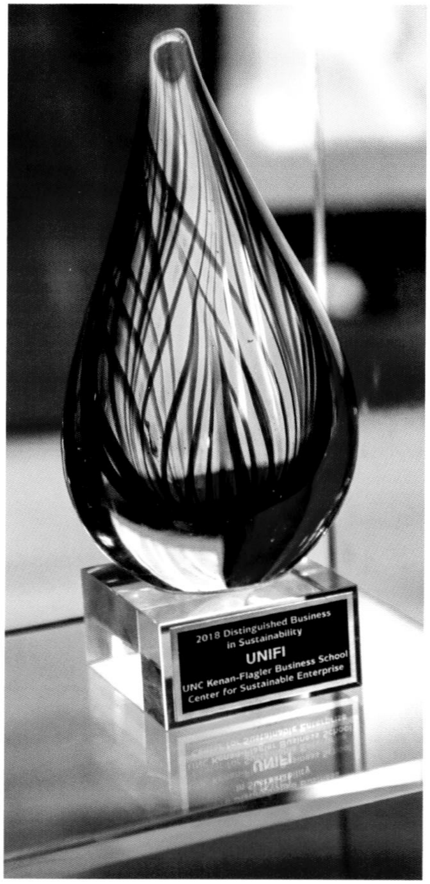

In business there are "different shades of green."

There are dollars, which ultimately are why someone would start a business in the first place—to generate a profit.

But nearly two decades into the 21st century, the concept of conducting business while being socially and environmentally responsible has reached a new level of awareness and importance, particularly at Kenan-Flagler.

"Our students believe in the greater good they are providing," says Olga Hawn, assistant professor of strategy and entrepreneurship and the Sustainability Distinguished Fellow at Kenan-Flagler. "Whether we will thank the millennials or older generations for their actions, there is no way back in sustainability, only forward."

Kenan-Flagler launched the Sustainable Enterprise Initiative in 1998 with professors Stuart Hart and James Johnson leading a program that included teaching, research, programs, service and outreach. The Center for Sustainable Enterprise was formally founded in 2001 and has been a strategic strength of the school.

Today over seven hundred MBA students have graduated with a concentration in sustainable enterprise, which is structured to complement the functional disciplines of marketing, operations,

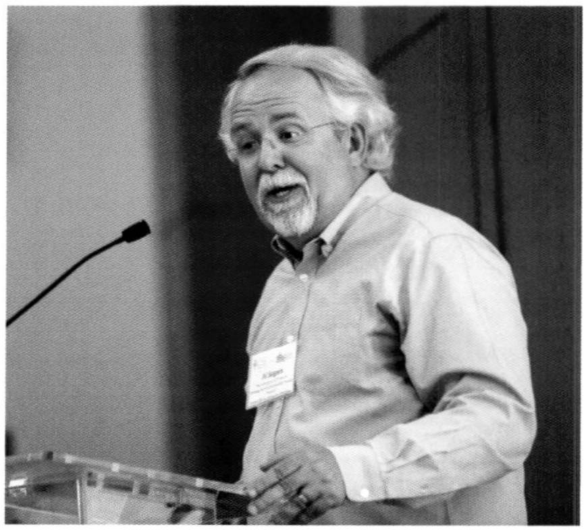

finance, entrepreneurship and consulting. The sustainable enterprise concentration is a sequence of elective courses during an MBA candidate's second year of study.

Dr. Al Segars came to Kenan-Flagler from Boston College in 1998 and served as faculty director of the CSE from 2004-18. Before Segars said "yes" to Carolina and Dean Paul Fulton two decades ago, he wanted to be sure Kenan-Flagler stood for something more than just teaching students how to make money. He was seeking a sense of community on campus where colleagues want to make the world a better place. He found that at UNC.

"It's been," Segars says, "a wonderful ride."

Kenan-Flagler was one of the first business schools to institutionalize sustainability as a curriculum and make it part of the school's identity, says Segars. "Staying engaged in the community and demonstrating the benefits of sustainability have been the keys to its long-term success."

Hawn has since taken the baton as CSE faculty director, and her sustainability strategy course that is open to undergraduate, MBA and PhD students has been immensely popular since being launched in 2016. Some of the highlights from the class include case studies on how Clorox and Wal-Mart go green, learning about green-washing by various companies, and a visit to Burt's Bees, which has a zero-waste policy among many other sustainability initiatives. Students also learn how to calculate the carbon footprint of a company, analyze current sustainability research and evaluate how-to guides that provide managers with step-by-step instructions on addressing sustainability challenges.

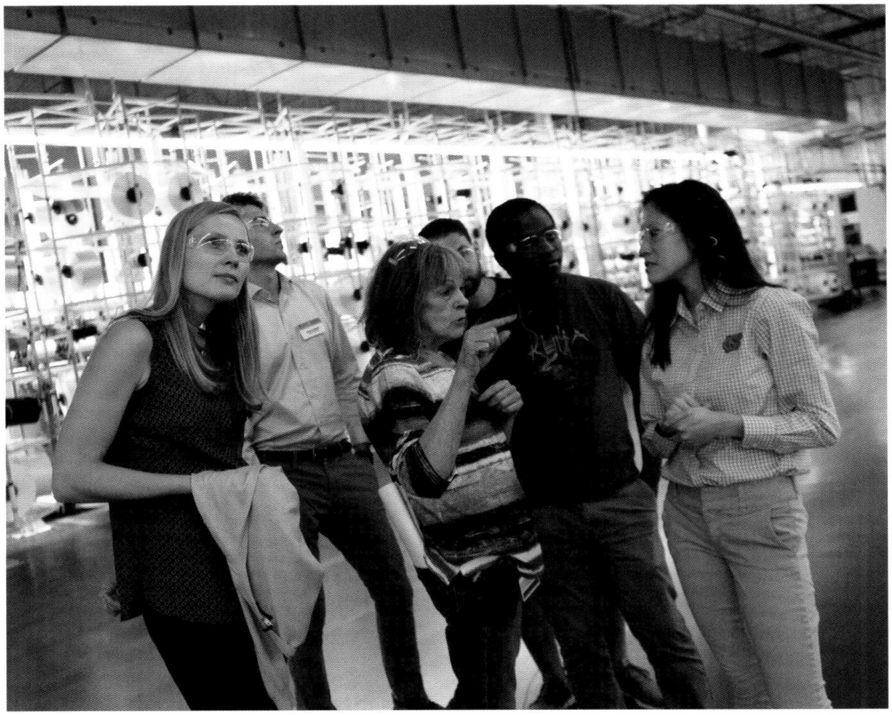

Dr. Olga Hawn (above left), director of the Center for Sustainable Enterprise, tours a manufacturing facility to inspect new "clean tech" initiatives; she followed Al Segars (opposite), who served as faculty director of the CSE from 2004-18.

In addition, students participate in a simulation, where as senior or middle managers, they face a sustainability challenge: Their clients inform them that they are going to buy only green moving forward. The students must get everyone in the company on board to respond to this challenge and learn about various techniques at their disposal and how hard organizational change is.

By introducing the principles of social responsibility in the lecture hall, Hawn hopes her students will search for these business practices in future employers. "Environmental practices are now becoming a part of consideration of jobs," she says.

Socialshots

MAC Online
Class of 2016
"Dirty Dozen"
unckenanflagler • Following
unckenanflagler When @joegibbsracing visits the #BSchool, they go all out! 😎🏁🏆
Excited to welcome #JGR president Dave Alpern back to UNC Kenan-Flagler. BUSI 406 students, you're in for an awesome class today!
#JGRatUNC #UNCUBP #marketing #NASCAR
unckenanflagler History in the making.
In 2015, we launched the online format of our world-class Master of Accounting program with 12 students who dubbed themselves 'The Dirty Dozen.' On Saturday, they'll turn their tassels and join the ranks of UNC Kenan-Flagler alumni. Today we installed their class brick in front of the McColl Building, cementing their place in Carolina history.
#UNCMAC #accounting #TARgram #AccountantsAreCoolerThanYouThink #GoHeels
30 likes
OCTOBER 6, 2016
OCTOBER 26, 2016
Add a comment...

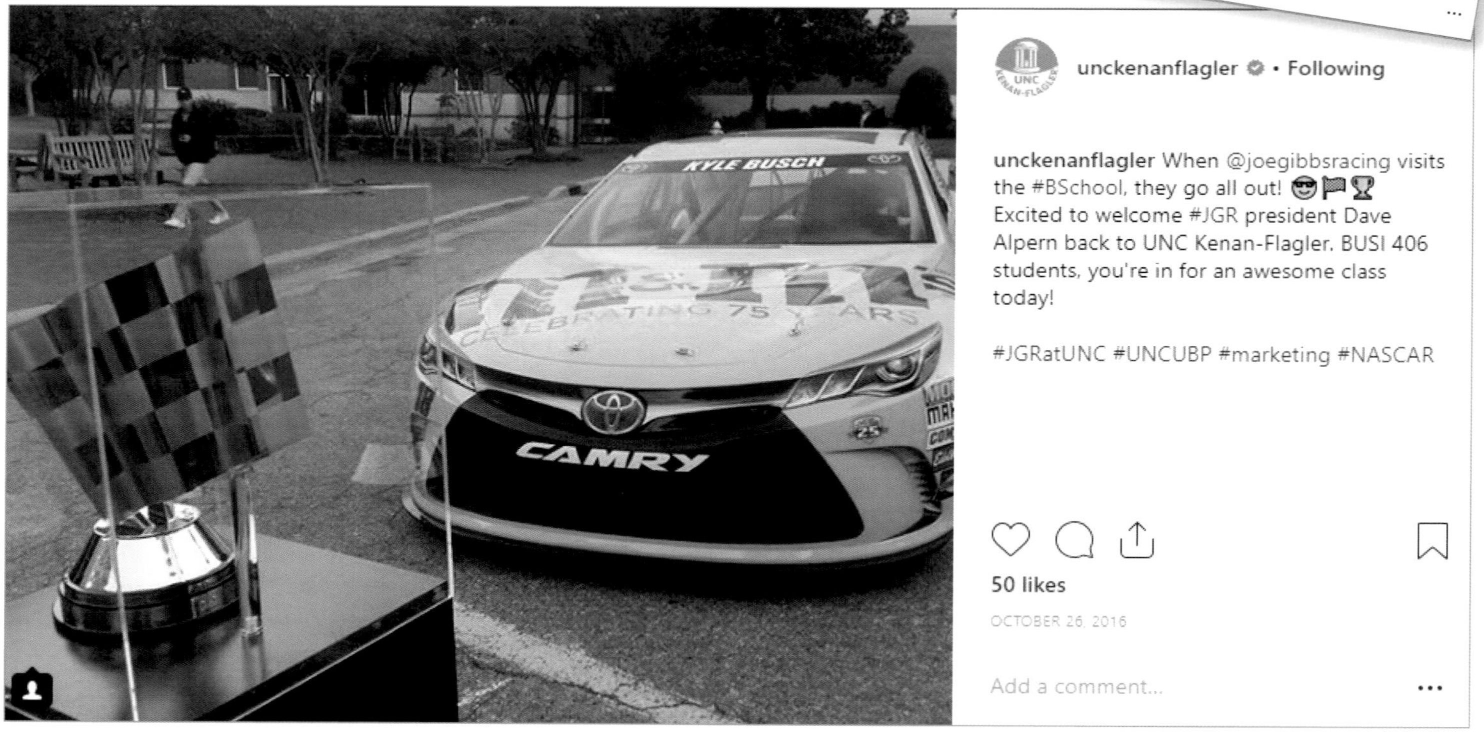

unckenanflagler • Following
unckenanflagler Congratulations fall class of 2017! We are so proud of you and look forward to all that you will accomplish in the future #UNCAlumni #ForeverHeels
.
.
.
#graduation #Classof2017 #Graduates #KenanFlagler
88 likes
DECEMBER 20, 2017
Add a comment...

unckenanflagler • Following
unckenanflagler Already reminiscing about Fall Break? Meet with UBP Global to start planning Fall Break 2019! Applications for fall semester #StudyAbroad open on Nov. 1! Where in the world will #kenanflagler take you? #BusiAbroad #TravelTuesday : @haleighglenn
113 likes
Add a comment...

THANK YOU
for your support!
UNC KENAN-FLAGLER
GIVING DAY
GIVING DAY FINAL RESULTS
POINTS DOLLARS
UNC 1,473 389,722
DUKE 1,094 348,461
1,188 Total Gifts
$389,722 Total Raised
BLUE vs BLUE
unckenanflagler • Following
unckenanflagler Together, we made history! More than 1,100 Tar Heels made a gift to UNC Kenan-Flagler during yesterday's #BluevBlue Challenge.
Because of YOU, we raised $389,722 for the Business School and #BeatDuke by 379 points! Now that's what we call a #GDTBATH! Your support helps us to continue our proud tradition of excellence in business education at Carolina. Thank you, Tar Heels!
#GoHeels #TARgram #Carolina
73 likes
MARCH 2, 2017
Add a comment...

Paying It Forward

Philanthropy

Doug Shackelford joins Bill and Sara McCoy in 2016 upon the opening of the student lounge made possible by the McCoys' generosity. The Donors & Scholars Dinner (opposite) is an opportunity for students to say "thank you" to the benefactors of scholarships and programs that directly benefit them.

One MBA student saw the price tag for a study-abroad trip to Europe and was resigned to thinking, "Maybe that's just something beyond my reach."

Another was juggling her studies with babysitting four toddlers to earn money to pay her tuition.

And still another holds back tears talking about the earning power her MBA will provide, giving her the resources to help send a younger brother to college and put toward medical expenses for her aging grandfather back home in the Philippines.

These three cases are just the tip of the iceberg in the largesse that philanthropy has meant to the evolution and existence of Kenan-Flagler Business School and its students. From the launch of the Business Foundation in 1946 to provide support to the school from the statewide business community to scholarships and fellowships available today, the Kenan-Flagler brand has been buffed and polished by the generosity of its extended family.

"People establish scholarships and fellowships for many reasons, and every reason is a heartfelt one, for the donor as well as for us at UNC Kenan-Flagler," says Dean Doug Shackelford. "These scholarships and fellowships help us compete for top students, provide unique study abroad opportunities and better prepare our graduates for career success."

One of Shackelford's favorite annual occasions is the Donors & Scholars Celebration that began in 2011 to connect the benefactors and recipients at a dinner and program. The event has tripled in size, and the 2018 function included 160 scholarship and fellowship recipients.

"Donors can see their investment in the next generation of business students, and our students learn, as recipients of someone else's philanthropy, the importance of paying it forward," says Shackelford, who challenges the students to work toward the day they can return and

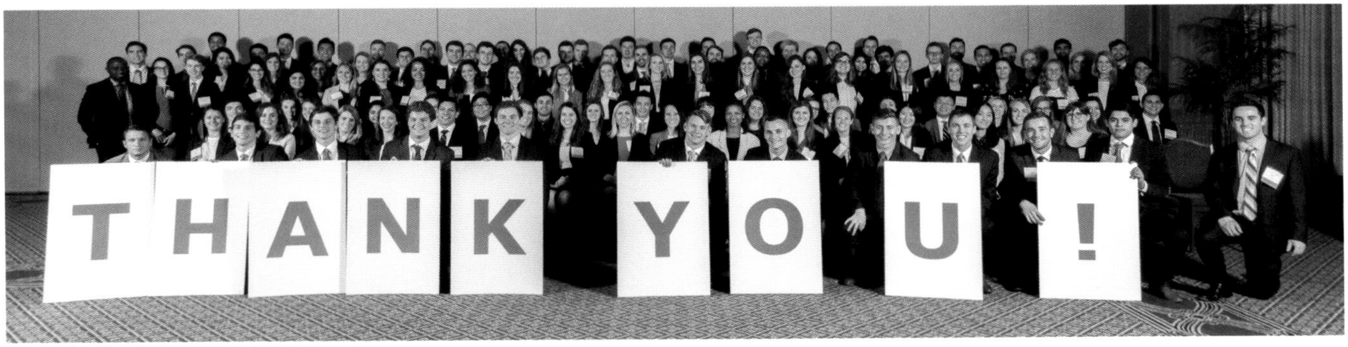

take the donors' seats.

That point hit home at the 2018 with Abbie Gration, whose education was augmented with a fellowship to the MAC Program. She thanked her benefactors for helping her get out of the babysitting business and said the debt she felt would "impact me the rest of my life.

"I feel a sense of responsibility that, when I'm older and wiser and not a poor graduate student, I can help financially," she said. "But there are ways I can give back right now."

Haleigh Glenn spoke from her heart at the 2018 dinner in thanking those who had funded the scholarship that allowed her to travel for six weeks to the Netherlands on a summer study abroad fellowship.

"When I first learned of the program and the cost, I just thought the idea of studying abroad was something beyond my reach," she said. But she heard of the scholarship program, applied and was accepted.

"When I landed in the Netherlands, I texted my mother to tell her I'd arrived," Haleigh says. "She texted back and said, 'You have officially gone further and done more in your twenty years than I will have done in my entire life.' It made me feel so incredibly proud and grateful as a first-generation college student."

Josephine Manlangit Halverson (MBA 2017) says she wouldn't have been able to attend graduate school if not for scholarship assistance.

"I would have had fewer opportunities to pursue a career that I'm passionate about and that's exciting to me," says Josephine, who matriculated at Kenan-Flagler with help from a T.W. Lewis MBA Fellowship and landed a job with Wal-Mart as senior manager for pricing strategy.

The philanthropy has taken many forms—from bricks and mortar to scholarships to something as varied as the Weatherspoon Lecture Series, created with a gift from longtime University and Kenan-Flagler supporters Van and Kay Weatherspoon. The series provides lectures by outstanding visiting scholars and world leaders from the fields of politics, education, business and government and has included talks by former president of Mexico Vicente Fox; publishing executive Steve Forbes; *New York Times* columnist David Brooks; former United Nations ambassador to Iraq and Afghanistan Zalmay Khalilzad; and journalists Cokie Roberts, Gwen Ifill and Tom Friedman. Van Weatherspoon is a 1954 Business School graduate who went on to a successful commercial development career in Charlotte. He and wife Kay (UNC '54) have been generous to a number of University concerns.

Ann Christian Goodno is Kenan-Flagler's longest-living consecutive donor, graduating with a degree in commerce in 1945 and making a contribution almost every year since. She was recognized in 2015 on the seventieth anniversary of her

Among many benefactors of Kenan-Flagler have been Maurice Koury (right), shown with long-time Carolina radio play-by-play announcer Woody Durham.

graduation with the naming of the Ann Christian Goodno Loyalty Society—which recognizes donors who have contributed to the Business School for two or more years in a row.

"I never thought anything about it, but I was shocked to read that gifts to the Business School—combined with other private support—fund twenty percent of its annual operating budget," Mrs. Goodno says. "If people don't give, I don't think the school could operate."

That tradition has continued through the decades.

Bill McCoy graduated from Carolina in 1955 with a business degree and went on a thirty-five-year career with BellSouth Corp., where he retired as vice chairman of the board. He spent four years from 1995 to January 1999 as vice president for finance for the sixteen-campus UNC System and then eighteen months from April 1999 to August 2000 as Interim Chancellor of the Chapel Hill campus. McCoy and his wife Sara provided a gift to name the William O. McCoy Graduate Lounge in the McColl Building. McCoy is also the 2002 winner of the school's Global Leadership Award and an emeritus member of the Kenan-Flagler Board of Advisors.

Steve Vetter (BSBA '78) and wife Debbie Vetter (BA '78) of Greensboro founded Ennis-Flint Inc., the world's largest manufacturer and distributor of road-marking materials for the highway safety industry. They sold the company and in 2017 used some of the proceeds to announce a $40 million gift to Carolina, including $10 million to support the Dean's Fellows Scholarship Program at Kenan-Flagler. The program focuses on attracting and nurturing an engaged community of leaders dedicated to the success of the Business School and each other. About twenty-five to thirty-five of the top students receive the Dean's Fellows designation each year, including many who have been admitted to other highly ranked schools.

Frank Sutton earned his BSBA in 1982 and set off on a business career that included buying and selling banks, opening convenience stores and starting an e-commerce company. He often relied on mentors he met along the way to help guide him to success. He and his wife, Shelayne, have five children, two of whom also graduated from UNC Kenan-Flagler.

The Suttons helped underwrite a fitness center in the basement of McColl Building in 2016, and Frank donates his time and expertise to an array of Kenan-Flagler students, most of them in the Adams Apprenticeship, a class of thirty-two diverse, entrepreneurially-minded students who form long-lasting relationships for mentoring and networking.

Coleman Ross (left, BSBA '65) and wife Carol (BA '64) helped set up and initially fund the Lewis M. Burton Master of Accounting Fellowship, to honor his friend Lewis Burton (BSBA '65).

"We had an incredibly strong group of professors when I was in school, but one thing I always believed that could have been improved on was more real-world exposure," Frank says. "There is a remarkable network of alumni wanting to give back, and this mentoring program is truly transformational. I see kids today learning as much outside the classroom as they are in the classroom. I think that's why we are attracting world-class students who want to start their own company or run a company. I'm just amazed at the talent we're getting."

Earl N. "Phil" Phillips Jr. (BSBA '62) funds the Phillips Ambassadors scholarship program to give students a chance to further their education with the kind of international travel he enjoyed as a young man.

"That opened my eyes to the world, and I have been traveling and exploring ever since," he said. "International travel is one of life's great educational experiences. I want Carolina undergraduates to experience that same thing."

The Phillips Ambassadors Program is one of the most generous and flexible scholarships for undergraduate study abroad at Carolina. The scholarship combines a financial award, an academic course, and a charge to students to share their unique study abroad experience with young people in their hometowns and with the Carolina community.

John Townsend was working at Goldman Sachs in the late 1980s when a fellow Kenan-Flagler graduate paid him a visit. Paul Rizzo at the time

Steve Vetter (second from left, BSBA '78), and wife Debbie Vetter (BA '78) of Greensboro were acknowledged in Kenan Stadium for their generous gift to support the Dean's Fellows Scholarship Program at Kenan-Flagler.

was dean of the school after a successful career at IBM. He was raising money and knew Townsend had the means to make a contribution.

"It honestly had never occurred to me," Townsend says. "Paul made me realize how important Kenan-Flagler had been to what I had achieved and would later achieve. He really made me start thinking about philanthropy, about how those of us with some resources are so vital to the operation of the school. He flipped the switch for me.

"Think about your balance sheet. All the assets on the left-hand side you enjoy because of what Kenan-Flagler gave you. The right hand is the liability that you owe. It's a very special place. Do a mental inventory of what you have received and what you have given."

Townsend acted on that philanthropic resolve again in October 2017 when the University announced a $50 million gift from the Townsend family to kick off the "Campaign for Carolina," a University-wide development initiative that seeks to raise $4.25 billion through the end of 2022. That gift includes $10 million to Kenan-Flagler.

"Carolina was one of the first organizations that we felt fortunate to support, and it's been such a rewarding place to continue to give to over the years," Townsend says. "It's wonderful to watch our contributions making a difference."

Building Toward The Future

New Space for Kenan-Flagler

The following three statements were made by Kenan-Flagler Deans Dudley Carroll, Paul Fulton and Doug Shackelford. Match the name with the quote.

* "Now we're in a position to compete against anybody. We had to overcome a lot. The accommodations in the old building were not anywhere near what prospective students and faculty were seeing at other schools."

* "We've expanded into the basement. We've expanded into the attic. We're at a point we have no offices for new faculty we've hired who are arriving in July. We have staff in three locations, we're renting space around town. We have no places for study rooms. We are very much in need of a new building."

* "Naturally neither the professor nor the student can do his best under such crowded conditions. We have but three laboratories, and in the morning, they are used for classrooms. This makes it impossible for the student to work his problems except at night."

Detect a theme here?

From the *The More Things Change Department* comes the issue of space for business education at Carolina. Whether it was Carroll speaking in 1940 (comment No. 3) .... Or Fulton in 1997 (No. 1) .... Or Shackelford in 2017 (No. 2) .... the issue of having enough space for students, faculty, classrooms, research, support and ancillary functions has always been on the front burner.

And so it is again as Kenan-Flagler enters its second century of operation.

School officials in the spring of 2018 got approval from the University to plan for a fifty-percent undergraduate enrollment increase over eight years, going from approximately four hundred business majors and minors in the junior and senior classes to six hundred in each class.

That's going to take significantly more space.

Architects have presented a plan for a new building with approximately 130,000 square feet of assigned space and an additional 10,000 of "shell" space for future expansion. It would be "L shaped" and positioned adjacent to the Business School parking deck's northwest side. The building would be bordered on the north side by Blythe Drive and to the west by the current forested area that, according to the University's master plan, will remain so in perpetuity. McColl and the new building would be connected at the northwest corner of McColl.

The Business School will go from having 22,000 square feet of teaching space to 50,000 and from 34,000 square feet of interactive space to approximately 50,000. McColl currently has eighteen classrooms,

This conceptual rendering from late 2018 shows the size and location of the proposed new Kenan-Flagler facility at lower-right, connected to the existing McColl Building.

and the expansion would double that capacity to thirty-six.

The projected cost is $145 million. Officials hope to get legislative approval and financial support in place by the summer of 2019. That would allow the school to move forward to the design stage later that year. Construction would take approximately two years for the new building and an additional twelve months for renovations to McColl.

"The new building will give the school a connection to main campus," says Kenan-Flagler Facilities Director Dave Moore. "It will help integrate south campus with main campus as there will be a main entrance and bus stop off Blythe Drive. An additional benefit of the building location will be to provide increased interaction and student opportunities with health affairs and the sciences. There will be a significant increase in space to support student services, study spaces and new ventures."

Among features planned are a "quiet study" lounge, outdoor study areas on the west side of the building taking advantage of the natural environment, and a sixty-percent increase in student study space. There will be outdoor dining with an overhang to ward off the sun and the elements and a café-bistro dining room as well as an IT services center for students that will be similar aesthetically to an Apple store. The plans also include significant renovations to the McColl Building student space and classrooms.

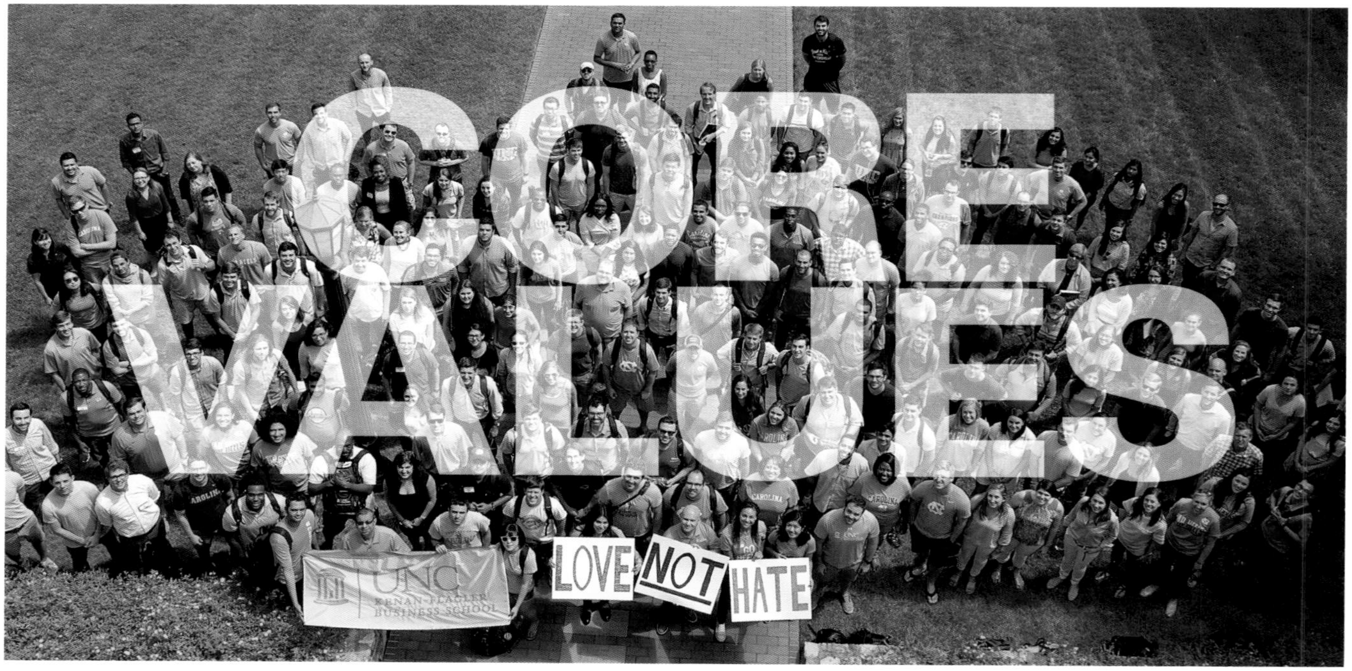

The Kenan-Flagler community lives by its core values: Excellence, leadership, integrity, community and teamwork.

EXCELLENCE

We strive for the very highest standards in everything that we do. We challenge each other to produce important new knowledge at the leading edge of our disciplines, to create an intellectually rigorous learning environment and to show uncompromising dedication to those we serve.

LEADERSHIP

In the 18th century, the people of North Carolina founded the University of North Carolina, the first state university in the nation. In the 20th century, UNC created one of the nation's first schools of business. In the 21st century, we will build on our heritage by providing innovative leadership in education and research and by inspiring and developing the leaders of the future.

INTEGRITY

We cultivate an environment of honesty, sincerity and trust in which we hold ourselves to the highest ethical standards. We believe integrity is the foundation of all moral character and is an essential trait for truly successful professional and personal lives.

COMMUNITY

From its earliest days, UNC has honored and cherished its special responsibility to serve the people of North Carolina. We at Kenan-Flagler extend this notion of responsibility to include service to the nation and the world through research, teaching and community leadership.

TEAMWORK

We create at Kenan-Flagler a unique atmosphere of collaboration, mutual support and genuine interest in each other's success. Our diverse mix of cultures, races and experiences provides a variety of perspectives and talents that, when united through teamwork, strengthens our ability to achieve our goals.

UNC KENAN-FLAGLER BUSINESS SCHOOL STAFF & FACULTY

Allison Adams
Leah R. Adeniji
Natalie Albertson
Jim Alessandro
Georgia A. Allen
Jeremy N. Allen
Kimberly Renee Allen
Allison Anthony
Alexander T. Arapoglou
Stephen V. Arbogast
Jamal "Jay" Arrington
Joanna Ashe
Mike Atkinson
Barbara Ann Aversano
Katrin Baker
Sridhar Balasubramanian
LaChaun J. Banks
Danielle Bass
Barry L. Bayus
Mike Beeler
Lisa Beisser
Cooper Smith Biersach
Dick Blackburn
Angela D. Bond
Yasser Boualam
Andrew Boysen
Callie Brauel
Gregory Brown
Amy Bugno
Pia Elizabeth Bunton
Dustin Burleson
Jeff Cannon
Mike Carroll
Tom Cawley
Les Chaffin
Sandra Chandler
Larry W. Chavis
Meredith Cheng
Jessica Siegel Christian
Michael S. Christian
Lennon D. Cianciulli
Patricia Collins
Bob Connolly
Jennifer Conrad
Whitney Corbett
Debra Corvey
Brittany Craig
Sarah Crockett
Devin Fratarcangeli Culbertson
David Culp
Jennifer Curasi
Jesse E. Davis
Travis Shelton Day
Leticia DeCastro
Andi Della Flora
Sreedhari Desai
Samantha E. Dickens
Alexander P. Dickey
Nicholas M. Didow Jr.
Lynn Dikolli
Isaac Dinner
Carrie Dobbins
Christy Dodson
Susan W. Drake
Timothy Dunham
Katie Dunn
Brian Edgar
Courtney H. Edwards
Jeffrey R. Edwards
Seyed Morteza Emadi
David G. Ernsthausen
Miranda S. Fearrington
Jessica Fleming
Tim Flood
Mark Forsyth
Alison Fragale
William Frasca
Jackie Fritsch
Paolo Fulghieri
Leah B. Fuller
Julie Gaudet
Melissa Hull Geil
Adam Z. Gerdts
Eric Ghysels
Vickie L. Gibbs
Katrijn Gielens
Maria J. Gill
Wendell Gilland
Stephen Anthony Glaeser
Alyssa Good
Meghan Gosk
Kyle Gray
Rajdeep Grewal
Tamala Grissett
Mustafa N. Gültekin
Melissa Gunnell
Douglas B. Guthe Jr.
Steven Hallman
Kelly W. Hammond
John R. M. Hand
Carrie S. Harbinson
Richard C. Hardy
Patricia Harms
Cyndi Hartmann
David Hartzell
Olga Hawn
Sandra Hedrick
Carol Ann Hee
Brad Hendricks
Matthew Hente
Amy Hepler
David Hetrick
Stacie B. Hewett
Steve A. Hicks
Melissa Hlavac
David A. Hofmann
Greg Hohn
Jeff Hoopes
Laura Howe
Alyson Hyman
Ashley Nicole Ivery
Pranav Jindal
James H. Johnson Jr.
W. Steven Jones
Kristopher O. Keller
Zoey Kernodle
Saravanan Kesavan
Kelly Starr Ryan King
David A. Knowles
Julia Kruse
Claudia Kubowicz Malhotra
Camelia Kuhnen
Eva Labro
Thomas LaDew
Lauren LaFemina
Wayne Landsman
Edward Brent Lane
Mark Lang
Susan Lebel
Erika D. Lewis
Huan Lian
Ursula E. Littlejohn
Lauren Xiaoyuan Lu
Christian T. Lundblad
Xiaoling (Charlene) Ma
Portia Made-Jamison
Stephanie L. Mahin
Arv Malhotra
Paul T. Marince
Kelsey V. Martin
Nicole D. Mason
Antonia Brisbourne Matthews
Edward Maydew
Leslie Goff McDow
Karen McFarland
Patia J. McGrath
Chenelle McInnis
Roscoe McNair III
Mark McNeilly
Leslie Melton
Shimul Melwani
Michael J. Meredith
Adam J. Mersereau
Cherie L. R. Michaud
Sarah Mier
Mabel M. Miguel
Anna Millar
Stephen P. Miller
Jason S Moon
Dave Moore
Noemi Morillo-Vasquez
Kaitlyn Murphy
Randy Myer
Tom Myrick
Rebecca J. Naples
Tina Narron
Atul Nerkar
Todd Northrup
Hugh O'Neill
Jack Oakes
Daniel O'Keefe
Candrice Oliver
Timothy E. Ott
Paige Ouimet
Brian Papajcik
Megan Parker
Ali K. Parlakturk
Matt Pearsall
Sarah Perez
Stephanie B. Peterson
Terri T. Pettigrew
Courtney C. Porter
Jeff Post
Michelle M. Pradhan
Russell Privett
Jana Raedy
Sandeep Rath
David Ravenscraft
Crystal Reed
Holly Rice
Danielle Richie
Shaydee Rivera
Melissa E. Robbins
Dave Roberts
Hank Robertson
Michelle Rogan
Miles C. Rosen
Markus Saba
Jason Sabow
Jacob S. Sagi
Jarrett Saia
Sam Sawyer
Allison Kate Hamer Schlobohm
Michael D. Schmidt
Heidi Schultz
Albert H. Segars
Ovul Sezer
Douglas Shackelford
Elad N. Sherf
C. J. Skender
Valerie D. Slate
Scott E. Smith
Chip Snively
Jim Spaeth
Karsen Lattimore Spain
Bradley R. Staats
Liz Stanson
C. Michael Stepanek
Dave Stevens, Sr.
Kara Stith
Mindy Storrie
Anne-Marie Summers
Jayashankar M. Swaminathan
Tim Switzer
Christina Synn
Shannon Taylor
Jeff Terry
Eric Thomas
Judy Jones Tisdale
Tracy Triggs-Matthews
Amy Z. Tufts
Amanda Tyus
Vikram J. Udeshi
Patrick Vernon
Natalie Viernes
David J. Vogel
Kaitlyn L. Vogt
Edwin K. Vosburgh II
Sherry Ford Wallace
Elizabeth Wallencheck
Kelly Weaver
Jacob West
Lael Whiteside
Lauren Humphrey Willets
Amanda Williams
Stephanie Barbee Williams
Kristin Elizabeth Wilson
Melissa J. Wilson
Amy Wittmayer
Allie Wooten
Anne B. Worthington
Courtney Wright
Kim Yates
Valarie Zeithaml
Ted Zoller

As of 10/2018 there were 407 full-time faculty and staff at UNC Kenan-Flagler Business School. Above is a listing of people who opted to be listed in this book.

DEANS & BOARD MEMBERS

Kenan-Flagler Deans

1919-50	Dudley Dewitt Carroll
1950-54	Thomas H. Carroll
1954	Arch Richard Dooley
1954-56	Richard J.M. Hobbs (Interim)
1956-76	Maurice W. Lee
1976-78	Harvey A. Wagner
1978-79	John P. "Jack" Evans (Interim)
1979-87	John P. "Jack" Evans
1987-92	Paul J. Rizzo
1992-93	Carl Zeithaml (Interim)
1994-97	Paul Fulton
1997-98	John P. "Jack" Evans (Interim)
1998-2002	Robert S. Sullivan
2002-03	Julie H. Collins (Interim)
2003-08	Steve Jones
2008-13	James W. Dean Jr.
2013-14	John P. "Jack" Evans (Interim)
2014-	Douglas A. Shackelford

Board of Advisors

George Alexander (MBA '11)
John Andrew Allison IV (BSBA '71)
Richard E. Allison Jr. (BSBA '89, MBA '95)
Jeffrey Alan Allred (BA '76, MBA '80, JD '80)
Phillip D. Ameen (BSBA '69)
Dwight W. Anderson (MBA '94)
Nathan R. Andrews (BSBA '93, MAC '93)
Sam B. Bowles (BSBA '97)
Kimberly P. Brunson (BSBA '83)
Brent Callinicos (BSBA '87, MBA '89)
David Milton Carroll (BSBA '79)
Susan E. Cates (MBA '98)
James T. Clark (BA '93, MAC '95, MBA '01)
Jan L. Davis (BA '73, MBA '79)
Ajit Dayal (MBA '83)
Alexander P. Dickey (BSBA '87)
Deborah H. Ellis (MBA '75)
Joi Ernst (BSBA '98)
Peter Fox
Paul Fulton (BSBA '57)
Allen E. Gant Jr. (UNC '70)
Meredith H. Garwood (BSBA '87, MAC '89)
Thomas J. Gawronski (BSBA '80)
Michael L. Griffin (BSBA '87)
Jeffrey A. Hoffman (MBA '93)
Rolf K. Hoffmann (MBA '87)
Leo S. Horey III (MBA '90)
James Jackson (MBA'82)
Robert A. Jones (BA '77, MBA '80)
Peter L. Keane (MBA '87)
Christopher A. Keber (MBA '02)
Francis X. Kelly
Frank Hawkins Kenan II (MBA '11)
Steven D. Krichmar (BSBA '80)
Stuart Wright Kronauge (BA '91)
H. Kelly Landis III (BSBA '79, MBA '82)
Lynn Diane Lewis (MBA '86)
Jason T. Liberty (MBA)
Eric A. Livingston (BA '92, MBA '11)
Anne Harris Lloyd (BSBA '83)
Tom Lutz (BSBA '87)
Charles McNairy (BA '97)
Nancy S. Millett (BSBA '83)
William M. Moore Jr. (MBA '67)
C. Toms Newby III (BSBA '89)
Kennedy C. O'Herron (BA '72, MBA '80)
William F. Paulsen (BSBA '69, MBA '71)
Michael J. Peterson (BSBA '81, MBA '87)
Earl Norfleet Phillips Jr. (BSBA '62)
Lansdon B. Robbins III (BSBA '87)
William L. Rogers (BSBA '68)
William G. Seymour (BSBA '64)
Kevin S. Smith (BSBA '90)
William N. Starling (BSBA '75)
Frank Cable Steinemann Jr. (BSBA '70)
W. Franklin Sutton (BSBA '82)
Patrick G. Trask (MBA '00)
Jeffrey K. Tucker (MBA '00)
R. Steven Vetter (BSBA '78)
Vanessa A. Wittman (BSBA '89)
G. Smedes York (MBA '68)

Emeritus Board of Advisors

Milton A. Barber III (BA '58)
Brent D. Barringer (BSBA '81)
Agnes R. Beane
Steven D. Bell (BA '67)
B. M. Boddie Sr.
Crandall C. Bowles
Robert Buckfelder (MBA '81)
Walter W. Buckley III (BA '82)
John W. Burress III (BA '58)
Wayland H. Cato Jr. (BSCOM '44)
William Cavanaugh III
Max C. Chapman Jr. (BA '66)
Amy J. Conlee (BSBA '75)
Daniel T. Cox (BA '68)
Steven M. Durham (MBA '86)
Robert C. Eubanks Jr. (BA '61)
Edward J. Fritsch (BSBA '81)
John J. Froehlich (MBA '03)
Mike T. Furuhata (MBA '55)
Joseph Galli Jr. (BSBA '80)
J. Alston Gardner (BA '77)
James S. Gold (BA '72)
Vernon D. Grizzard Jr. (BSBA '75)
W. C. Hamner Jr.
William B. Harrison Jr. (BA '66)
Patrick G. Hartley (BSBA '76)
George W. Henderson III (BA '70)
Joseph C. High (BSBA '76)
Luther H. Hodges Jr. (BA '57)
Donald C. Ingram (BSBA '67)
Charles M. Johnson III (BA '75)
Don R. Johnson
George H. Johnson (BSBA '58)
Betty Kenan
Thomas S. Kenan III (BA '59)
Libby Ho Hwa Leung (MBA '83)
Thomas W. Lewis Sr. (MBA '73)
Ann M. Livermore (BA '80)
R. Charles Loudermilk Sr. (BSBA '50)
Peter G. Mallinson (BA '81, MBA '83)
William M. Matthews (UNC '73)
Hugh L. McColl Jr. (BSBA '57)
William O. McCoy (BSBA '55)
John O. McNairy (BSBA '71)
Stevie S. McNeal (MBA '87)
Tom Moser (BSBA '69)
Frank T. Nickell (BSBA '69)
Peggy S. Nielson
John C. O'Hara Jr. (MBA '79)
Gary W. Parr (BSBA '79)
Todd McNeill Pope (BA '87)
Julian H. Robertson Jr. (BSBA '55)
Nelson Schwab III (BA '67)
Peter M. Scott III (BSBA '72, MBA '77)
Sherwood H. Smith Jr. (BA '56)
John L. Townsend III (BA '77, MBA '82)
Edwin A. Wahlen Jr. (MBA '72)
Thomas J. Ward (ABJO '77)
Van L. Weatherspoon (BSBA '54)
Allen Wilson (BSBA '77)
Leonard Wood (MBA '72)
Edwina D. Woodbury (BSBA '73)
Charles E. Zeigler Jr.

Alumni Council

Atul Aggarwal (MBA '89)
Evan Balafas (MAC '05)
Alex Bean (BSBA '07)
Diana Berry (MBA '15)
Brad Bertinot (MBA@UNC '14, MAC '16)
Tonya Brady (BSBA '94)
James Brandau (MBA '10)
Patrick Brennan (MBA '13)
Cole Buckfelder (BSBA '08, MBA@UNC '14)
Bishop Byerly (BSBA '07)
Pete Canalichio (MBA '90)
Gabe Catala (BSBA '07)
Mary Elizabeth Catala (BSBA '07)
John Chapman (BSBA '00, MBA '08)
Jason Colgate (MBA '09)
Anthony Cummings (MBA '97)
Greg Damron (MAC '97)
Scott Davis (BSBA '84)
Rich Doggett (MBA '95)
Mark Donnolo (MBA '93)
Mark Edwards (BSBA '83)
Stuart Friou (BSBA '88)
Mary Moore Hamrick (MBA/JD '87)
Scott Hauser (BSBA '07)
Chris Heimers (MBA '13)
Kurt Hockmeyer (MBA '06)
Barry Holloway (BSBA '73)
Nora Jabbour (BSBA '06, MBA '14)
Alexander Jackson (MAC '16)
Bob Kadlec (BSBA '85)
William Keesler (BSBA '08)
Indra Lahiri (MBA '09)
Mac Lewis (BSBA '94)
AraLu Lindsey (BSBA '83)
Chris Mallin (MBA '15)
Michael Marr (BSBA '82)
Betsy Matthew (EMBA '95)
Brian McBroom (BSBA '88)
John McMichael (MBA '93)
Charlie Mercer (MBA '09)
John Murchison (JD '02, MBA '02)
Laura Oslick (MBA '12)
Tim Palmer (BSBA '13)
Jack Partain (BSBA '13)
Kendra Perlitz (MBA '11)
Allison Phillips (MBA '05)
John Puskar (MBA@UNC '18)
Amanda Rabideau (MBA '11)
Cindy Rahman (BSBA '03)
John Rhodin (MBA '92)
Carl Rice (MBA '94)
Brett Scodova (MBA@UNC '14)
Margo Shepard (BSBA '78)
Louise Smith (BSBA '06, MBA@UNC '13)
Barron Stroud Jr. (BSBA '88, JD '91)
Chris Thomas (BSBA '84)
Dianne Thomas (BSBA '82)
Deron Weston (MBA '00)
Jim White (MBA '06)
Genna Zimmer (BSBA '14)

Foundation Board of Directors

Betsy Battle (ABJO '76)
Gregory Brown
Stephen Cumbie (BA '70, MBA '73)
Adam Z. Gerdts (BA '00, MBA '14)
Patrick G. Hartley (BSBA '76)
David Hofmann
Francie Keenan (BSBA '76)
John McColl (MBA '91)
Adam Mersereau
John C. O'Hara, Jr. (MBA '79)
Douglas A. Shackelford (BSBA '80)
Steven Skolsky (BA '78)
David W. Stevens
Brien White (BA '99)

ALUMNI AWARD WINNERS

Leadership Award
2018 R. Steve Vetter, BSBA '78
2017 Stephen M. Cumbie, BA '70, MBA '73
2016 William N. Starling Jr., BSBA '76
2015 Lonnie Craven Poole, Jr., MBA '64
2014 William M. Moore, Jr., MBA '67
2013 Steven D. Bell, BA '67
2012 John P. Evans
2011 Julian Robertson, BSBA '55
2010 Erskine B. Bowles, BSBA '67
2009 Maurice J. Koury, AB '48
2008 Leonard W. Wood, MBA '72
2007 Wayland H. Cato Jr., BSCOM '44
2006 R. Charles Loudermilk Sr., BSBA '50
2005 Hugh L. McColl Jr. BSBA '57
2004 Van L. Weatherspoon, BSBA '54
2003 Rollie Tillman Jr., BSBA '55
2002 William O. McCoy, BSBA '55
2001 Paul Fulton, BSBA '57
2000 Paul J. Rizzo, BSCOM '50
1999 Frank H. Kenan, BSCOM '35 (posthumous award)

Global Leadership Award
2017 Allen E. Gant, Jr., UNC '70
2016 Raj Rajkumar, MBA '93
2015 Jeffrey K. Tucker, MBA '00
2014 Ajit Dayal, MBA '83
2013 Rolf K. Hoffmann, MBA '87
2012 Peter McMillan, BSBA '81
2011 Peter G. C. Mallinson, AB '81, MBA '83
2010 Derick S. Close, MBA '90
2009 Mick Hawk, MBA '90
2008 Jack N. Behrman, MA '45
2007 Paul Fulton, BSBA '57
2006 John D. Kasarda, PhD '71
2005 William B. Harrison Jr., AB '66
2004 John G. Medlin Jr., BSBA '56
2003 J. Alston Gardner, AB '77
2002 Owen G. Kenan (posthumous award)
2001 Earl N. "Phil" Phillips Jr., BSBA '62
2000 Lovick P., AB '44, and Elizabeth T. Corn
1999 David S. Van Pelt, BSBA '63

Dwight W. Anderson Young Alumni Award
2018 Nick Black, MBA '13
2017 Scott A. Quilty, Executive MBA '15
2016 Allison M. Hughes, MBA '14
2015 Jim Jones, MBA '06
2014 Ashok S. Jayaram, MBA '11
2014 Phaedra Boinodiris, MBA '08
2012 Callie Joyce Brauel, BSBA '09
2011 Joi M. Corrothers, BSBA '98
2010 Amit Singh, Executive MBA '03
2009 Henry M. T. Jones, MBA '99
2007 Sindhura Citineni, BSBA '04
2005 Courtney A. Brown, BSBA '97
2004 Kayrn A. Withers, BSBA '96
2003 David W. Jernigan, BSBA '00
2002 Elizabeth Klompmaker Moshier, BSBA '87, MBA '92
2001 Jeffrey K. Tucker, MBA '00
2000 Dwight W. Anderson, MBA '94
1999 Derick S. Close, MBA '90

Alumni Merit Award

2018
Meredith Hawley Garwood, BSBA '87, MAC '89
Joseph C. High, BSBA '76
Jason T. Liberty, MBA

2017
Lewis M. Burton, BSBA '65
Vanessa Wittman, BSBA '89

2016
Susan E. Cates, MBA '98
C. Scott Hultman, Executive MBA '08
Richard "Stick" Williams, BSBA '75

2015
H. Paul Chapman, BSBA '74
Janet L. Davis, MBA '79
Richard L. Michaux, MBA '73

2014
William J. Armfield, IV, BSBA '56
Michele G. Buck, MBA '87
Gary L. Monroe, MBA '98
Charles Edgar Sams, Jr., BSBA '71

2013
William D. Perreault, PhD '73
Cam Patterson, Executive MBA '08
H. Kel Landis, III, BSBA 1979, MBA '82
Jeffrey A. Allred, MBA '80
Coleman D. Ross, BSBA '65

2012
Anne Harris Lloyd, BSBA '83
Tesa L. Oechsle, OneMBA '06
Lee Ainslie III, MBA '90
Duke Steinemann, BSBA '70

2011
Allaudeen Hameed, PhD '92
C. Martin Nassif, BSBA '61
Penny Oslund, Executive MBA '90
Thomas W. Lewis, MBA '73
John A. Allison, BSBA '71

2010
Nancy S. Millett, BSBA '83
David Kirkpatrick, Executive MBA '91
John C. O'Hara Jr., MBA '79
Jason Kilar, BSBA '93

2009
R. Trent Gazzaway, BSBA '90, MAC '91
Ronald L. Martin, OneMBA '04
Donna J. Dean, MBA '78
William G. Seymour, BSBA '64

2008
William F. Ezzell Jr., BSBA '73
Roland T. Rust, MBA '77, PhD '80
Claire Babrowski, Executive MBA '95
Tom Harvey, MBA '72
David M. Carroll, BSBA '79

2007
Diane E. Wilfong, BSBA '83
Jesko A. von Windheim, Executive MBA '96
Ralph L. Falls Jr., BSBA '63
Dwight W. Anderson, MBA '94

2006
Philip D. Ameen, BSBA '69
Valerie M. Parisi, Executive MBA '04
William N. Starling, BSBA '75
Thomas M. Belk Jr., MBA '81

2005
Thomas M. Brantley, AB '73
Elizabeth B. Matthew, Executive MBA '95
Daryl G. Brewster, MBA '82
Gary W. Parr, BSBA '79

2004
Richard J. Rendleman, PhD '76
Sanford A. Cockrell III, BSBA '82
Phail Wynn Jr., Executive MBA '89
Brent Callinicos, BSBA '87, MBA '89
Charles S. Ackerman, BSBA '55

2003
Kimberly P. Ellis, BSBA '83
Edwina D. Woodbury, BSBA '73
Christopher T. Speh, Executive MBA '91
George Smedes York, MBA '68

2002
William Lee Rogers, BSBA '68
S. Philip Harris, BSBA '54
Susan K. Acker, Executive MBA '97
Thomas L. Jones, MBA '77
Robert H. Litzenberger, PhD '69

2001
Van L. Weatherspoon, BSBA '54
M. Allen Wilson, BSBA '77
M. Nixon Ellis, Executive MBA '92
Leonard W. Wood, MBA '72

2000
R. Charles Loudermilk Sr., BSBA '50
Thomas W. Hudson Jr., BSCOM '46
John L. Townsend III, MBA '82

1999
William O. McCoy, BSBA '55
S. Thomas Moser, BSBA '69
William M. Moore Jr., MBA '67
Richard W. McEnally, PhD '69

FUNDS ESTABLISHED BY DONORS TO BENEFIT UNC KENAN-FLAGLER BUSINESS SCHOOL

The 1916 Foundation Fund
The A. Donald Christopher Scholarship Fund
The A.L. Hobgood Jr. Scholars Endowment
The Absher Family Fund for Accounting Excellence
The Alexander Thorpe Family Fund
The Alfred C. Starling Scholarship Fund
The Alvin M. Bodford Undergraduate Assured Admission Scholarship Fund
The Andy and Jennifer Rose Scholarship Fund
The Ann Lewallen Spencer and the Lewallen Family Dean's Endowed Faculty Fund
The Anna Maria Poulos Scholarship Fund
The Anthony, Caroline and Louis Berini Scholarship Fund
The Archie K. Davis Management Lecture Series Endowment
The Arthur Andersen Faculty Fund
The Assured Admit Scholarship for Excellence
The Bank of America Faculty Development Fund
The Bank of America MBA Fellowship
The Barry Roberts International Fund
The Battle Family Foundation Kenan-Flagler Business School Fund
The Belk Distinguished Professorship
The Benjamin Cone Research Term Professorship in Business
The Bob and Mindy Jones Family Assured Admit Scholarship
The Bob and Mindy Jones Family Global Immersion Fund
The Bob and Teresa Scheppegrell BSBA Study Abroad Scholarship
The Boyd White Harris Jr. Family Distinguished Professorship
The Braxton E. Barrett Sr. Scholarship Fund
The Burgess Family Endowment Fund
The Burlington Industries MBA Fellowship
The Burress Faculty Development and Support Fund
The C. Knox Massey Professorship in Business Administration
The C. Martin Nassif Master of Accounting Fellowship Fund
The Callinicos MBA Fellowship
The Calvin Atwood MBA Fellowship
The Carl and Janice Brown Preferred BSBA Scholarship
The Carl and Janice Brown Upperclass Academic Scholarship
The Carl and Susan Baumann Fellowship Fund
The Carl Clinton Scott Scholarship Fund
The Carolina Business Faculty Fund
The Carolina Way Leadership Fund
The Carolyn and Harold Anderson MBA Premier Fellowship
The Center for Excellence in Investment Management
The Center for Real Estate Development Endowment
The Charles C. McKinney Faculty Development Fund
The Charles E. Sams Jr. MAC Scholarship Fund
The Charles Glenwood Hawley Scholarship Fund
The Claude and Eleanor George Fund for Teaching and Learning
The Clifford Earl Bullard Jr. Faculty Excellence Fund
The Clyde L. Stutts and Rufus Edwards Stutts Scholarship Fund
The Coca-Cola MBA Scholars Fund
The Coleman D. Ross Master of Accounting Fellowship
The Collins Dawson Endowment
The Crist W. Blackwell Distinguished Professorship
The D. Ralph Huff III MBA Fellowship in Real Estate
The Dalton L. McMichael Sr. Professorship
The Danny R. Newcomb and Ernst and Young LLP Fund
The David D. and Carol Ann Flanagan Fellowship
The David E. Hoffman Memorial Fund
The David E. Hoffman Professorship
The David M. and Virginia C. Knott Distinguished Professorship
The David S. and Christine C. Moss Scholarship
The David S. Van Pelt Family Distinguished Professorship of Marketing
The Dearborn Family MBA Fellowship in Real Estate
The Deloitte and Touche Research Fellowship Fund
The Dixon Hughes Goodman Alumni Endowment
The Donald Charles and Donna Williard Ingram Faculty Excellence Fund
The Dr. Luther Wade Humphreys Jr. Scholarship Endowment
The Dr. Richard "Dick" Levin Faculty Excellence Fund
The E. Jackson Sapp Scholarship
The Eddie C. Smith Jr. Leadership Initiative
The Edison E. Marley Undergraduate Business Scholarship
The Edmund B. Ross III BSBA Endowment
The Edward J. and Vicki J. Fritsch MBA Fellowship
The Edward M. O'Herron Jr. Fund for Distinguished Faculty
The Edwin A. Wahlen Jr. Fund for Faculty Excellence
The Edwina D. Woodbury Business Endowment
The Ellison Distinguished Professorship
The EMBA Class Gift Endowment
The EMBA Class of '99 in Memory of Don Segneri Fund
The Emily Pleasants Sternberg and Mary Pleasants Bossong MBA Fellowship Fund
The Erdossy Family Endowment for Real Estate Center Faculty Support Fund
The Erie Windsor Cass and Jessamine Brown Cass Undergraduate Scholarship Fund
The Ernest E. Mayo Undergraduate Research Fund in Finance
The Ernst and Young Professorship of Accounting
The Ernst Kemm Endowment Fund
The Eugene T. Barwick Scholarship Fund
The Evans MBA Fellowship
The Ewing Schleeter Harris BSBA Scholarship
The F. Trammell Crow MBA Fellowship for Leadership in Real Estate
The Forensic Accounting Distinguished Professorship
The Frank and Shelayne Sutton BSBA Excellence Fund
The Frank Ervin Young Jr. and Mae T. Young Undergraduate Business Fund
The Frank H. Kenan Institute of Private Enterprise Award
The Frank Hawkins Kenan Award
The Fred B. James Memorial Scholarship
The Freddy and Susan Robinson Scholarship in Accounting Fund
The Friends of The Kenan Foundation Asia Fund
The Fulton Global Business Distinguished Professorship
The G. Martin Poole Study Abroad Endowment
The G. Morrison Creech and Elizabeth J. Creech Family Assured Admission Scholarship
The Gary Armstrong Undergraduate Enrichment Fund
The Gene Clark Memorial Scholarship
The George H. Johnson Fund for Business
The Gerald Barrett Faculty Award

The Gerald D. Bell Distinguished Professorship
The Glaxo Distinguished Professorship
The Glen Raven Dean's Excellence Fund
The Glen Raven Mills, Inc. Faculty Development Fund
The Greer and Bryan Pope Global Experiences Fund
The Gregory C. Edmister Memorial Fund
The H. Allen Andrew Professorship in Entrepreneurial Education
The H. Kelly Landis III Faculty Fund
The Hampton Shuping Memorial Prize
The Hampton Shuping Memorial Scholarship
The Harold Q. Langenderfer Distinguished Professorship of Accounting
The Harris Family Fellowship
The Harry W. Cherry Accounting Education Fund
The Harry W. Cherry Accounting Faculty Development Fund
The Helen Craig Wardlaw Fund
The Henry Latané Doctoral Fellowship
The Henry Latané PhD Banquet Fund
The Horey Family MBA Fellowship
The Hugh and Frances McColl Faculty Development Award in Business Administration
The Hugh L. McColl Jr. Distinguished Leadership Professorship
The Independent Insurance Agents of NC Scholarship
The Information Technology Fund
The International Telephone and Telegraph Corporation Scholarship
The Investors Title Insurance Company Assured Admission Undergraduate Scholarship
The Ira Walter Hine Scholarship Fund
The Isaac Dean Gurley Business Endowment Fund
The J. Taylor Rankin Memorial Fellowship
The Jack Behrman "Pay It Forward" India Fellowship
The Jack Behrman and Dick Levin Award
The Jackson Anderson Scholarship Fund
The James C. and Ethel M. Crone Fund in Tax Excellence
The James H. Toy Scholarship
The James K. McLean Scholarship
The James Wilford Clark Jr. Undergraduate Scholarship
The Jane and Lucien Ellison MBA Fellowship Fund in Real Estate
The Jane H. and William J. Armfield IV Dean's Discretionary Fund
The Jason Ray BSBA Global Scholarship
The Jay E. Klompmaker MBA Fellowship
The Jeff Garwood Student Excellence Fund
The Jeffrey A. Allred Distinguished Professorship
The Jeffrey F. Buckalew MBA Fellowship Fund
The Jerry Warsky MBA Fellowship
The Jesse C. Morris Jr. Scholarship Fund
The Jimmy W. Garrell-Tabor City Endowment Fund
The Joe Summers Floyd Jr. Fund in Undergraduate Teaching
The John B. Stedman Sr. Fund for Social Entrepreneurship
The John C. Whitaker Jr. Undergraduate Business Program Fund
The John Duke Baldridge Jr. and William Paul Baldridge Scholarship
The John G. Slater MBA Fellowship
The John L. Brantley/Deloitte and Touche Fellowship Fund
The John R. Alexander and Sarah Jane Alexander Fund
The John Stedman Endowment
The Joseph C. Ramage Family Endowment
The Joseph Cooley and Kathleen Cullins High Koinonia Scholarship
The Julian Price Professorship in Finance
The Juliber-Wrenn Scholarship
The June and L. Gordon Pfefferkorn Jr. BSBA Study Abroad Scholarship
The Kay and Van Weatherspoon Distinguished Professorship
The Kenneth Bartlett Howard BSBA Scholarship
The Kenneth Felton Howard Jr. Undergraduate Scholarship
The Kenneth Rhudar Miller Undergraduate Global Learning and Leadership Fund
The Kit and Turner Bredrup Faculty Excellence Award Fund
The KPMG Professorship of Professional Accounting
The KPMG Research Fellowship
The L. David and Barbara D. Berryhill, Jr. Fund
The L. Worth Holleman Jr. Graduate Scholarship Fund
The Lee P. Shaffer II MBA Fellowship
The Leonard and Kira Wood Diversity Fund in Real Estate
The Leonard W. Wood Foundation for Excellence in Real Estate
The Lewis G. Holland Scholarship
The Lewis M. Burton Master of Accounting Fellowship
The Lewis S. Morris MBA Fellowship
The Lichtin MBA Fellowship
The Lincoln Financial Group Faculty Development Fund
The Litzenberger Family Foundation Fund
The Long Family UK Experience Scholarship
The Lovick P. Corn Fellowship
The Lovick P. Corn Fund for Global Business Education
The Luther H. Hodges Leadership Center
The M. Allen Wilson Endowment for the Center for Tax Excellence
The M. Nixon and Josephine Taylor Ellis MBA Fellowship
The M. Wayne DeLozier Doctoral Endowment
The M.W. "Dyke" Peebles Jr. Faculty Development Fund
The MAC Millennium Class Gift Endowment
The Macon G. Patton Distinguished Professorship
The Management Development, Inc. MBA Fellowship
The Mann Family Distinguished Professorship in Business
The March Floyd Riddle BSBA Scholarship
The Marion Dixon BSBA Scholarship
The Marvin B. Smith Jr. Memorial Scholarship
The Mary Beth (Cheshire) Fee MAC Legacy Fellowship
The Mary Farley Ames Lee Distinguished Professorship
The Mary K. Brown Memorial Scholarship Fund
The Mary Lou Hague Memorial Scholarship
The Maurice V. Polk Memorial Scholarship
The Maverick Capital Premier MBA Fellowship Fund
The MBA Class Gift Endowment
The MBA Class of 1990 Graduate Scholarship Fund
The MBA Class of 1991 Endowment Fund
The MBA Class of 2002 Alumni Endowment
The MBA Class of 2005 Fellowship for Excellence in Leadership
The MBA Fellowship in Memory of Buck Williams
The MBA Reinvestment Fund
The McMichael Family Study Abroad Scholarship
The Meade H. Willis Chair of Investment Banking
The Medlin Excellence Fund
The Medlin Scholarship for Business and the Liberal Arts
The Melville Brice Rose III Memorial Scholarship
The Michael J. Peterson Scholarship Fund
The Michael R. Hilton Graduate Fellowship
The Michael W. Haley Distinguished Professorship
The Michaux Family MBA Premier Fellowship for Real Estate Students
The Monk Family Student Excellence Fund

The Mr. and Mrs. James E. S. Hynes Fund for MBA Study Abroad
The Mr. and Mrs. John L. Townsend III Faculty Development Fund
The N. Courts Cooledge Family Endowment
The N.C. Trucking Association Fellowship
The Nancy and Michael Millett Dean's Excellence Fund
The Nat T. Harris Faculty Development and Support Fund
The Norman Block Award Fund
The Norman M. Black III Family Faculty Excellence Fund
The Norman McKinley Black Jr. Student Excellence Fund
The Norona Family Global Experiences Scholarship Fund
The North Carolina Real Estate Educational Foundation Professorship in Real Estate
The North Carolina Treasury Management Association MBA Fellowship Endowment
The P. Rao and Venku M. Chatrathi Doctoral Scholarship in International Business Fund
The Pace Poag Endowment Fund
The Parker Family – Goldman Sachs Scholars U.S. Veterans Fund
The Patricia Dowdy Draughon Study Abroad Scholarship
The Patrick and Cathleen Trask MBA Fellowship
The Paul Fulton MBA Fellowship
The Penny Oslund EMBA Fellowship Fund
The Peter G.C. Mallinson MBA Fellowship
The Phillip Hettleman Professorship
The Phillip W. Wilson/KPMG Scholarship Fund
The Phillips Ambassadors
The Pirouz Family Global Experiences Scholarship
The Poole Family Leadership Skills Fund
The Professor Jack Behrman 'Pay it Forward' India Fellowship
The R. Lawrence Leigh MBA International Education Fund
The R. Leslie Johnson Accounting Fund
The R. Owen Mitchell MBA Fellowship
The R. Steven Vetter MBA Fellowship
The Ralph H. Bowden UNC Ethics Fund
The Ralph L. Falls Jr. Endowment Fund
The Randee and Dave Hartzell Excellence in Real Estate Fellowship
The RBC Centura Distinguished Professorship
The Reynolds/Langenderfer Endowed MAC Fellowship
The Richard "Dick" Levin Distinguished Professorship
The Richard and Susan Allison Assured Admit Scholarship
The Richard Carpenter Endowment
The Richard H. Jenrette Business Education Fund
The Richard H. Jenrette Fellowship Awards
The Robert C. Davis Scholarship Fund
The Robert C. Davis Undergraduate Assured Admission Scholarship
The Robert D. and Emily S. Bayliss Family Scholarship Fund
The Robert G. Culp Jr. MBA Fellowship Endowment
The Robert G. Sanford/PricewaterhouseCoopers Fellowship
The Robert Gilliam and Katherine Wilcox Kittrell MBA Fellowship
The Robert March and Mildred Borden Hanes Professorship
The Robert W. Long Jr. Scholarship
The Robin Bradford Reynolds Scholarship
The Rollie and Mary Windley Tillman Endowment
The Rollie Tillman Jr. Development Fund
The Ron Terwilliger Award for Excellence in Real Estate Development
The Roy and Alice H. Richards Bicentennial Professorship
The Roy O. Rodwell Distinguished Professorship
The Russell Browning Family Dean's Discretionary Fund
The Ruth K. and Robert D. Coleman, Jr. Scholarship Fund
The Sailash and Bhavna Patel MBA Fellowship
The Sanford A. Cockrell III/Deloitte Scholars Fund
The Sarah Graham Kenan Fund
The Scholarship in Memory of Hal Kearns Reynolds
The Schomburger Family Scholarship
The Schrum-Boulware MBA Fellowship Fund
The Senkbeil Real Estate Lecture Series
The Sion A. Boney Jr. Endowment Fund
The Stacia L. Wood Social Impact Summer Grant
The Stephen M. Cumbie MBA Fellowship for Real Estate Students
The Steve F. Warren MBA Fellowship
The Steven D. Bell and Leonard W. Wood Distinguished Professorship
The Steven H. Kapp MBA Fellowship
The Steven L. Bean MBA Fellowship
The Sustainability Chair
The T. W. Lewis Distinguished Professorship
The T. W. Lewis MBA Fellowships
The Thomas H. Vance Faculty Fellowship Fund
The Thomas Hart Norwood Scholarship
The Thomas L. Teague MBA Fellowship
The Thomas M. Belk MBA Fellowship
The Thomas W. Dana III Undergraduate Scholarship Fund
The Thomas W. Hudson Jr. Graduate Scholarship
The Thomas W. Hudson Jr. MBA Fellowship
The Thomas W. Hudson Jr./Deloitte and Touche LLP Distinguished Professorship
The Thomas Willis Lambeth Distinguished Chair in Public Policy
The Tiger MBA Fellowship
The Tom Reddin Innovation Fund
The Toni and Rush Wilson MBA Premier Fellowship
The Townsend Family Professorship
The Tracy A. Leinbach MBA Fellowship Fund
The Triangle Advertising Federation Scholarship
The Tricia and Tom York Goldman Sachs Scholars Fund
The Ullrich Family Scholarship Fund for Study Abroad
The UNC Kenan-Flagler MBA Class of 1968 Faculty Excellence Fund
The Van and Kay Weatherspoon Business Endowment
The Vernon and Carol Grizzard Fund
The W. Benton Pipkin of the Class of 1926 Faculty Development Fund
The Wade S. Dunbar Jr. Undergraduate Scholarship
The Wayland H. Cato Jr. Leadership Scholars Program Endowed Scholarship
The Wayne and Melissa Judkins MBA Scholarship
The Weatherspoon Distinguished Faculty Scholars Endowment
The Wells Fargo Center for Corporate Finance
The Wells Fargo Distinguished Professorship
The Wells Fargo Fund for Undergraduate Excellence
The Whit C. Purvis Endowed Fund
The Willard J. Graham Distinguished Faculty Chair
The William D. Parmelee Faculty Excellence Fund
The William G. Daughtridge Jr. Study Abroad Fund
The William H. and Laura L. Rogers Faculty Fund
The William H. and Laura L. Rogers Leadership Initiative Endowment
The William L. Rogers Dean's Discretionary Fund
The William M. Rawls Scholarship Fund
The William R. Kenan Jr. Entrepreneurship Fund
The William R. Ludwick Business Scholarship
The William Starling Life Sciences MBA Fellowship
The Wittman MBA Centennial Fellowship
The York Family Goldman Sachs Fund

CENTENNIAL CORNERSTONE SOCIETY MEMBERS

Anonymous
John and Betty Allison
Richard and Susan Allison
Dwight and Julie Anderson
Howard and Sharon Averill
Todd and Jessica Barr
Kimberly Brunson
Phyllis Slick Cowell
Steve and Sheryl Durham
Marsha and Tom Dugan
Jack and Pat Evans
Paul Fulton
William R. Hackney III
Jon and Angie Hilsabeck
Harry and Parker Jones
John and Kay Kelly
Tom S. Kenan III
Mrs. Frank H. Kenan
Pierre and Laurie Lapeyre
Andrew and Lynn Lewis
Jason and Erica Liberty
Thomas and Dana Lutz
Nancy and Mike Millett
Steve and Jennifer Miller
Bill and Sandra Moore
Robert and Melanie Niblock
Tom Newby and Maisie O'Flanagan
Michael J. Peterson
Carter and Bet Pope
John and Nancy Pope
William L. Rogers
Bill and Emmaday Seymour
Bill and Dana Starling
John and Marree Townsend
Bruce and Katie Van Saun
Steve and Debbie Vetter
Vanessa and Drew Wittman
Ira and Marcia Wagner
Susan Cates and Scott Warren

Donors qualify for the Cornerstone Society with an unrestricted, expendable gift of $25,000 or more to the Fund for UNC Kenan-Flagler.

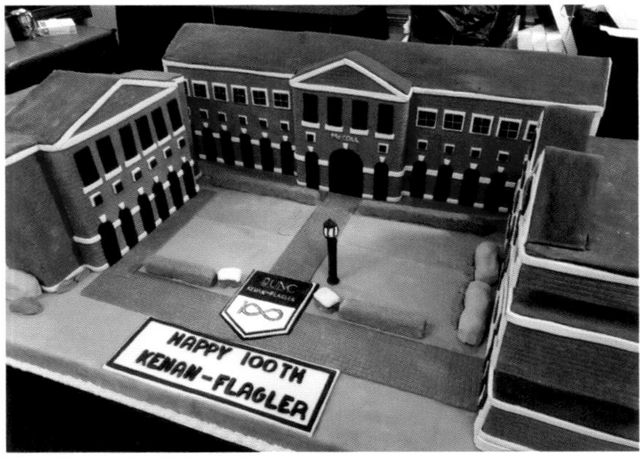

FACES OF KENAN-FLAGLER

(From Gatefold following page 16)

First row (L-R):
Henry Flagler, Leslie Morton, Pete Canalichio, Eddie Sams, Ann Hildebrand, Erin Nilon, Adam Gerdts, Alison Fragale, Veronica Gomes, Katie Venable, Jack Kasarda, Rollie Tillman, Cliff Bullard, Nancy Millett, C.D. Spangler, David Hofmann, Robert Hanes, Bill Rogers.

Second row:
Ann Marucheck, Anne-Marie Summers, Doug Shackelford, Tom Hudson, Leila Kerzic, Winton Green, Jeff Saturday, Alyssa Patel, Dudley Carroll, Tiffanie Johnson, Frederic Merrick, Larry Redell, Edwina Woodbury, Eli Joyner, Kenny Selmon, Ajit Dayal, Brett McFarland, Thomas Belk.

Third row:
Joseph High, Lee Shaffer, Chantel Adams, Harvey Wagner, Ben Rosen, Brad Staats, Ann Wang, Caroline Ririe, Helen McGill, Patrick Gomez Menzies, David Cohen, Christian Lundblad, J.M. Hobbs, Michelle Kimbrough.

Fourth row:
Carl Zeithaml, Katy DeCoursey, Allen Fine, Segun Olagunju, Nannie Davis, Hugh O'Neill, Christine Lasway, Douglas Day, Chris Smith, Don-Ho Chien, Marquita Brazier, Virginia Harrison, Sridhar Balasubramanian, Eddie Smith.

Fifth row:
Jan Davis, John Allison, George Keller, Jay Klompmaker, Tom Kenan, Jay Swaminathan, Ann Goodno, Libby Leung, Jeff Terry, Juan Cofield, Jim Inscoe, Leo Horey, Bill Starling, John Ashcraft, Michael Peterson, Matthew Lyde-Cajuste, George Watts Hill, Phaedra Boinodiris.

Sixth row:
Sherry Wallace, Donna Dean, Stephen Bell, Abner Efird, Richard Jenrette, Erskine Bowles, Gwendolyn Earnshaw, Phail Wynn Jr., Billy Carmichael, Shimul Melwani, David Ravenscraft, Rebecca Stewart, Greg Poole, Jana Raedy, James Short Jr., Kane Nakamura, Jen Stutsman, Frank Kenan.

INDEX

(Boldface denotes photo)

INDEX

PHOTOGRAPHY

Thanks to the following photographers and sources for the images included in this book. All other images are from UNC Kenan-Flagler Business School archives.

Steve Exum: McColl Building exterior 1, Carroll Hall 6-7, Doug Shackelford 10, McColl Building stairs 14-15, campus buildings 41-43, DuBose Home 78, 83 and 84; McLean Hall 85, Shackelford 96, Loudermilk Hall 106, bell ringers 104-05, Frank Kenan portrait 125, Henry Flagler bust 126, Kenan Center entrance 144, Business Cares 165, McColl Building flags 175.

John Gessner: Veterans Association 109, Global Scholars Academy and Dr. Jim Johnson 146-48, Ready-Fire-Aim winner 176.

Ryan Montgomery: Campus aerial 2-3.

North Carolina Collection, Wilson Library, UNC: Vintage campus 18, Dudley Carroll portrait 22, William Kenan campus 134.

UNC General Alumni Association: Campus map 40.

Mike Furuhata: 1950s era photos 44-45.

Jerry Wolford: Hugh McColl 62.

Maury Faggart: Paul Rizzo 65.

IBM: Paul Rizzo 72.

Southern Historical Collection, Wilson Library, UNC: Paul Hardin letter 67.

Flagler Museum, Palm Beach, Fla.: William Rand Kenan Jr. and Flagler-Kenan wedding 110-11, Flagler 112-13 (two); historical images 118-19 (five); Breakers postcard 120.

Lila Photography: Kenan Family 119.

ACKNOWLEDGEMENTS

You just never know in this world of business where an idea is going to germinate. In late July 2016, I had a meeting with Allen Wilson, the president of Old Chatham Golf Club just east of Chapel Hill, to talk about gathering and preserving the story of the club that just happened to have been conceived in the late 1990s by Paul Rizzo, a graduate and former dean of the Kenan-Flagler Business School. Knowing Allen was an ardent Tar Heel sports fan, I showed him a book I had authored that was literally just days off the printing press—a richly illustrated book on Kenan Stadium.

"Well, let me throw something out," said Wilson, a longtime partner with the global accounting firms of Arthur Anderson and Grant Thornton. "In a couple of months, I start to work at Kenan-Flagler Business School. The dean, Doug Shackelford, is a longtime friend, and I'm starting a new position there as vice president for strategy and innovation.

"In three years, the school turns one hundred. A centennial book would be perfect. You should submit a proposal."

It turns out that Adam Gerdts, Kenan-Flagler's associate dean of advancement, was already looking toward 2019. Wilson brought the idea through the front door, where it found support from Gerdts and his associate Becky Naples, the executive director for advancement services.

After several months of proposals, meetings and giving the idea time to work its way through channels, we were ready to go in early 2017. And here comes Paul Rizzo again—I was literally at his funeral service in March 2017 when I received an email from Becky: "We're a go!"

The process of writing and assembling this book over two years was fascinating and fulfilling as it took me out of my wheelhouse of golf and college athletics. But the truth is, a good story is a good story, no matter the venue. And there were plenty to tell in considering a century at Kenan-Flagler.

I thank Shackelford and his team that begins with Allen, Adam and Becky for entrusting this project to me. Becky in particular as my primary contact through the evolution of the book was supportive, helpful and pleasant while juggling what seemed to be a thousand balls as the hundred-year birthday drew nigh.

The Marketing and Communications staff was vital as well, beginning with Chief Marketing Officer Jim Alessandro. Director of Global Media Strategy Allison Adams brought a wealth of institutional knowledge to developing the manuscript, fact-checking and offering direction. Associate Director of Multimedia Will Frasca was invaluable for his supply of photos of modern life around Kenan-Flagler.

Also from the faculty and staff, Jeff Terry, Dave Stevens and Dave Hartzell were particularly helpful, and Jack Evans brought more than four decades as a professor, dean, and interim dean to bear in helping edit the manuscript and suggesting where holes needed filling.

This book being published in 2019 marks the ten-year anniversary of my most crucial employee hire--that of the lovely and talented Sue Pace. She's a terrific wife and and a brilliant partner in producing these books. This is the tenth book we've orchestrated together, me with the words and photo assembly and her marrying it into an attractive and elegant package.

The result is something I hope does the school and its graduates proud. And the good news it's in a format that will endure a hundred years from now. I'm not sure we can say that about a film or PDF. Amid the cloud and 5G and texting and Instagram, happily there remains a healthy appetite for paper and ink, words and images with enough girth you'll wince if the whole thing falls on your toe.

"You can never get a cup of tea large enough or a book long enough to suit me," the British writer C.S. Lewis once mused.

We could have filled four hundred pages, but there was a deadline looming.

Lee Pace, January 2019

About the Author

Lee Pace is a 1979 University of North Carolina School of Journalism graduate who has worked as a freelance writer, publisher and broadcaster in Chapel Hill since 1987.

He and his wife Sue, a graphic designer and also a Carolina graduate, have collaborated on coffee-table books in recent years for Pinehurst Inc., the Country Club of Charleston, Grandfather Golf & Country Club, Secession Golf Club and Forsyth Country Club.

Pace also has a long connection with the Tar Heel football program, having written his "Extra Points" column since 1990 and reporting from the sidelines for the Tar Heel Sports Network since 2004. In 2016 he released *Football in a Forest—The Life and Times of Kenan Memorial Stadium.*

"Our graduates' job is to go back and make their families, companies, communities and countries better. If that is what we're achieving, then we are providing a great social good."

Dean Doug Shackelford